D1625965

IRELAND'S
COASTLINE

EXPLORING ITS NATURE AND HERITAGE

IRELAND'S
COASTLINE

EXPLORING ITS NATURE AND HERITAGE

RICHARD NAIRN

The Collins Press

FIRST PUBLISHED IN 2005 BY

The Collins Press,
West Link Park,
Doughcloyne,
Wilton,
Cork

British Library Cataloguing in Publication data.

Nairn, Richard, 1952-
    Ireland's coastline : its nature & heritage
    1. Coasts - Ireland 2. Natural history - Ireland
    3. Coastal ecology - Ireland
    I. Title
    577.5'1'09415

ISBN 1903464501

Cover and text design by Anú Design, Tara
Typeset by Anú Design, Tara
Printed in Ireland by Colour Books

This publication has received support from the Heritage Council
under the 2005 Publications Grant Scheme

Contents

Foreword

A couple of years ago I was sent a new book – or rather, an old one made new by translation from Irish into English. *The Shores of Connemara*, by Séamus Mac an Iomaire, is virtually unique in our culture: a book about the sea and its creatures by an intuitive naturalist born into a fishing community. The *currach* and its pots and nets, the rockweeds and shellfish, were as much a part of his life as the sound of surf and wind.

I have delighted in Mac an Iomaire's book, partly for its glorious contrast to the usual solemnities of science and partly as proof that a good many of the 'mere Irish' must have known a good deal about the sea; above all, for its unaffected, exuberant observation of the strange and wonderful animals of the shore.

His book pops up at several points in the present work, for the enthusiasm of Mac an Iomaire has spoken as magically to its author as it has to me. As a roamer of tidelines, a watcher at pools, Richard Nairn, too, has passed through the looking-glass that separates us from the shifting, quick-silver world of the intertidal zone. He has given us the first ever comprehensive guide to Ireland's most dynamic frontier with nature.

On this well-worn island the margin between high and low tides can be seen as the last authentic stretch of wilderness, its life explored most fully on sufferance of the moon. As a sailor, ornithologist and explorer of Ireland's oceanic battleground of a coast, Richard is particularly well equipped to paint the picture whole. But above the shore, at a distance from the last bungalow, is a littoral also shaped by a largely forgotten human past: of shell middens and kelp ovens, eroding green paths and little churches lost in the sand. Along with seals and otters and seabird colonies, he is attentive to the human story of the coastline, remembered in the details of ancient stone settlements and of traditional boat design.

After its long historical interlude of indifference to the sea, Ireland has reawakened to its interest and promise at entirely new levels of appreciation: a fresh interface with the natural world; a playground; a realm for enterprise. Our coastline, with its richly diverse habitats and species, is a threshold of imagination, for which this book is a valuable guide and companion.

Michael Viney

Preface

My life, like that of so many other Irish people, has been intertwined with the coastline, the border between land and sea. As a child, I listened to the low sound of the foghorns warning shipping of the sandbanks off Dublin Bay. A great-uncle of mine was a retired sea captain. He had a telescope mounted in his attic window, with which he watched the passing ships, noting each one by its shape and markings. My father, who served as a naval officer, taught me and my siblings to swim and sail and fish. He also taught us a love and respect for the sea in all its moods.

As a student I was inspired by the writings of Frank Frazer Darling and Ronald Lockley and I longed to live like them on an uninhabited island. After graduating in Natural Sciences from Trinity College in Dublin, I found employment as a nature reserve warden in Northern Ireland. The spartan accommodation, which went with the job, was an isolated house on the end of a magnificent sand dune spit in Dundrum Bay. Ever present here were the sounds of the waves, the calls of waders in winter and the moaning of seals on the bar in summer. The seals caught my imagination for several years and later I joined a boat-based expedition around the entire Irish coast to census these fascinating animals.

At Dundrum, I learnt the basic natural history of coastal ecosystems and how they can be managed for conservation. Here also I met Bill Carter, of the University of Ulster, who was to become one of the world's foremost authorities on the coastal environment until his tragically early death. Moving back to the south, I became enmeshed in the Irish Wildbird Conservancy (now called BirdWatch Ireland) and was fortunate to carry out some interesting studies of coastal birds, including a survey of breeding waders on the unique sandy machairs of the west coast. About this time too I began to monitor the winter wildfowl and waders of the small estuary of Broadlough near Wicklow, a study which is still ongoing today.

On overseas trips to the Arctic and Africa, I have become acutely aware of how valuable the coastline of Ireland is to our island nation. And yet we know so little about it. What controls the blooms of plankton which sometimes turn the sea bright red? What is the capacity of the coastal waters to absorb the sewage effluent which we pump into it on a daily basis? How will the almost unknown populations of fish in the ocean deeps respond to heavy commercial trawling? What causes the continual process of coastal erosion, which we see on the east coast? Why do schools of whales sometimes beach themselves in apparent mass suicide? The answers to some of these questions must inevitably remain mysteries but we are slowly beginning to understand the sea and its interaction with the land.

As well as my own ramblings, this book is a summary of the work of many other people who have devoted their energies to studying the Irish coast in all its aspects. To them I owe my thanks for the use of their hard-won knowledge. In particular, I would like to thank: Simon Berrow, David Cabot, Kendrew Colhoun, Mark Costello, Tom Curtis, John Davenport, Brendan Keegan, Jon Moore, Stephen Newton, Oliver Ó Cadhla, Karl Partridge, Cilian Roden, Michael Viney, and many others more expert than me. I am especially grateful to Brendan Dollard, Michael Gibbons, Oscar Merne, Donal Murphy, Paul Murphy and Jim Wilson, who read and helped to improve particular chapters. Needless to say, any mistakes in the book are entirely mine.

I thank all my colleagues in *NATURA* environmental consultants over the last six years – Frank Burke, Clare Byrne, Nuala Carr, Elaine Dromey, Katharine Duff, Julie Fossitt, Maeve Flynn, Vicky Jones, Colin Kelleher, Maria Long, Paul Murphy, Anne Newton, Nuala O'Reilly, Vinch Sacre, Helen Sheridan, Rhian Smith, Faith Wilson – who have tolerated my frequent indulgences in book research and writing when I should have been concentrating on the job in hand. Anne Newton typed parts of the manuscript and acted as first editor for the rough cut text. Rhian Smith prepared the maps, which add so much useful information for the visitor to the coast.

I am grateful to various people for searching out or providing their own pictures for the book. These included Jaimie Blandford, Simon Berrow, Eddie Dunne, James Fairley, Julie Fossitt, Críostóir Mac Cárthaigh, Bente Larsen (Viking Ship Museum), Donal MacPolin, Seamas MacPhilib (National Museum), Thomas McErlean (University of Ulster), Patricia McLean (Ulster Museum), Dymphna Moore (Royal Irish Academy), Richard T. Mills, Oscar Merne, Nigel Motyer, Oliver Ó Cadhla, Eugene O'Kelly, Aidan O'Sullivan (University College Dublin), Tony Roche (DOEHLG) Sean Pierce, Paddy Sleeman, Alyn Walsh, David Walsh, Padraig Whooley, Noel Wilkins, Faith Wilson, Geoff Sarratt, Sara Smyth (National Photographic Archive). Ros Harvey inspired me with her stunning paintings of coastal landscapes.

The Marine Institute is acknowledged for sponsoring the production of the maps in Chapter 9. I am especially grateful to Pauline Ní Flaherta, who went to great trouble to search out information on tourism and leisure uses of the coast.

The professional layout and design was entirely the work of Karen Carty and Terry Foley (Anú Design) who went to endless trouble to ensure that the pictures were of the best quality.

Much of this book was written over successive summers, while gazing out on the Atlantic Ocean from the kitchen of a house in Rosbeg, west Donegal, kindly lent by Brian and Olivia Farrington. My family – Wendy, Rowan, Derry, Hazel and Tim – have enjoyed the wild coasts with me and have given me the space and support which I needed to get these ideas on paper. To them, I dedicate the book.

Richard Nairn
Wicklow
March 2005

Picture Credits

The following photographs are reproduced with the kind permission of the trustees of the Museums and Galleries of Northern Ireland by the photographer R.J. Welch:

p. 10	Fair Head, County Antrim
p. 104	Whale at Magilligan, County Derry
p. 136	(above) *Currachs* near the Aran Islands
p. 146	(above) Ardglass, County Down
p. 147	Ballycastle, County Antrim
p. 153	Rathlin Island, County Antrim
p. 163	Tory Island, County Donegal

All other photographs are credited alongside the picture. Those photographs with no credit are by the author.

Acronyms

CDB	Congested Districts Board
CMRC	Coastal and Marine Resources Centre
CZM	Coastal Zone Management
DBSC	Dublin Bay Sailing Club
GIS	Geographic Information System
GMT	Greenwich Mean Time
IDRA	Irish Dinghy Racing Association
ISA	Irish Sailing Association
ISKA	The Irish Sea Kayaking Association
IWDG	Irish Whale and Dolphin Group
IWeBS	Irish Wetland Bird Survey
NHAs	Natural Heritage Areas
NPWS	National Parks and Wildlife Service
PCBs	Polychlorinated Biphenols
PDV	Phocine Distemper Virus
RDS	Royal Dublin Society
SAST	Seabirds at Sea Team

Author's Note

While every effort has been made to ensure accuracy in the information supplied, no responsibility can be accepted for any damage or loss suffered as a result of error, omission or misinterpretation of this information. The author and publisher shall have no liability in respect of any loss or damage caused arising from the use of this book. This includes – but is not limited to – loss or damage resulting from missing signs, future changes in routes, accidents and lost or injured persons.

Introduction

Ireland is at the edge of Europe and Ireland's coastline is a long and complex fringe where the land and sea embrace one another. The nature of Ireland is so inextricably bound up with the coast and sea that no place on this small island is divorced from the marine influence. So too, the history of Ireland is a maritime heritage and, over the millennia, its people have carved out a living on its seas and shores as much as from its land.

Imagine a boatload of early explorers arriving on a wild and uninhabited part of the Irish coast some 8,000 or 9,000 years ago. Their boat is made of the hide of animals stretched over a wooden frame. Their sail is made from seal skins, which they have managed to trap on a rocky beach and their clothes from the skins of animals, which they have hunted in the forests. With them they carry weapons tipped with flint which has been worked to a sharp

The most northerly sand dunes in Ireland at Trawbreaga Bay, County Donegal.

point, for they are not sure if they will meet resistance on this remote western shore. Landing on a sandy beach they find no evidence of human occupants, but the coast is richly endowed with wildlife. It is easy for the strangers to harvest oysters, mussels and other shellfish at low tide, to use nets on the river mouth to catch migratory salmon and eels, and to collect the eggs of birds nesting on the nearby cliffs. Firewood is plentiful as the forests stretch away inland as far as the eye can see. But these are mysterious and unexplored places and it is safer to settle on the sand dunes where their boat gives them easy access along the coast and a ready escape route should they be attacked. At night they sit around a great fire feasting on shellfish and tossing the empty shells into an ever-growing heap.

In the early 1970s, I stood beside just such a heap of shells in the middle of a sand dune at Dundrum, County Down. Across the dune face ran a dark band of fossil soil representing a

Glashedy Island, County Donegal.

period of settled climatic conditions when the dunes were well vegetated. On this brown sand were fragments of flint untouched by human hand since a Stone Age craftsman had chipped them from a rock he had picked up on the beach. I felt the sharp edge of the flint and marvelled at how this same coast had supported human inhabitants over the millennia, almost since the end of the last Ice Age.

Even today, though we have moved from flint chips to silica chips, we are still drawn to the coast, as if by some magical force. John Masefield touched on this in his famous poem, 'Sea Fever':

> *I must go down to the seas again,*
> *for the call of the running tide*
> *Is a wild call and a clear call,*
> *that may not be denied.*
> *All I ask is a windy day with*
> *the white clouds flying*
> *And the flung spray*
> *and the blown spume,*
> *and the seagulls crying.*

The writer and marine biologist, Rachel Carson, believed that we have a deep attachment to the shore, 'the place of our dim ancestral beginnings'. She wrote in *The Edge of the Sea*:[1] 'When we go down to the low-tide line, we enter a world that is as old as the earth itself – the primeval meeting place of the elements of earth and water, a place of compromise and conflict and eternal change.' She was one who not only 'understood' the ecology of the sea and the coast, but could also 'sense with the eye and ear of the mind the surge of life, beating always on its shores – blindly, inexorably pressing for a foothold'.

This same combination of 'science and sense' was admirably displayed by the Irish writer Séamus Mac an Iomaire, whose book, *The Shores of Connemara*,[2] is a unique combination of natural history and fishing lore which demonstrates that nature and human uses of the coast are intricately linked. In fact, if one

Mweenish Island, County Galway.

believes that man is part of nature then ecology becomes not just a science but a way of life.

Almost everyone in Ireland can claim to live in a coastal environment as there is nowhere in this small island which is more than 100 kilometres from the sea. In fact, more than half the population of Ireland lives within ten kilometres of the coast. The rain-laden westerly winds, which blow in from the Atlantic Ocean, are probably the single greatest influence on the Irish climate. Most people have at some time enjoyed a visit to the seaside or a meal of seafood. Fisheries are a significant part of our natural resources, the majority of our imports and exports travel by ship and we dispose of much of our waste water to the sea. Whether or not we are conscious of the fact, we are a maritime people, dependent on the seas around us for much of our existence.

This book is an attempt to celebrate the beauty and diversity of life on the coastline of this island. I have included many personal experiences to show that this is just one view

'Undertows rushing and tumbling on the shingly shore.'

of the coastline and should not be considered an academic textbook. Each reader will find his or her own viewpoint. I have tried, with the inspiration of Séamus Mac an Iomaire, to blend nature and human heritage into a single story.

Mac an Iomaire was in hospital in America with tuberculosis when he wrote these lines about his native home, the island of Mweenish in Connemara. I visited that special place recently and, when I stood there by the cabin door, I understood exactly what he felt.

I can see now in my mind's eye the cabin by the shore, the high spring tides accosting me at the doorway, undertows rushing and tumbling on the shingly shore near the side of the house, the healthy salty taste of the wind blowing around me and the continuous pulsing of the breakers reaching my ears through the severe winter. I thought there was nowhere on the surface of the earth which bettered it for beauty and adornment, and it was hard to beat for fun and pastime.

1

Shape of the Shore

Omey Island, County Galway. 'A rope of closely interwoven strands' (Jaimie Blandford).

Defining the Coast

In reality Ireland is a small maritime island perched on the north-western edge of the European continental shelf. It has been estimated that 90 per cent of the Irish territory is actually under the sea. In the catchphrase of the Marine Institute, it is under-explored, under-developed and underwater. The key to this major resource is the coastal zone where land and sea are interwoven. But defining the coast has left many eminent scientists tied in knots.

The core of the coastline is that continuous zone between the tides where, twice each day, the sea ebbs and flows onto the land. Either side of this zone is an area where the sea has a direct influence on the land and vice versa. However, the limits of the coastal zone are difficult if not impossible to draw. Physical, biological and cultural factors all have a role to play and, anyway, the coast is a dynamic area, which defies precise definition.

If the width of the coast is a mystical dimension, the length is somewhat easier to define. Estimates for the total length of coastline around the island of Ireland vary from 7,000 to 7,500 kilometres, depending on whether the minor islands are included. A recent calculation using a Geographic Information System (GIS) found the figure of 7,524 kilometres to be the total length of coast.[1] Despite the small size of Ireland, its coastline is longer than many larger European countries such as France and Spain. Taking the length of coastline as a percentage of land area, only Greece, Denmark and the UK are in the same league as Ireland when comparing relative length of coastline. In human terms, over 50 per cent of the Irish population lives in coastal municipalities with only Denmark, among EU countries, exceeding this proportion.

On the north, east and south coasts the shoreline is relatively straightforward but in the west the indentations are so great that it is sometimes difficult to follow. Nearly half of the total length of the Irish coast is found on the western side between Kerry and Donegal. The cartographer Tim Robinson, in his essay 'Setting Foot on the Shores of Connemara',[2] describes the coast as 'a rope of closely interwoven strands flung down in twists and coils across an otherwise bare surface'. No scientific term can adequately describe the complexity of the Connemara coastline where, according to Robinson, 'land and sea not only entwine their crooked fingers but each element abandons particles of itself temporarily or permanently to the clutch of the other'.

Length of Coastal Features

The coast can be subdivided into hard (rocky) and soft sections (glacial cliffs, shingle, sand and mud) with some 3,000 kilometres of the Republic of Ireland being classified as soft coast.

Portnoo, County Donegal. Sandy beaches occupy about one-third of the Irish coastline.

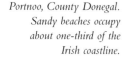

Slieve League, County Donegal. These are among the highest sea cliffs in Europe.

Over half of this length is considered to be at risk from erosion. The length of sandy coast in Ireland has been calculated at 2,382 kilometres, much of which is backed by sand dunes. In the mid-1800s, Kinahan and McHenry[3] estimated that coastal sand dunes and sand sheets (machair) in Ireland occupied about 15,500 hectares. Most of the dunes are found in the northern half of the island – in Counties Antrim, Down, Derry, Donegal, Sligo and Mayo – with over 40 per cent in Donegal alone.

Estuaries are a significant feature all around the Irish coast. Mud and saltings together occupy about 784 kilometres of coastline but significant areas of sand are also contained in the estuaries. The largest estuarine areas are the Shannon/Fergus, Lough Foyle, Strangford Lough, Cork Harbour, Castlemaine Harbour and Dundalk Bay. All of the major cities, Belfast, Dublin, Waterford, Cork, Limerick, Galway and Derry, are located on large estuaries or bays.

Rocky shores probably make up the largest proportion of the coast including cliffs, which account for about 828 kilometres. These vary from the dramatic high rocky cliffs of the west and north coasts to the lower more continuous cliffs of the south and east coasts. The longest cliff coastlines are in Counties Cork, Kerry, Clare, Mayo and Donegal. These include some of the highest sea cliffs in Europe at Slieve League, Achill Island and Cliffs of Moher. Soft sea cliffs, comprised mainly of glacial till, form at least 250 kilometres of the Irish coast.[4]

Artificial structures make up a surprisingly large part of the coastal length. At least 300 kilometres are protected by sea wall. Over one-third of this length is in County Cork alone, where sea walls were built in the nineteenth century to protect coastal roads. Much of the inner Shannon Estuary is bordered by sea walls, built in the 1800s to prevent flooding of coastal farmland. The island of Ireland has approximately 200 harbours, both large and small, 600 small piers and slips and many hundreds of rock revetments, breakwaters or gabions, which have been built to try and stop coastal erosion.

Hook Head, County Wexford. A lobster lies in a wave-cut crevice formed in the limestone beneath the oldest lighthouse tower in Ireland (Nigel Motyer).

(left) Flat-bedded limestone on the Aran Islands form a wave-cut platform.
(below) Rathlin Island, County Antrim with white chalk boulders in the foreground and black basalt cliffs behind (Sean Pierce).

Geology and Landscape

There are few better places than the coast to study geology, where the structures and the contacts between different rock types are usually fully exposed. During my student days in the early 1970s, I spent a very enjoyable summer on the coast of south Donegal mapping the Carboniferous rocks, west of Killybegs. I admit that I spent as much time admiring the stunning landscapes as I did unravelling the complexities of the geology but it left an indelible impression on me and I have returned frequently to the area ever since.

In fact, the Carboniferous period was one of the least complex of geological times, as it left behind a series of mainly flat-bedded limestones and shales, which outcrop around Dublin, in west Clare and Galway Bay and between Killala Bay and Donegal Bay. We must imagine Ireland in those times covered by shallow

tropical seas in which large masses of corals and other marine organisms lived. As they died their hard parts accumulated and formed deep deposits on the sea bed. These eventually became buried and lithified to form sedimentary rocks. I have walked across the rocky shores on these limestone coasts, at Hook Head in Wexford or at Streedagh Point in Sligo, and seen wonderful fossil remains of large corals, extinct shellfish such as brachiopods and a curious animal called the crinoid that was like a stalked starfish. The Carboniferous rocks tend

The photographer Robert J. Welch sits astride a fallen dolerite column at Fair Head, County Antrim (Ulster Museum).

running in a mainly east-west direction. Some of the river valleys of the south west were flooded by rising sea level after the last Ice Age and now form the great bays of Castlemaine, Kenmare, Bantry, Dunmanus and Roaringwater, separated by the finger-like peninsulas of Dingle, Iveragh, Sheep's Head and Mizen Head. The sandstones are frequently lifted into spectacularly upright strata pointing to the sky and forming long band-like features in the coastal landscape. The coast around Sneem in County Kerry is a good example of this, with a string of small islands where the strata have become isolated from the mainland.

The granites and metamorphic rocks of Donegal and Connemara are among the hardest of rocky coastlines and often form prominent headlands such as Slyne Head, Slieve League and Malin Head. The Leinster Granite, which forms the spine of the Wicklow Mountains in the east of the country, meets the sea at Killiney and Dalkey, in County Dublin, where it forms the cliffs of White Rock. At Carnsore Point, in the extreme south-east corner of County Wexford, a distinctive pink granite forms large boulders on the shoreline.

The north-east corner of Ireland has a unique combination of rocks with black sheets of basalt overlying white chalk, most easily seen in the cliffs of Fair Head and of Rathlin Island. They are among the most recent of rocks, in a geological sense, and arose because volcanic activity caused an outpouring of lava onto the surface, cooling to form the basalt columns which are best known from the world-famous Giant's Causeway. This basalt cap protects beneath it the softer chalk, which was eroded off most of the remainder of the Irish landscape.

Recent Coastal Sediments

Of course, there are many places where the hard rocks are masked by drift or glacial sediments, which are mainly composed of boulder clay. These include much of the east coast between Belfast and Wexford and parts of the south and

to erode more easily than, say, granites but in places they form dramatic cliffs. The Cliffs of Moher are the most famous but those of the neighbouring Aran Islands and of Loop Head are equally exciting, especially on a stormy day. The limestones and shales usually form flat beds, the softest of which erode to form horizontal ledges. Other classic Carboniferous headlands are at Downpatrick Head in north Mayo and Muckross Head in south Donegal.

In the south and south west, Old Red Sandstones are the dominant rock types with folds

(left) Malin Head, County Donegal. The raised beach to the right of the picture was formed when sea level was higher after the last Ice Age; (below) sedimentary cliffs formed of glacial sands and gravels near Barna, County Galway.

and Donegal. Even within the last century there have been very stormy periods when coastal sand dunes became quite mobile and whole villages have sometimes been buried by sheets of moving sand, as at Horn Head, County Donegal, or lost to the sea by marine erosion, as at Rosslare Point, County Wexford.

In some parts of the west coast blanket bog, which is normally a mountain feature, occurs at sea level. Examples of lowland blanket bog are found in places such as south Connemara and south Mayo, where high rainfall combined with poor drainage produce coastal peatland formations. It is extraordinary to stand on the high tide line, in a place like Bellacragher Bay, near Achill Island, and be surrounded by bog vegetation on one side and seaweeds on the other.

west coasts such as west Waterford and the Shannon Estuary. The classic glacial features are the small rounded hills called drumlins, which form swarms of islands in such places as Strangford Lough and Clew Bay. The islands here are often surrounded by low cliffs, formed by wave action over the millennia.

Sand dunes and sand sheets, deposited by the wind within the last few centuries, are found extensively in counties such as Wexford, Kerry

In some parts of the south and west coasts it is not unusual to find peat below high water mark, draped in seaweed and washed by the tides. This is because of the continuing rise in

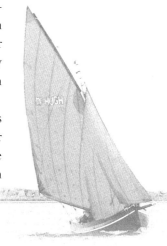

sea level as Ireland's land mass readjusts to the melting of ice sheets at the end of the last Ice Age, some 10,000 years ago. On the north coast there are raised beaches, perched many metres above present sea level. So the read-justment of land and sea is uneven in its effects as the northern part of the island is rising and the southern part sinking relative to modern sea level.

Winds

We live beside the North Atlantic – not the Mediterranean, nor the Caribbean. Wind and rain are a normal part of everyday life here. Sometimes it may be difficult to tell the dif-ference between summer and winter, except by length of daylight. In many coastal districts, especially where they face the open ocean, the wind is a constant feature of life. Any trees that grow here are heavily sculptured by the wind. Sand from the beaches can be carried far inland and the salt in the winds even affects the acid-ity of coastal lakes. Traditionally, buildings in the windier parts of Donegal were thatched, with a rounded ridge and gable to make the roof more aerodynamic in the strong winds.

The Beaufort Scale of Wind Force

Beaufort Number	Brief Description	Indications on land	Wind velocity in knots	Wind velocity in metres per second
0	Calm	Smoke rises vertically	less than 1	less than 0.3
1	Light air	Direction of wind shown by smoke but not by wind vanes	1-3	0.3-1.5
2	Light breeze	Wind felt on face: leaves rustle; ordinary vanes moved by wind	4-6	1.6-3.3
3	Gentle breeze	Leaves and small twigs in constant motion; wind extends light flag	7-10	3.4-5.4
4	Moderate breeze	Raises dust and loose paper; small branches are moved	11-16	5.5-7.9
5	Fresh breeze	Small trees in leaf begin to sway; crested wavelets begin to form on inland waters	17-21	8.0-10.7
6	Strong breeze	Large branches in motion; whistling heard in telegraph wires; umbrellas used with difficulty	22-27	10.8-13.8
7	Near gale	Whole trees in motion; inconvenience felt when walking against the wind	28-33	13.9-17.1
8	Gale	Breaks twigs off trees; generally impedes progress	34-40	17.2-20.7
9	Strong gale	Slight structural damage occurs (chimney pots and slates removed)	41-47	20.8-24.4
10	Storm	Seldom experienced inland; trees uprooted; considerable structural damage occurs	48-55	24.5-28.4
11	Violent storm	Very rarely experienced; accompanied by widespread damage	56-63	28.5-32.6
12	Hurricane	Extremely rare in Ireland; severe coastal erosion and structural damage	64 and over	32.7 and over

Even though it is not possible to see the wind itself, it is possible to estimate its speed by watching its effect on the sea surface, on trees or on flags. To standardise these observations we use the Beaufort Scale of Wind Force, which was introduced by an Irishman, Admiral Francis Beaufort, in the nineteenth century.

The windiest place in Ireland is the very northerly point at Malin Head in Donegal. Here winds are moderate to fresh for about half the time and strong or higher for a further quarter of the time. The wind speed is not constant but varies throughout the day. High winds can occur at any time but, on average, wind speed reaches a maximum in the afternoon

between 1300 and 1500 GMT. This is a result of heating of the land surface, which increases the mixing of air bodies. The variation in wind speeds is greatest on sunny days when the land heats up more quickly.

Gales are most frequent in January and can average as high as 57 days per year at the most exposed coastal locations, such as Malin Head, County Donegal. A high frequency of gales is also experienced at other prominent headlands such as Belmullet, County Mayo (29 days per year) and Roche's Point, County Cork (32 days per year). Calm days are rare on the west coast but can occur up to 3 per cent of the time on the Irish Sea coast.

The principal winds blow from between south and west on the compass. This pattern varies enormously from place to place and from day to day but it is true that northerly and north-easterly winds are least common on the Irish coast. The most familiar situation is to watch the clouds scudding in from the Atlantic on the damp oceanic winds.

Wind on the sea causes the water to oscillate and waves moving across the open ocean cause a swell in the seawater as it hits the coast. The impacts of erosion by wind-driven waves on

Thatched house at Malin Head, County Donegal showing the traditional rounded profile which was designed to be more aerodynamic in the strong winds.

Galway Hooker under full sale at Kinvara, County Galway.

softer coastlines are well known, and these are described in Chapter 8. But strong onshore winds can also have constructive effects. Most sand dunes and the unique machair plains of the north-west coast were built by the action of winds carrying sand from the beaches (see Chapter 3).

Currents

The most important current of all is the Gulf Stream, which flows, like a river in the ocean, across the Atlantic from the Gulf of Mexico to north-west Europe, wrapping the coasts from Ireland to Norway in its 'warm embrace'. It originates in the Gulf of Mexico, from where tropical seeds and marine turtles are sometimes carried across the Atlantic to strand on Irish beaches. Most seas at the same latitude as Ireland (for example, Newfoundland) freeze over in winter. Without the warming influence of the Gulf Stream Ireland would have much more severe winters and a more extreme climate in general.

Knowledge of the circulation of water around the island of Ireland is incomplete but the general pattern is well known. A persistent current at about 500m depth follows the continental slope between the Bay of Biscay and the south-west coast of Ireland, continuing north along the west coast of Ireland. Another persistent current moves across the mouth of the English Channel towards the south coast of Ireland, where it splits in two. One stream turns westward and around the south-west coast while another enters the Irish Sea between Wexford and south Wales. Yet another current stream enters the Irish Sea from the north between Antrim and south-west Scotland.

Fronts

The water that flows in these coastal currents is not uniform as one descends to the sea bed. Seawater is normally mixed but, during the summer months, there is a tendency for water bodies to stratify into different vertical layers, separated by temperature and density. Fronts develop where mixed water meets stratified water and these are fairly consistent in their position relative to the coast. The Irish Shelf Front separates coastal waters from those of the Atlantic Ocean off the south-west coast. Thermal fronts in seawater bring with them an abundance of phytoplankton which form the base of the food chain for higher groups

Thermal fronts cause the upwelling of productive cold water which attracts feeding whales and seabirds, as here on the west coast of Cork (Padraig Whooley).

(left) Trawbreaga Bay, County Donegal at low tide. (below) The daily ebb and flow of the tide controls the lives of these sanderlings.

such as fish, seabirds and marine mammals. The south-west coast of Ireland in summer has some of the densest feeding concentrations of seabirds, dolphins and porpoises in Europe.

Another front occurs between south-east Ireland and the coast of south Wales. Known as the Celtic Sea Front, it is one of the main oceanographic phenomena supporting the large seabird colonies of Wexford and Pembrokeshire. Between County Down and the Isle of Man, an important front occurs in summer, generating significant food resources for fish, seabirds and basking sharks. The phytoplankton produced in the frontal areas can often be transported by onshore winds into the shallow coastal bays and estuaries where they can form concentrations which are harmful to shellfish, especially where these are farmed in high densities.

Tides

The constant ebb and flow of the tide is one of the overriding features of life on the coast. It dominates the marine life of the shore from barnacles to brent geese and it controls the activities of those people who use the sea for their profession or recreation. It is a major factor in the use of coastal ports, in fishing and sailing, and it helps to flush out waste water from enclosed bays and estuaries. The gravitational pull of the sun and moon on the earth's surface produce a disproportionate movement in the ocean waters. The oceans of the world are divided into natural basins and the seawater moves around these in response to the turn of the earth and the gravitational forces.

Waves, generated by the tides, move across the world's oceans such as the Atlantic. As they reach the continental shelf they increase in height and are further accentuated as they enter funnel-shaped bays such as Bantry Bay or estuaries such as that of the Shannon. The maximum tidal range around the Irish coast is about 2-4 metres but this increases to 4-5 metres in restricted waters such as the Shannon Estuary. Tidal amplitude can reach extremes during periods of low atmospheric pressure and under strong onshore winds. A combination of these factors in early February 2002 caused serious coastal flooding in a number of urban areas along the Irish Sea coast.

The difference between high and low tide each day varies according to the phase of the moon, with the greatest range occurring twice per month after the full moon and the new moon. The greatest tidal range (or amplitude) is known as the spring tide (no connection with the season of spring) while the least is called the neap tide. Knowledge of the dates of spring and neap tides is especially valuable to those people who are making a living from marine resources or studying marine biology. It can also reveal some of the secrets of the marine world. On one of the lowest spring tides of the year each August, I love to wander on the lowest part of rocky shores where the giant kelp beds wave lazily back and forth in the waves.

Waves

Surfers know all about the meteorological conditions which produce big waves. The west of Ireland is one of the world's best surfing coasts with a fetch (unbroken ocean) stretching to America. On the continental shelf south and west of Ireland wave heights range from 3 to 5 metres in January and 2 to 4 metres in June. This ocean swell is driven onto the coast by predominantly south-westerly winds forming the breakers so much sought after by the surfers in such places as Castlegregory, County Kerry and Rossnowlagh, County Donegal. Larger waves occur more frequently off the north and west coasts. In the nineteenth century the people of the Donegal coast could forecast the weather from the waves:

A set of waves in sheltered waters of the Irish Sea.

What is singular is that those immense waves are not always caused by storms or the force of the wind; on the contrary such convulsions can be seen in the calmest weather, and it is well known by the seaboard men that when such a rock 'speaks', a great fall of rain is approaching; another rock is the index for high wind; another for dry weather, and one for frost or frosty weather. So acquainted were the observing among the people with the workings of these rocks and the manner in which the waves broke, the particular roar for different states of the weather, that each rock was a weather guide in itself.[5]

Storm conditions may drive these waves onto the coast with a tremendous energy release, changing the shape of sandy beaches and dunes in a few hours and sculpting the cliffs and islands of the more prominent parts of the coast. Séamus Mac an Iomaire gives a lyrical, if breathless, account of big waves in *The Shores of Connemara*.[6]

> *Big surf rising in high walls, drawing back and folding, swelling and running and rushing at each others' heels, doffing their white crests as they approach the shore bursting and falling on top of one another, mixing and making whirlpools and boiling in one big commotion, until their strength and pressure is exhausted and used on the hard granite edge of the island which stands boldly against it since time immemorial.*

Atlantic breakers can reach 5 metres in height after a big storm.

17

Coastal Habitats

The variety of coastal landscapes and habitats is one of the most enchanting features of the Irish coastline. From the island-studded bays of west Cork to the basalt cliffs of Antrim, the earth's history has determined the shape of the shore. From the most exposed storm beaches of the west coast to the sheltered muddy shores of the east coast, there is an infinite variety of sediment, vegetation and animal life. However, we notice that certain features are repeated again and again. Sand dunes often form a long hooked shape at the mouths of rivers. The same small group of specialised plants is usually found growing on a saltmarsh. A rock pool in Donegal will usually contain a similar complement of marine animals to one in Cork. So we can recognise particular habitats which are common to many parts of the coast and which respond in similar ways to exposure and shelter from the ocean.

The most widely-used classification of habitats in Ireland is that prepared for the Heritage Council.[7] The major subdivision is between marine (that is below high water mark) and coastlands (above high water mark). Vegetation is the normal character by which land habitats are defined. This scheme is not entirely satisfactory, as there is inevitably some overlap between marine and terrestrial systems and many of the boundaries are 'grey areas'. It is difficult, for example, to place saltmarshes in this classification as they are dominated by plants, yet are covered by some high tides. However, the system, described overleaf, is designed as an easy-to-use method for describing and classifying habitats and comparing them with similar habitats elsewhere.

For the marine and intertidal habitats, the classification of the Marine Nature Conservation Review is the most widely used in Ireland and Britain as it uses a combination of substrate type, vertical zonation, degree of wave exposure and animal communities.[8] Irish marine communities are quite varied because Ireland lies at the edge of two zones in the oceans – at the northern limit for warm water species and at the southern limit for arctic species.[9] The extension of the warming Gulf Stream up the

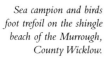

Sea campion and birds foot trefoil on the shingle beach of the Murrough, County Wicklow.

west and around the north coast allows some of the warmer water species to live here when they are absent from the cooler east coast waters of the Irish Sea. One large marine species, the crawfish (*Palinurus vulgaris*), demonstrates this effect well. It is predominantly a southern species in Europe but is found all along the west coast of Ireland and western Scotland, although it is largely absent from the Irish Sea. The warm waters of the Gulf Stream also prevent the arctic species such as the squid *Sagittatus sagittatus* from extending into western Irish waters, although it occurs seasonally in the Irish Sea.

Simplified List of Coastland Habitats in Ireland

(adapted from Fossitt 2000[10])

HABITAT TYPE	CHARACTERISTIC PLANT	TYPICAL EXAMPLE
Sea Cliffs and Islets		
Rocky Sea Cliffs	Thrift, Bladder Campion	Horn Head, County Donegal
Sea Stacks and Islets	Red Fescue, Lichens	Rathlin Island, County Antrim
Sedimentary Sea Cliffs	Various	Blackwater, County Wexford
Brackish Waters		
Lagoons and Saline Lakes	Tassleweed	Lady's Island Lake, County Wexford
Tidal Rivers	Common Reed	River Shannon at Limerick
Saltmarshes		
Lower Salt Marsh	Glasswort, Cord Grass	Fota Island, Cork Harbour
Upper Salt Marsh	Saltmarsh Rushes, Sea Purslane	Bull Island, Dublin Bay
Shingle and Gravel Banks		
Shingle and Gravel Banks	Sea Sandwort, Sea Beet	The Murrough, County Wicklow
Sand Dune Systems		
Embryo Dunes	Sand Couch, Lyme Grass	Magilligan Point, County Derry
Marram Dunes	Marram Grass, Sea Holly	Castlegregory, County Kerry
Fixed Dunes	Red Fescue, Bent Grass, Dog Lichen	Brittas Bay, County Wicklow
Dune Scrub and Woodland	Gorse, Burnet Rose, Sea Buckthorn	Murlough, County Down
Dune Slacks	Creeping Willow, Silverweed	Inch Strand, County Kerry
Machair	Red Fescue, Ribwort Plantain, Daisy	The Mullet, County Mayo
Coastal Constructions		
Sea Walls, Piers and Jetties	Various	Shannon Estuary, County Limerick
Fish Cages and Rafts	Usually None	Bantry Bay, County Cork

There have been quite comprehensive surveys of littoral (between high and low tide marks) and sublittoral (below low tide) zones surveys around the Northern Ireland coast[11] while the BioMar survey sampled a wide variety of locations around the coast of the Republic.[12] The main types of marine habitats on the coast are summarised in the following table.

Simplified List of Marine Habitats Around Ireland

(adapted from Wilson and Lawler 1996[13])

Habitat Type	Characteristic Species of Plants and Animals	Typical Example
Littoral (Between High and Low Water)		
Exposed Bedrock and Boulders	Black Lichen (*Verrucaria*), Brown Rib-Weed, Barnacles	Mizen Head, County Cork
Moderately Exposed Bedrock and Boulders	Brown Seaweeds, Limpet, Periwinkle	Bray Head, County Wicklow
Sheltered Bedrock and Boulders	Knotted Wrack, Oarweed	Connemara Inlets
Limestone Pavements	Purple Sea Urchin	Burren Coast, County Clare
Caves	Encrusting Sponges	Rathlin Island, County Antrim
Cobble	None	Bloody Foreland, County Donegal
Shingle	Sandhoppers in weed at strand line	Beaches near Loop Head, County Clare
Coarse Sand	Amphipods, Worms	Fanore, County Clare Killiney, County Dublin
Sand	Tellin, Cockle	Dublin Bay
Mud	Peppery Furrow Shell, Baltic Telling	Cork Harbour
Estuaries	Ragworm	Shannon Estuary
Sublittoral (Below Low Water)		
Bedrock and Boulders, Strong Current	Hydroids, Anemone (*Sagartia*), Breadcrumb Sponge	Lambay Island, County Dublin
Bedrock and Boulders, Lesser Current	Dead Man's Fingers, Plumose Anemone, Feather Star	Rockabill Island, County Dublin
Bedrock and Boulders, Slight Current/Waves	Cuvie Weed, Papillate Sponges, Sea Fan	Mullaghmore, County Sligo
Cliffs and Overhangs	Sponge (*Dercitus*), Soft Coral	Lough Hyne, County Cork
Cobble, Shell Gravel, Mixed	Brittlestars (*Ophiocomina* and *Ophiothrix*)	Dalkey Sound, County Dublin
Clean Coarse Sand	Sand Eel	Kish Bank, off County Dublin
Medium Sand	Heart Urchin, Masked Crab	North Lambay, County Dublin
Maerl Beds	Algae such as *Dictyota Dichotoma*, Amphipod, Crustaceans	Kilkieran Bay, County Galway
Muddy Sand	Sea Pen (*Virgularia*), Burrowing Anemone	Dublin Bay
Mud	Brittlestar (*Amphiura*), Dublin Bay Prawn	Galway Bay, Lambay Deep

2

Rocky Shores and Islands

The area between high and low tide marks is perhaps the core of the coastline because it is the interface between land and sea. It is known by various names, such as the 'intertidal area', 'the littoral zone' or 'the foreshore'. It is a hugely variable habitat, depending on a combination of rock or sediment type, the degree of exposure to waves and the variable inputs of nutrients (for example from rivers). In this account the main subdivision is between rocky (or hard) shores and sediment (or soft) shores. The soft shores are described in Chapter 3 (sandy) and Chapter 4 (muddy).

Rocky Shores

Rocky shores include those formed of solid rock (bedrock) or loose rock (boulders and cobbles). The angle at which the rock strata lie has a significant influence on the type of shore which develops. For example, upright strata, as occur in the Old Red Sandstones of Kerry, produce deep gullies and long, narrow rock pools. Flat-bedded strata, such as the Carboniferous limestones and shales of north Clare, tend to produce platforms of rock with broader, shallower rock pools. Sheltered areas of rocky shore

will have small pockets of sand which hold animal communities more typical of depositing shores. Boulders and loose rock increase the degree of shelter available to animals and plants and hence the diversity of the communities.

Seaweeds and lichens form parallel bands near high water mark on a rocky shore.

The Splash Zone

Just above the limit of the highest tides is the splash zone that, on rocky shores, is invariably dominated by lichens. Few other plants could survive the extreme conditions of high salt content from spray, high temperatures, drying effects of wind, absence of fresh water and soil.

Lichens are often abundant on rocky surfaces in the spray zone.

Cover of lichens in the splash zone is often extensive and the dominant colours are yellow, grey and black. The bright yellows and orange colours of *Xanthoria* result from the orange pigment, which protects the lower algal cells from extreme sunlight. The black lichen *Verrucaria maura* is capable of tolerating brief periods of salt water cover and is edible by grazing animals after softening in water. All lichens are very susceptible to pollution and can be killed by oil pollution or by some of the chemicals used to disperse oil spills. Few flowering plants can survive in these extreme conditions, but occasional plants of thrift and sea plantain may gain a foothold in cracks and crevices.

The Intertidal Zone

On most rocky shores the algae (or seaweeds) form distinct zones that lie parallel to the high tide mark. It takes a little practice to learn the distinguishing features of the brown seaweeds, but they are probably the most important components of the rocky shore habitat. On the upper shore, the dominant seaweeds are channel wrack and spiral wrack. Among the weed,

acorn barnacles encrust the rock surfaces and rough periwinkles move about at high tide grazing on lichens and algae. Very exposed shores are often dominated by mussels, which cling onto cracks and crevices in the rock and may form dense colonies. Limpets are also able to cling tightly to rock surfaces using their large fleshy foot.

One of my favourite pastimes, on summer trips to the west coast, is to clamber barefoot among the rocks at low tide on a local estuary. The sensation of the slippery seaweed between the toes has to be felt to be appreciated. Pull aside the curtain of brown weed and underneath is a whole world waiting to be discovered. Visit again at high tide with a snorkel and mask and the weedy world becomes like a forest with fronds waving back and forth in the tidal currents. Shore crabs race away to cover. Small fish dart in behind the weed curtains and periwinkles graze like sheep on the algae covering the rocks.

The middle zones of the shore are characterised by the knotted wrack and bladder wrack. The knotted wrack is especially typical of more sheltered shores. Red seaweeds such as Carragheen moss and dulse may grow densely attached to the rocks or to larger seaweeds. Typical animals of the mid-shore area are the flat and edible periwinkles. These are much sought after by winkle collectors in such places as the Salthill coast of Galway city. In older parts of the city, such as The Claddagh, winkle collecting is passed on from one generation to the next and some families even have traditional territories on the shore.

Common inhabitants under the shelter of the seaweeds are the shore crab and edible crab, the latter moving down into deeper water as it becomes mature. Anemones are abundant in rock pools and on exposed shores, the most common being the beadlet anemone, which can survive at low tide by withdrawing its tentacles. The snakelocks anemone and others cannot do this, so they are usually restricted to

22

the lower shore and to rock pools. The dog whelk is a carnivore that roams about at high tide attacking and eating barnacles, limpets and mussels. Its own thick spiral shell gives it protection from other predators such as crabs and shorebirds. The empty shells of dog whelks are often taken over by hermit crabs, which lack a hard shell of their own.

The lower shore on a rocky substrate is characterised by the serrated wrack with bladder wrack in the more sheltered areas. A red seaweed *Corallina officinalis* survives best on the lower shore where it lives in the shelter of the brown seaweeds. Here, too, the encrusting sponges may form large sheets or mounds on the rock surface. A common species is the

(Clockwise from top left) Brown seaweed [or wrack] often covers the rocky shore with a thick blanket; mussels and barnacles survive on very exposed coastlines by anchoring themselves to the rock surface; rock pools provide endless fascination for those who take the time to watch (Nigel Motyer); *a short spined sea scorpion fish lies in wait for prey in a bed of jewel anemones* (Nigel Motyer).

Slieve League, County Donegal. Light grazing allows heather to survive in the thin soils.

breadcrumb sponge, which tends to prefer crevices to avoid drying out. The surfaces of some of the larger seaweeds may be covered with mats of an organism called a bryozoan, which looks like a fine white mesh netting. It is, in fact, a colony of tiny animals that create chambers made of calcium carbonate and filter the seawater for food. An enormous range of strange and colourful animals may live on a typical rocky shore and ultimately these are dependent on one another and on the sea for their survival.

Rocky Sea Cliffs

It is hard to imagine a more exhilarating experience than standing on the top of a western cliff as the full force of the Atlantic Ocean dashes all its energy on the rocks far below. Some of the highest and most spectacular cliffs in Europe are found on the Irish coast at such places as Fair Head, County Antrim; Horn Head and Slieve League, County Donegal; Achill Island and Clare Island in County Mayo; Aran

Islands, County Galway; Cliffs of Moher and Loop Head in County Clare; Brandon Head, Seven Sisters and Valentia Island in County Kerry; Mizen Head and the Old Head of Kinsale in County Cork. The more inaccessible cliffs tend to have the most interesting vegetation as they are remote from grazing pressures. Typically bare rock, loose boulders or scree make up a high proportion of the surface, but lichens may be extensive. Wherever ledges and crevices form in the rock, then a thin soil will accumulate and typical plants of the spray zone will establish, such as sea pink, sea campion, sea plantain, rock spurry and scentless mayweed. These tend to form dense, spongy cushions, especially where they are grazed by rabbits or sheep. Any grassland that takes hold is likely to be dominated by red fescue but, where seabird colonies add fertiliser, a more enriched community containing docks and bracken may take over.

The absence of competition from more vigorous grasses, herbs and shrubs and the lack of grazing favours the occurrence of some rare plants on remote cliff sites. Robert Lloyd Praeger was very interested in the presence of some rare arctic-alpine species on north-facing cliffs such as Brandon Head in County Kerry. He was fearless in his pursuit of these specialities and was known to have walked across the so-called 'Deadman's Path' on the north face of Clare Island, County Mayo, without the aid of any ropes or other safety equipment. This type of natural history pursuit is not encouraged today.

Soft Sea Cliffs

Some cliffs are formed primarily of loose sediments such as clays, sands and gravels, while more commonly a layer of mixed boulder clay often overlies a rocky basement. Typical examples occur around Kilmore Quay and Blackwater Head in County Wexford, St. John's Point in County Donegal and many of the islands in Clew Bay in County Mayo. In many places, such as the cliff path north of

24

(left) Sea pink or thrift forms dense spongy cushions on clifftops (Julie Fossitt)*; (below) kittiwakes nest on the cliffs within the harbour at Dunmore East, County Waterford.*

Greystones, County Wicklow, the boulder clay is continually undermined by the sea and slumps easily. The steeper, more unstable cliffs are generally devoid of vegetation, but some may hold extensive swards of maritime grassland and heath.

I once had the unusual job of evaluating the vegetation of the cliffs at Dunmore East, County Waterford where there was a risk that they might collapse onto the dock below. The most significant feature here is the colony of nesting kittiwakes, which carry on their noisy breeding activities within metres of a busy port road and to the fascination of members of the public. To avoid disturbing the birds my colleagues and I made use of a mechanical hoist to lift us to the upper edge of the cliff. Here we could make a detailed description of the vegetation. The softer, more unstable parts of the cliff are based on glacial deposits and have a dense scrub-like vegetation which is dominated by such plants as ivy and bramble.

25

Soft sea cliffs made of boulder clay in Clew Bay, County Mayo.

(Below from left) Cave on the Atlantic coast of County Clare (Eugene O'Kelly)*; Sponges thrive in the absence of competition from seaweeds in caves and beneath overhangs; a blow-hole on Inishmaan, Aran Islands.*

Soft coastal cliffs have a special importance for invertebrate animals. The key factors here seem to be the availability of bare ground, presence of extensive pioneer vegetation, seepages and other hydrological features and physical attributes such as soil type, topography and aspect. Because they are poorly consolidated, there are frequent slumps or landslips caused by heavy rain, percolating ground water or by wave action. This creates new bare ground which is ideal terrain for visual hunters such as tiger beetles, ground beetles, jumping spiders, nest sites for burrowing bees and wasps and warm basking areas for a variety of insects.

An example is found on the north-west coast of the Great Saltee Island, which is formed of glacial till, and regularly slumps into the sea. It is estimated that there are at least 250 kilometres of soft sea cliff in Ireland.[1]

Sea Caves

In certain rock types, the action of the waves causes the collapse of strata or the erosion of caves at the tidal level of the shore. Where a complete ceiling exists, the resulting shade and reduced desiccation allows certain species to proliferate in the absence of competition from the common seaweeds that require light. Especially abundant here are sponges, sea squirts, bryozoans, barnacles and spirorbid tubeworms. Most are encrusting species because there is immense energy as the waves surge in along the walls of a cave. I know one cave on the Wicklow coast where the spray comes back out of the rocks for a distance twice or three times the length of the cave. In calmer conditions the water makes sucking and blowing noises like a child with a lollipop. Some caves are important refuges for breeding grey seals in the autumn months. The white-coated pup is born on a beach at the head of the cave (often in complete darkness) and will remain there for about three weeks until it is weaned and takes to the sea. Cave-breeding seals occur at Lambay Island on the Dublin coast, Saltee

Islands off Wexford and on the remote cliff coast of Slieve Toohy, County Donegal.

Where the roof has collapsed at the back of a cave, a blow-hole may be created. This feature, often known by such names as 'Puffing Billy', may send a jet of spray into the air during strong swell or storm conditions. There are a number of blow holes in the karst limestone of the Aran Islands, where the opening to the sky is a rectangular shape. These blow-holes have such descriptive names as Poll na bPéist (hole of the monster), Poll Dubh (black hole), Poll Gorm (blue hole) and Poll na Feamainne (Hole of the Seaweed).

Rocky Sea Inlets and Bays

The highly indented shape of the Irish coastline has produced a complex and varied selection of sea inlets and bays. Some of these were formed when sea level rose and drowned a river valley or low-lying coastal wetland. The great inlets of the southwest, from Dunmanus Bay to Dingle Bay, are known by the geographical term 'ria' meaning a drowned river valley. Other inlets were formed by the actions of glaciers during the last Ice Age. Most spectacular of these is the long, narrow fjord of Killary Harbour, which forms the boundary between the counties of Mayo and Galway. It is 15 kilometres long, but only a few hundred metres wide. A glacier must have scoured the bottom as it moved towards the sea, taking large volumes of rock and gravel with it. Just outside the entrance, the depth reduces dramatically and there are a number of rocky islands giving a profile that is typical of the

The deep and narrow inlet of Killary Harbour, County Galway is the only true fjord in Ireland.

fjords of Scandinavia. Carlingford Lough, on the north-east coast, is also a good example of a fjord, although it is wider and less dramatic.

Other coastal areas show the depositional actions of the ice sheets where small rounded hills of boulder clay known as drumlins occur in groups or swarms. The greatest number of drumlins in Ireland occurs in a broad band stretching from County Down to County Mayo. At either end of this band are the two drowned drumlin landscapes of Strangford Lough and Clew Bay. The inner part of Galway Bay also has some drumlin features with low islands linked to the mainland by narrow gravel causeways. Other large bays, which can be regarded as single coastal cells, include Donegal Bay, Belfast Lough, Dundrum Bay, Dundalk Bay, Dublin Bay and Roaringwater Bay. More enclosed natural harbours with major river inputs, such as the Shannon/Fergus Estuary, Cork Harbour, Dungarvan Harbour, Tramore Bay, Wexford Harbour and Lough Foyle, are considered as estuaries.

Special Rocky Shore Sites

The habitats of a large sea inlet such as Strangford Lough mirror the seabed habitats of the Irish Sea itself.[2] The sediment size varies from large boulders and cobbles, in the areas where tides and currents are strongest, to fine sands and muds at the most sheltered inner reaches. In between are areas of coarse sand and some mixed with rock fragments and shell debris. Rock and sand are continually being eroded from the edges of the drumlin islands and headlands by the action of waves. The finer muds can be carried in suspension by even the slowest of tidal movements.

At the northern end of the 30-kilometre long Strangford Lough, enormous expanses of mud are exposed at low tide with distances of up to 5 kilometres between high and low water mark. Here there are significant beds of the eelgrasses. The animal communities on the bed of the Lough reflect the varied substrates. In 'the Narrows' at the entrance to the Lough currents can reach up to 8 knots and encrusting

Seawater pours over a rock sill at low tide in Strangford Lough, County Down, creating unusual conditions for seashore life.

Lough Hyne, County Cork.
This tidal lake is probably
the best studied marine
environment in Ireland.
'The Rapids' at the narrow
entrance can be seen at
the top of the picture
(Richard T. Mills).

forms such as sponges and soft corals predominate. Where the Lough widens out, currents slow down to about 3 knots and the mobile sands are colonised by sea cucumbers and dog cockles. In the deeper areas coarse sands are virtually covered by a living carpet of brittlestars.

In the western and central parts, where currents decline to about 1 knot, one of the unique communities of Strangford Lough is found. The main species here is the large horse mussel, which lives attached to the empty shells of former generations of mussels partly buried in soft mud. The living mussels are encrusted by a huge variety of life, including hydroids, sponges, barnacles, sea squirts and polychaete worms. Other mobile species such as variegated scallops and porcelain crabs live in the shelter of the mussel community. Recent dredging of scallops has caused major damage to these horse mussel beds and all of the rich community which they support. As the lough shallows around the islands and reefs, greater shelter allows dense colonies of sea squirts to dominate the seabed. Finally, in the most sheltered areas, where only the finest silts occur, animal

life is predominantly of the burrowing type. This includes the Dublin Bay prawn and burrowing brittlestars. These communities have evolved with the evolution of the seabed habitats.

Another virtually land-locked, although much smaller, sea inlet is Lough Hyne, County Cork. The most important features here are the deep water (average 40 metres), high salinity (close to that of seawater outside) and 'the Rapids', where the tidal current surges across a rock sill. Lough Hyne has been studied intensely by marine biologists for over a century and over 250 scientific publications have resulted from this work. A number of clear zones have been identified in Lough Hyne, including the littoral zone between high and low water mark; the shallow sublittoral rocky areas down to about 2 metres below low water mark; the fine mud zones covered with broken shells of molluscs and the red seaweed *Audouinella floridula*; the mud-burrow zone with numerous animals such as the Dublin Bay prawn; and the very deepest parts which are occupied by worm tubes standing up out of the mud.[3,4]

Clare Island, County Mayo. This view was made famous by the photographer Robert J. Welch who was part of a ground-breaking biological survey undertaken by the Royal Irish Academy in the years 1909-11.

Lough Hyne was the site for some of the earliest field experiments, which were to transform marine biology.[5] For example, it was noticed that the common mussel was abundant in both the most sheltered parts of the Lough and on the most exposed, wave-lashed rocks outside, but was uncommon everywhere in between these two extremes. To find the cause, the researchers transplanted mussels into the intermediate locations and found that they were rapidly eaten by crabs and starfish – predators which were uncommon at the more extreme sites.[6] This convinced the biologists that certain key organisms – predators, herbivores and competitors – had a determining role in the structure of the marine communities. Some of these experiments were achieved with the ingenious use of rather simple equipment. To map the movement of seawater as it entered the lough, researchers used baby's feeding bottles filled with warm jelly and set at different depths on a rope. In the cool water, the jelly began to set but as the bottles were deflected by the current the jelly set at an angle, reflecting the current velocity. Green dye was also released in the entrance to the lough in order to track the currents around the lough. Pipes deployed at different depths were used

to measure the degree of mixing of the dye in the water. The magic of those early days at the Lough Hyne marine laboratory is captured in a humorous way by Trevor Norton[7] in his book *Reflections on a Summer Sea*.

Also in Cork, the rocky inlet of Kinsale Harbour and its approaches has been well studied by the late Dr Brendan Keegan and a team of marine biologists from Galway.[8] The sediments of the inlet vary from exposed bedrock to clean sand with pockets of silt-clay carried down the Bandon River. The bottom sediments are colonised by a highly diverse, species-rich marine fauna that has been subdivided into four main assemblages. On the shoreline (littoral), a rich variety of seaweeds harbours a diverse animal community including typical barnacles, mussels and limpets on the more exposed upper shores with sponges, bryozoans and the blue-rayed limpet on the lower shore only. The natural ridges and hollows in the bedrock provide shelter for anemones (*Actinia* and *Sagartia*) and dog whelks normally associated with deeper water.

Clare Island, County Mayo, was the site of the famous survey of 1909-11, led by Robert Lloyd Praeger, which produced a stunning inventory of marine flora and fauna. In recent years a *New Survey of Clare Island* has been produced, also by the Royal Irish Academy. Volume 3 of the New Survey is concerned with Marine Intertidal Ecology[9] and a significant proportion of this is devoted to the study of molluscs including limpets and mussels, in one of the most exposed locations in Europe. One of the study sites on the island, at Leckacanny, faces into the full onslaught of Atlantic swell and, to add to the difficulties of studying it, the upper zone is regularly coated with a slime of blue-green and red algae. Barnacles and mussels are the dominant animals in these conditions, where severe wave energy would dislodge any but the most closely fixed life forms.

Other bays and inlets which have a long history of marine biology research and survey

include Cork Harbour, Galway Bay and Dublin Bay, but these are described in Chapters 4 and 5.

Birds of Rocky Shores

One of the most widespread, though least conspicuous, birds of rocky shores is the rock pipit. This little songbird flits about within the splash zone where it finds a combination of marine and terrestrial invertebrate food between the tidelines. Rocky shores are often used as high-tide roosts for large concentrations of waders from nearby estuaries. Those waders that spend the majority of their time feeding on these rocky shores tend to congregate in smaller numbers. Rocky and bouldery shores, encrusted with mussels and barnacles, are a favourite habitat for the curlew and oystercatcher. Around the weed-covered pools and shingle shores the observant birdwatcher will see small flocks of turnstone, purple sandpiper, ringed plover and dunlin. The turnstone, as its name suggests, feeds by overturning stones and seaweed in search of small invertebrates. Occasionally, after winter storms, a large bank of kelp and other brown seaweed is cast up on exposed beaches, as in Quilty, County Clare. Here the weedy debris begins to decompose, attracting flies and sandhoppers and providing a feast for many of the small waders as well as pipits, pied wagtails and starlings.

Until recently little was known about the distribution and numbers of these rocky shore waders in Ireland. A partial survey was carried out on parts of the west coast in the 1980s[10] indicating that there were significant numbers

(left) Low spring tides expose the thick beds of kelp which carpet the rocky shores on many Atlantic coasts; (right) purple sandpiper is one of the typical winter birds on rocky shores where it feeds in the intertidal zone (Sean Pierce).

of waders outside the estuaries and bays. Then, in winter 1997/98, a more extensive survey of non-estuarine waterfowl species was organised throughout Ireland.[11] Although coverage on this survey was limited on the west coast, the results confirm the importance of the non-estuarine areas. Oystercatcher and curlew are the most widespread and numerous species, probably because they feed on the hard-shelled molluscs like mussels and periwinkles that are so common on rocky shores. Ringed plover and sanderling are especially common on west coast beaches. Redshank and turnstone are widespread on all coasts in relatively small numbers. The most restricted of the regular species on rocky shores is the purple sandpiper, which hardly ever appears on sand or mud, but seems to focus on rocky shores with good cover of brown seaweeds. Here they move about rapidly in pursuit of small shellfish and crustaceans like crabs and shrimps. When roosting at high tide they are quite difficult to spot as their dark colours hide them very effectively against the weed.

Barnacle Goose

While some waterbirds favour sheltered bays and estuaries, others prefer the more exposed rocky shores. Brent geese move from feeding in mudflats during the early winter to searching for green algae on rocky shores, as the food resources become depleted. The remote and mainly deserted islands and headlands of the west coast are valuable habitats for another of Ireland's wild goose species. This is the barnacle goose, so called because at one time it was believed that the bird and the shellfish were two stages in the life cycle of the same animal. There has clearly been some confusion over the centuries between the two black and white species of geese, the brent and the barnacle, as the former were also known as barnacles to early hunters. However, they are quite distinctive in their appearance, habits and migrations, despite both being members of the genus *Branta*. The barnacle geese that winter in Ireland are from a population which breeds on the north-eastern coast of Greenland. They are relatively long-lived birds with a low breeding success and low mortality which makes them ideal subjects for long-term population studies, such as those carried out in Ireland by David Cabot.[12,13] This study, which is still ongoing, has focused on the wintering geese on the Inishkea Island group of County Mayo, although the flocks increasingly visit the mainland to feed. Here, despite a steadily increasing world population, the Inishkea area reached its carrying capacity for geese in the 1970s and has only slightly increased since.

I have been fortunate to share a few days with these magnificent geese on the deserted islands

(left) Barnacle goose feeding on short grazed maritime grassland; (below right) Inishtrahull, County Donegal, the most northerly land in Ireland, is one of the islands used regularly by wintering barnacle geese (Sean Pierce).

Lissadell, County Sligo is one of the few mainland locations regularly used by wintering barnacle geese. The nearby cliffs of Benbulbin resemble the landscapes where the geese breed in East Greenland.

of the Inishkeas. From the vantage point of the old village street, abandoned in the 1930s, I watched thousands of geese moving across the island pastures, which are totally exposed to the high winds off the Atlantic Ocean. These fields are patterned by the old 'lazy bed' cultivation ridges, which probably date back to the nineteenth century and show that the islands were once intensively farmed.[14] The birds are undisturbed now except by the occasional visit from a passing fishing boat and they share these old pastures with sheep and cattle owned by the former island families. Amazingly the cattle, which graze the islands, have developed a habit of hoovering up the droppings left by the geese, as these contain a high nutrient and mineral content and are valuable winter feeding for the stock. The barnacle geese fly between the various islands in the archipelago, their strong quills scything the air as they move overhead in a V-shaped formation.

A whole string of similar grassy islands, from Inishtrahull in north Donegal to the Maharees, and occasionally the Blaskets in County Kerry,

are winter haunts for small flocks of barnacle geese. These flocks are censused approximately every five years by aircraft and the results show a steadily rising population in line with the remaining wintering areas in Scotland.[15] One of the few mainland haunts used by the barnacle geese is around Lissadel in County Sligo. Many times, I have stood here on one side of an ordinary hedgerow, while on the other side, hundreds of arctic breeding geese 'talk' to each other as they graze the short grass. Here the birds prefer the larger coastal fields within sight of the magnificent cliffs and scree of Benbulbin.

Such landscapes must be familiar in outline to the geese, as their breeding grounds in East Greenland include similar tall cliffs and scree above the ice-filled glacial valleys. In 1984 I was fortunate to join an Irish expedition following the geese back to their breeding grounds in the coastal valleys of Jameson Land at about 72 degrees North on the Greenland coast.[16] Here the geese choose to nest in small colonies high on cliff ledges where they are out of reach of their main predator, the arctic fox. Nevertheless,

(top) A family party of chough flies in to feed in a sand dune area on the west coast; (right) chough in flight (Eddie Dunne).

Chough

One of the characteristic sounds of west coast headlands and islands, for me, is the call of the chough, a rare member of the crow family. Many times I have watched these marvellous birds soaring, tumbling and spiralling on the updrafts from a cliff or feeding on the cliff pastures or sand dune grasslands. Distinguished firstly by its bright red bill and legs, the chough is a specialist of Atlantic coastlands because it relies for food on probing the soil and sandy shores for invertebrates. The influence of the warm Gulf Stream means that Ireland's west coast rarely if ever experiences frozen ground and the chough can feed unhindered in this chosen habitat throughout the year. However, it does rely on short grassland or heath for feeding and the exposure of cliff-top grassland to high wind and salt spray tends to keep it short. Grazing of this habitat by sheep or rabbits, as on the Great Blasket Island, produces an ideal sward for the chough. Along the northern Irish coast, where grazing pressures are reduced and scrub invades the grassland, populations of chough are virtually extinct.[17]

David Cabot has shown that there is a very low breeding success and much of this can be attributed to predation of the goslings by arctic fox and by aerial predators such as raven, gulls and the beautiful gyr falcon. As the short arctic summer draws to a close, the goose flocks move off to their autumn staging ground in Iceland before arriving in the wintering areas of western Scotland and western Ireland during October. The sight of a skein of wild barnacle geese flying in off the Atlantic Ocean directly from Iceland to land on an Irish coast is one to stir the spirit.

In spring individual pairs of chough hold breeding territories along stretches of cliff where they often choose to nest on a ledge within a crevice or cave. Ruined signal stations and Norman castles are also popular nest sites for chough. Unusual nesting places are occasionally found, such as the old slate mines of Valentia Island, where artificial caves have created a suitable habitat for the birds. In late summer it is common to see family parties of chough moving about on top of the cliffs or performing aerial acrobatics in the strong updrafts at the cliff face. As autumn moves into winter, the families coalesce into larger winter flocks, which move around between traditional feeding areas. These areas are clearly crucial to the survival of the population as flocks of between 50 and 100 birds are common in some places. Such areas include large sand dune systems, machair plains and sandy beaches. Here they move along the strand line like waders turning over the seaweed, to pick up the sandhoppers and other delicacies which they find there. The choughs also form communal night roosts in winter.

Birds of Prey

Ireland's largest falcon, the peregrine, is found thinly distributed on remote headlands and islands around the Irish coast. These spectacular flyers prefer to nest on some of the most inaccessible crags and in traditional locations, which have been used for many centuries. Here they prey on rock doves and smaller seabirds, especially kittiwakes and, when the opportunity arises they take passing racing pigeons. These must seem like easy pickings to a bird that can dive at speeds over 150 kilometres per hour. The other common falcon of Ireland's coastlands is the kestrel, which is equally at home among the cliffs and crags, also nesting in deserted buildings and towers. In the mid-nineteenth century Irish naturalists were well used to seeing two magnificent species of eagle on the Irish coastline. William Thompson[18]

A peregrine falcon nests on the sea cliffs of Bray Head, County Wicklow.

recorded significant populations of golden eagle and the larger white-tailed sea eagle nesting on many islands and headlands. Unfortunately, by the end of the nineteenth century both species were in severe decline due to human persecution, especially poisoning.[19] Today, we are left to imagine these magnificent raptors soaring above the cliffs and beaches but, with a re-introduction programme for the golden eagle underway at Glenveagh National Park in Donegal, it is quite possible that the remoter Irish coastline will be re-occupied by eagles over the coming decades.

Seabird Colonies

Few sights in nature can compare with the spectacular concentration of birds in a large seabird colony. The most sheer and inaccessible cliffs are chosen because they provide refuge from ground predators such as fox and stoat. Among the most characteristic cliff-breeding species are kittiwake, razorbill and guillemot, their clamouring calls echoing around the cliffs as they reflect from the rock surfaces. Kittiwakes appear to cement their nests to the vertical rock surface while the razorbills and guillemots occupy narrow ledges without making any proper nest at all. Among the jumble of boulders and crevices at the foot of the cliff, other seabirds such as the shag and black guillemot find suitable nesting places.

(Clockwise from left) Roseate tern at Rockabill, County Dublin (Oscar Merne); Richard Nairn at the gannet colony on Great Saltee, County Wexford; nesting gannets with downy chick (Oscar Merne).

Fulmars prefer to nest in narrow ledges, often on soil or among vegetation, near the tops of the cliff. On the grassy slopes above the cliff top there are colonies of the larger gulls and occasional groups of cormorant. However, the most precipitous cliff sites are reserved for the largest Irish breeding seabird, the gannet, which is found in only five colonies around the Irish coast. On certain steep slopes on islands and headlands, several seabird species, including puffin, storm petrel and Manx shearwater, nest in underground burrows, the latter two emerging only at night when they are safe from aerial predators.

The excitement of visiting a large seabird colony is typified by my first trip with a group of bird ringers to the Saltee Islands off south Wexford. As we approached the larger island the numbers of feeding seabirds around the boat increased markedly. Climbing up from the landing place we could smell the distinctive seabird guano which pervades the island air. Then, on a walk along the cliff top, the secrets of the island cliffs were revealed. The large mixed colonies of razorbill, guillemot and kittiwake packed into impossibly narrow ledges while the feeding birds flew to and from the cliff face carrying fish from the ocean. At the highest cliffs on the southern tip of the island an expanding colony of gannets nests in tightly packed regularity. Their sharp sword-like bills provide ample deterrent to prevent neighbours from encroaching on the small area around each nest. Camping on the island through several summer nights, we became accustomed also to the night-time calls of gulls and Manx shearwaters, to the sunburn and the salt winds, and to the rhythm of island life.

Most of the really big seabird colonies are on island cliffs. Some are isolated islands such as Rathlin and Lambay while more are part of island groups such as the Blaskets and Skelligs of County Kerry. Most of these islands have been visited at one time by Oscar Merne. His review of Irish seabird islands showed that several Irish islands held substantial parts of the

*(Clockwise from top left)
A fulmar hangs in the
updrafts near its clifftop
nest (Oscar Merne); a puffin
stands on the slopes at the
top of the cliff (Oscar Merne);
the cormorant colony on
Lambay Island, County
Dublin; a cormorant dries
its wings in the sun to
improve their waterproofing.*

world population of species such as storm petrel, Manx shearwater and gannet.[20] The first national census of seabirds, known as Operation Seafarer, was carried out in 1969-70.[21] A second inventory of seabird colonies was prepared in the mid-1980s and this considerably improved our understanding of Irish breeding seabird populations.[22] This showed, in addition, that Ireland holds significant parts of the British and Irish populations of cormorant, razorbill and roseate tern. A third international census called 'Seabird 2000' has been organised in Ireland by Stephen Newton and the changes which it records provide another fascinating insight to seabird population dynamics.[23]

A century ago, the fulmar was a rare sight in Irish waters. Two great ornithologists of the nineteenth century, Ussher and Warren[24] concluded that this species 'seldom or never comes to the shores of Ireland except by accident'. They believed that, 'though apparently avoiding the vicinity of land, fulmars have been often seen by the Rev W.S. Green and

Black guillemot, a widely dispersed nesting seabird on rocky shores (Sean Pierce).

Mr Holt, who accompanied him, when they went out from ten to twenty miles west of the Irish coast'. It was on the north-west coast that the first nesting of fulmar was recorded, on the north Mayo cliffs in 1911 and in Donegal in 1912. Following this colonisation, fulmars spread quickly around the Irish coast and by the first full census in 1969-70, over 19,000 pairs were estimated. This remarkable population boom was part of a general expansion of the species from its arctic base to the south, all around the coasts of north-west Europe. Some biologists believe that the expansion of the breeding range was fuelled by the discarded waste from whalers in the North Atlantic and then from the trawlers of Europe's expanding fishing fleet. Whatever the reasons, the longevity and low mortality of adult fulmars have certainly made them permanent occupants of most seabird colonies in Ireland.

One of the single most important seabird colonies in Ireland is Lambay Island off the coast of County Dublin. To reach the island a boat is chartered from the nearby harbour of Skerries or Rogerstown pier. Lambay is a privately owned bird sanctuary and was the location for an early natural history survey in 1905-1906, led by the naturalist Robert Lloyd Praeger.[25] The western side of the island, which faces the mainland, is low and fertile, while the northern, eastern and southern parts are rocky and surrounded by substantial cliffs. The abundant seabirds and eggs on these cliffs were harvested by the then owner, Lord Revelstoke, during the Second World War (1939-1945) for export to help with food shortages in Britain. Lambay's seabirds have been the subject of a special study during the 1980s and 1990s.[26] The island holds the largest cormorant colony in Ireland or Britain and the largest colonies in Ireland of razorbill, guillemot, shag, herring gull, great black-backed gull and kittiwake.

Even up to the mid-1980s significant gaps remained in our knowledge of Irish seabird colonies. To fill one of these gaps, all the islands in the Blasket group were censused by a team

of twelve ornithologists in 1988.[27] As well as the first accurate census of seabirds on the islands, this expedition suggested the breeding of Leach's storm petrel, a very rare seabird in the north-east Atlantic. Taped recordings of the birds' calls were broadcast in the night air attracting them to fly into mist nests from which they were recovered, examined, ringed and released. In May to July 2000 another group of hardy ornithologists camped on the Blaskets and on Puffin Island and, using tape recorded calls and climbing equipment, they checked a large sample of the burrows for occupancy to reach a meaningful estimate of the huge storm petrel and Manx shearwater populations which are largely unseen by the casual day visitor.

The Seabird 2000 project has, for the first time, provided a true population estimate of black guillemot, one of the most widely dispersed of Irish breeding seabirds. Easily distinguished by their bright red feet, these dapper black and white birds are mostly found in sheltered rocky coastlines where they nest in crevices, and even in holes in harbour walls. They differ from many of the other seabirds in returning to nesting colonies as early as the end of March, so the census work is quite specific and must be concentrated in the early morning when the birds are most obvious near the nest sites. Now we know there are at least 4,500 black guillemots in the island of Ireland.[28] They are mainly seen in isolated pairs, although small colonies do nest in preferred habitats, such as the harbour wall in Bangor, County Down.

Also on the east coast, a tiny island of Rockabill, County Dublin, holds the largest single colony of the rare roseate tern, comprising 85 per cent of its breeding population in north-west Europe. This colony has been intensively studied over the past decade and, since the lighthouse keepers were withdrawn in the late 1980s, a wardening scheme has been provided here by BirdWatch Ireland and the National Parks and Wildlife Service. Following serious declines in the Irish and British population of these sensitive birds in the 1970s, numbers recovered slowly to about 870 pairs in 1999.[29] The terns have taken to wooden nest boxes all over Rockabill and this has allowed a much greater breeding success, as the tiny chicks are sheltered from predators and bad weather. The presence of full-time wardens on Rockabill has allowed detailed scientific monitoring of the birds to be carried out. Close observation of the fish food brought back to the nests shows that sand eels are the predominant food exchanged between adults, but that substantial amounts of sprat and occasional juvenile herring are delivered to the small chicks. While feeding chicks the adults catch their food within a 10-kilometre radius of the colony. By August, many of the terns have already left their nesting site and are feeding and roosting on the Kish lighthouse and in other parts of Dublin Bay, where the shallow sandy waters provide the fish they need to fatten up for the long migration back to West Africa.

Seabird Ringing

The scientific study of seabirds has been much improved since the introduction of large-scale ringing or banding. This involves trapping the bird unharmed, placing a uniquely numbered metal ring on its leg and releasing it to return to its normal behaviour. Subsequent recoveries of these ringed seabirds have proved conclusively where they spend the winter months, how long they survive and have also demonstrated the interchange between different breeding colonies. For example, most guillemots, ringed on Great Saltee Island off Wexford move south in winter to the Bay of Biscay off western France but the adult birds remain closer to Ireland returning to the colonies in early spring. Similarly, juvenile gannets disperse greater distances than the adults, many wintering off north-west Africa. Irish sandwich terns regularly migrate as far as South Africa, even reaching Durban in the Indian Ocean.[30]

(left) Doulus Head, County Kerry. The horizontal rock strata form ideal nesting places for guillemots and razorbills but any eggs lost in storms drop straight down to the seabed (Nigel Motyer); *(right) Razorbills migrate south to warmer waters in winter.*

Information on the causes of mortality can be gleaned by examining the ringing returns. For example razorbills and guillemots die in significant numbers each year through drowning in monofilament drift nets. Only one attempt has been made to quantify such mortality in Ireland when Tony Whilde counted 763 razorbills and guillemots removed from fishing nets in one summer at ports around Galway Bay.[31] These birds were thought to originate from the Cliffs of Moher but there was insufficient information to assess the impact of the drownings on the huge colonies.

Ringed or marked seabirds have also been helpful in determining the origins of the populations affected by natural disasters. In the autumn of 1969 thousands of razorbills and guillemots were picked up on beaches all around the Irish Sea. Although the tissues of these birds contained high levels of the industrial bi-products polychlorinated biphenols (PCBs), the actual cause of death was thought to be starvation due to prolonged autumn gales.[32,33]

Large numbers of cormorants have been ringed at the colonies on Little Saltee Island since the 1960s. In winter many Irish-bred cormorants migrate to the waters of France, Spain and Portugal. Here they have been found in the oil spilled from such shipping disasters as that off north-west Spain in late 2002. Other cormorants disperse around the Irish and British coastline and many move into fresh waters where they feed on salmon and trout, among other fish, thus bringing them into direct conflict with angling and fisheries' interests.

Grey Seals

Another animal that has a habit of getting into conflict with fisheries is the grey seal. There are few more fascinating marine animals than seals. Seen close up, they have remarkably large, almost human eyes, they are close to humans in body size and, like us, they have a complex social life. They also seem to be nearly as curious about us as we are about them. But seals live in two worlds. They are intelligent air-breathing mammals, which breed on land but they spend more than half their lives in the sea. They are superbly adapted to the coastal environment in which they live. Their body shape is highly streamlined for swimming with no protrusion except for flippers, which are short and powerful. The ears and nipples are retracted into cavities in the body wall. Unlike whales and dolphins they have a fur coat, or pelage, for insulation against the cold water. But they share with cetaceans the thick layer of fat, known as blubber, beneath the skin. This can be up to 6 centimetres thick.

To catch fish seals have to be adept at diving and to do this they have evolved several unique features. Dives can last between four and eight minutes and, to survive, seals carry large reserves of oxygen attached to haemoglobin in the blood and myoglobin in the muscles. They can also make a rapid exchange of carbon dioxide for oxygen when they come to the surface, thus stocking up for another long dive. This allows them to make a series of relatively short dives, replenishing their oxygen supply in between. For longer dives they can reduce the depletion of oxygen from the blood by slowing the heart rate to just a few beats per minute and, by doing so, can stay underwater for up to 30 minutes.

After such extreme exertion, seals have to spend more time on the surface recovering the lost oxygen in the blood and muscles. They also spend long periods each day hauled out on land resting and digesting their food. During the breeding season more time is spent on land – giving birth, suckling the newborn pup, mating and moulting the fur coat. Such haul outs are usually in traditional sites and give us the best opportunities to observe seals and seal behaviour closely.

Grey seal, showing the typical long straight profile of the head and large blotches on the fur.

A grey seal in its underwater habitat. Large reserves of oxygen in the blood allow these mammals to dive for long periods (Nigel Motyer).

Seal Habitats

Although mixed haul outs of both seals are not uncommon outside the breeding seasons, each species favours particular habitat types for the breeding assemblies. Grey seals seek out the more remote and exposed coasts, especially on deserted islands and cliff coastlines. Harbour (or common) seals, by contrast, prefer the sheltered waters of sandy bays and the low rocky shores which are often found in inlets and estuaries (see Chapter 4). The reasons for this disparity in habitat choice is probably linked with the vulnerability of each species to predation, disturbance and hunting in the past. The grey seal pup is confined to land for up to three weeks after birth while the harbour seal pup can swim almost immediately it is born. Those grey seals born on accessible coasts do not usually survive because of human interference (or predation by land mammals). Thus, natural selection has probably given an advantage to those which breed on the remoter coasts.

The differences in the season of pupping between the two species may also be connected with this dependence on land. The harbour seal breeds in mid-summer while the more vulnerable grey seal pups are born between September and December, which is often a wild and stormy period of the year. Perhaps the storms have protected those pups born on remote islands and headlands as hunters and fishermen would have been unable to land there. So, the habitat type often gives a hint to the species of seal that can be expected there.

The largest haul out of grey seals in Ireland is found on the remote Inishkea Islands off the coast of Mayo. Here, on a sandy bay on the northern island, up to 1,000 seals have been counted by David Cabot. A large number of these are immigrant Scottish seals as the total breeding population on the Inishkeas is estimated to be not more than 693 animals. This is based on a detailed series of counts of pups carried out in the islands by Oliver Ó Cadhla in the autumn of 1995.[34] He found that the pupping season began with the first pregnant females coming ashore in September, peaked in October and continued until December. It is quite an experience to crawl quietly up to one of these large haul outs and listen to the noise and communication between the animals as they vie for space on the shore.

The other large grey seal assembly occurs on the Blasket Islands. Here, several hundred animals now haul out on Trá Bán, the beach, where islanders used to play hurley a century ago. There are smaller breeding groups of grey seals in a variety of locations including Rathlin Island, County Antrim; Slieve Toohy, County Donegal; Saltee Islands, County Wexford and Lambay Island, County Dublin. Some of these animals give birth in caves and the pups do not see the sunlight until they take to the water after about three weeks. Many pups, however, are washed into the sea by storms or die as a result of separation from their mothers in the first few weeks.

Seals are often accused of causing serious damage to fisheries, either by eating significant quantities of commercial fish or by causing damage to fish in nets and to fishing gear. However, few detailed studies of the problem have been carried out. A recent study at Youghal, County Cork and Dunmore East, County Waterford, showed that the average incidence of seal damage to monkfish landings was only 10 per cent and that crabs and skinners caused much more damage to these fish in the nets. Occasionally the seals themselves become tangled and drown in the nets. These are usually immature animals and are known as bycatch seals. Their post-mortem analysis gives us additional information on their diet. There is a striking predominance of whiting

(above) A cuckoo wrasse is a typical inshore fish of rocky shores (Nigel Motyer); (left) Trá Bán on Great Blasket Island, County Kerry where a large group of grey seals hauls out to breed in the autumn.

in the stomachs of grey seals in the Celtic Sea but faecal samples collected at haul-out sites suggest that flatfish are dominant in the Irish Sea area.[35]

One of the most interesting findings of research in the Irish Sea has been the new information on movements and interchange between grey seal colonies. Many individuals were identified by photographing the markings on their heads, which have a combination of light and dark blotches. Resightings of these individuals shows that the greatest number of movements is between colonies off Wexford and south-west Wales, with no interaction recorded between the Wexford sites and those off north Dublin, including Lambay Island.

Seal Legends

Seals regularly feature in Irish storytelling, as seal mothers nursing human children, as the reincarnation of fishermen lost at sea or as females luring unsuspecting seafarers to their deaths. These legends were collected by the author David Thomson on his travels in western Ireland and Scotland and retold in his classic book, *People of the Sea*.[36] One of the more believable tales is of five fishermen who were swept out to sea in a storm off the coast of north Mayo. After several days of drifting out into the Atlantic and living on raw fish, which they had caught in their nets, they saw a seal and attracted it close to the boat by throwing fish to it. Eventually the seal set off and they followed it until they came within sight of land and were rescued by a coastguard in south Donegal. The men eventually walked back to their home parish arriving in the middle of a wake, which was being held to mark their loss at sea.

Many of these legends contain a mixture of truth and imagination but reveal the respect that coastal communities had for these intelligent mammals. The desertion of many offshore islands, such as the Blaskets or the Inishkeas, and the cessation of hunting, has led to a recovery in seal populations in these remote haunts, as the 'people of the sea' reclaim their natural habitats.

Coastal Otters

Once, on a wild headland in Donegal, I was watching a pair of choughs when an otter bounded along a fence line and disappeared down a cliff into the sea. In the busy fishing

An otter feeding on a western shoreline. They often swim to offshore islands (Éamon de Buitléar).

*(left) An otter cub emerges
warily on a rocky shore
(Éamon de Buitléar);
(below) a Tom Pot blenny
peers out of its rocky crevice
(Nigel Motyer).*

harbour of Wicklow town, an otter regularly feeds along the back of the piers in the early morning light. On the Aran Islands I have picked up the unmistakable loping track of an otter on a sandy beach only to lose it in the tide further along. Most of all, the distinctive spraints (or droppings) with their musty smell, can often be found in prominent places where they are left as territorial markers or coded messages for other otters to find.

Despite their popular association with lakes and rivers, otters in Ireland are just as common on the coast and in the sea. They will even swim to offshore islands and are quite active by daylight in little disturbed areas of the west coast. They love to feed among the kelp of rocky coasts where they can easily catch rock fish and crabs. They will collect shellfish from the rocks or scavenge for debris on the strandline. However, at some stage each day, they seek out a source of freshwater as they need to wash the salt from their fur to improve its water-proof qualities. Pat Smiddy, who has walked most of the coasts of Waterford and east Cork as part of his work as a Conservation Ranger, regularly finds concentrations of otter spraints near the mouths of streams and rivers.

The diet of coastal otters on the west coast of Ireland has been studied by James Fairley and his colleagues at the National University of Ireland, Galway. They collected otter spraints on a monthly basis over a full year around the shores of Inishmore in the Aran Islands, and analysed the hard remains – mainly fish bones and scales.[37] Not surprisingly, they found that the otters were feeding mainly on the commonest rock fish such as rockling and wrasse, which together made up about 70 per cent of the food. Less frequent items included eel, sea scorpion, blenny, various shellfish and the purple sea urchin, which lives in rock pools on the limestone shores of the west. The preferred prey is common, slow-swimming and is mainly found on rocky shores among the dense beds of seaweed. The otters use these as cover in the same way that predators on land lie up in dense vegetation. In a more sheltered location on the south shore of Galway Bay a similar study found that the otters took a greater diversity of fish prey and more smaller items such as goby and butterfish.[38] The researchers concluded that otters generally avoided feeding in sandy shores where fish were perhaps less abundant and harder to catch and, where prey was abundant, they took the largest and most nutritious items available.

The otter is more common and widespread in Ireland than in any other European country and this may, in part, be linked with the long and varied coastline, much of which is relatively undisturbed and rich in fish prey. Watching otters requires great patience and these techniques have been perfected by the film-maker Éamon de Buitléar. In his ground-breaking films of these sensitive animals, he has captured some won-derful close-up images of otters with their young on the coasts of Counties Mayo and Galway. He has shown that storms at sea can cause young otter cubs to drown where there is no shelter available.

Island Mammals

Paddy Sleeman has been studying badgers for many years on several island sites including Fota Island, County Cork; Coney Island, County Sligo and Rutland Island, County Donegal. He is convinced that some of these groups of mammals have developed characteristics that are unique to their isolated homes. On Coney Island, most of the badgers have white noses, while the usual colour is black. On Rutland, the animals are so much smaller in body size than mainland animals that they were originally mistaken for mink.

Conversely, some other mammals have significantly larger forms living on islands. James Fairley, the doyen of Irish mammal studies, admits to 'something of a shock' when he weighed the first long-tailed field mouse which he caught on Rathlin Island, County Antrim, in 1963. On the mainland any over 25 grams in weight are regarded as big while, of the seventeen field mice that Fairley trapped on Rathlin, only three weighed less than 30 grams. A more extensive study, carried out by Pat Kelly, a student of Fairley, found that Irish field mice from a range of island and mainland sites fall into several distinct groups.[39] Those from mainland sites and also from Achill Island, which is joined to the mainland by a bridge, were all rather similar. However, mice trapped on a total of eleven offshore islands were rather similar to each other, in size and weight. The biggest of Ireland's field mice come from Rathlin and the Great Blasket Island, County Kerry. Individuals from the Great Blasket also have larger hind feet and this, Fairley postulates, may be an advantage in moving about on the steep slopes on this island. Overall, Fairley believes that the

A badger on Coney Island, County Sligo, with the white nose which is characteristic of this isolated population (Paddy Sleeman).

absence of ground predators, such as fox and stoat, on many of the offshore islands has allowed natural selection to favour the larger sized animals, as there is no advantage in being small to escape underground.[40]

A famous population of house mice lives on the North Bull Island in Dublin Bay. This three-mile long sand dune spit developed as a result of the building of the Bull Wall in the early nineteenth century. Initially it was joined only by a wooden bridge but, in 1965, it was linked to the mainland by a causeway. At the beginning of the twentieth century it was discovered that many of the house mice on the island had a sandy colour to their coats. This was taken to be a form of protective colouring which the mice had evolved to avoid the attention of predators such as kestrels and short-eared owls. The presence of these sandy-coloured mice was confirmed recently by James Fairley but he has also demonstrated that there

is a huge natural variation in the colour of this household pest and that it is not valid to describe the sandy variety as a separate race.[41]

Island Flora

The flora of offshore islands held a fascination for many early naturalists because of the quest to understand how the plants had reached their isolated destination. This is exemplified by Robert Lloyd Praeger who gives in his autobiography, *The Way that I Went*,[42] a table of the number of plants found on six major Atlantic islands. He believed that 'the figures will not be much increased by future work'. He considered that the discrepancies mean, 'that variety of habitat, not size, is the important thing'. He also concluded that distance from the mainland was unimportant and that 'either the flora arrived on the islands before they became separated, or else the plants succeeded

(left) A harebell on a west coast island; (right) typical cliff flora on the east coast.

in the course of time in crossing the intervening channels'.

These conclusions, perhaps regarded as obvious to modern ecologists, were quite new in the late nineteeth and early twentieth centuries. We have only to think of the momentous outcome of Darwin's studies on the origin of species in the Galapagos Islands in the Pacific Ocean to understand why islands were at the cutting edge of scientific discussion of the time. Such puzzles were part of the reason for Praeger's drive to undertake major surveys of such places as Lambay Island, County Dublin and Clare Island, County Mayo. The Clare Island Survey became one of the most complete accounts of the natural and human history of any island in Europe. The island is almost completely cliff bound and measures several kilometres across at its widest point. Over the three-year period (1909-1911), more than 100 naturalists, including volunteers from all over Europe, took part in the survey which was co-ordinated by Praeger. In all, some 3,219 species of plants were listed, 585 of which were new to Ireland, and 11 new to science – mostly algae and fungi. The total fauna recorded comprised 5,269 species, 1,253 of which were new to Ireland and 109 new to science. It was one of the greatest achievements of Praeger's life and of Irish natural science.[43]

3

Sand and Shingle Shores

Blowing sand is trapped by the marram grass growing at the top of a Mayo beach.

As the power of the sea erodes the exposed rocky headlands and cliffs, it produces large quantities of sand and cobbles that are deposited in sheltered bays and shingle beaches. These sediments are worked and reworked by the marine currents and eventually end up on a sandy beach or on a storm beach. Such habitats have characteristic plants and animals that are repeatedly found around the coastline.

Soft Shores

The eventful history of a single sand grain, as described evocatively by marine biologist Rachel

Carson in her book *The Edge of the Sea*,[1] could easily apply to an Irish sand grain.

Before it was sand, it was rock – splintered by the chisels of the frost, crushed under advancing glaciers and carried forward with the ice in its slow advance, then ground and polished in the mill of the surf. And long ages before the advance of the ice, some of the rock had come up into the light of the sun from the black interior of the earth by ways unseen and for the most part unknown, made fluid by subterranean fires and rising along deep pipes and fissures. Now, in this particular moment of its history, it belongs to the sea's edge – swept up and down the beaches with the tides or drifted alongshore with the currents, continuously sifted and sorted, packed down, washed out, or set adrift again, as always and endlessly the waves work over the sands.

The term 'soft shores' is a little misleading as many of these coastlines are comprised of stones of various sizes. However, they have at least the common feature that most are found in sheltered areas where the sea is depositing rather than eroding. The sediment is generally unstable in that it can be moved by tidal currents, by storms or by the wind. Compared to rocky shores, these soft muddy and sandy coastlines look at first barren and devoid of life. However, because of the unstable nature of the surface, most of the animal life is of the burrowing type. The proportion of soft coastline varies from county to county with Donegal, Mayo, Kerry and Wexford high in the sandy beach stakes.

Beach sand becomes part of a seasonal cycle of movement between the shallow inshore waters and the strandline at the top of the beach. If there is a river entering the sea, its mouth may move backwards and forwards over a longer cycle of years, causing erosion on one side and accretion on the other only to be followed by the reverse situation a few years later. Where the sandy beach is wide the wind will do its work and blow the sand into dunes behind the shore. These can take many forms, from the familiar marram-covered sandhills of the south and east to the sand plains or machair of the northwest.

Larger sediment size, from gravel and shingle up to boulders, produces a typically steep beach front and a distinctive flora and fauna. Sand, shingle and muddy shores are generally considered as soft coastlines when compared with rocky shores and cliffs because they are made up of mobile sediments and are easily eroded or changed by tidal currents.

Shingle or Gravel Shores

Shingle beaches and gravel shores are usually formed on exposed or moderately exposed shores, where pebble or cobble-sized material may be transported by waves. The most extreme examples of this occur on the west coast where Atlantic storms carry large stones many metres above the normal tidal level, often throwing them over onto roads and fields behind the shoreline. There are some fine storm beaches at Dunmanus Bay and Crookhaven in west Cork, Cromane Point, County Kerry between Loop Head and Spanish Point in west Clare, on the Aran Islands of Inishmore and Inishmaan, on the islands of Clew Bay and the Inishkea Islands in County Mayo. In Donegal, an impressive series of storm beaches at Bloody Foreland, made up of granite boulders up to the size of a football, jut out into the Atlantic. On the south and east coasts shingle beaches are no less common, but they are usually tamer barrier-type beaches, such as those at Lady's Island Lake in south Wexford and the Murrough in north Wicklow. Lower energy gravel shores are typically found in the outer parts of large estuaries, such as the Shannon Estuary.

As the stones are constantly moving up and down the beach with wave action, they become smoothed and rounded by abrasion against one another. Because of the mobile nature of

(Clockwise from top left) Sea-kale was once widely harvested as a vegetable but is now quite rare; shingle beach near Malin Head, County Donegal; a dunlin, still in breeding plumage, having just arrived in Ireland from its arctic nesting area; scentless mayweed growing on a shingle beach.

the substrate, the intertidal areas of the shingle and gravel are typically impoverished, with respect to both plants and animals, although some opportunist amphipods may colonise them, especially where rotting seaweed accumulates. In gravelly estuary shores, only burrowing molluscs with thickened shells, such as cockles, can survive. The spaces between the gravel and pebbles are usually filled with sand, which supports tiny worms and other microfauna. Larger stones can serve as attachment sites for brown seaweeds such as bladder wrack.

Where the gravel or shingle is piled up above the level of most high tides, a patchy vegetation may develop in the summer months.[2] Typical species are sea campion, scentless mayweed, sea

(left) After a storm, the strandline may be littered with the egg-like shells of the heart urchin; (right) saltwort grows in summer on the buried strandline of rotting seaweed.

beet, sea sandwort and various species of orache. A large perennial plant, sea-kale, used to occur widely on shingle but it was harvested extensively as a vegetable in earlier centuries and it has now become quite rare. In fact these disturbed and shifting shores were probably the natural habitat of many ancestors of our cultivated vegetables such as spinach beet, beetroot, chard, mangold, carrot and radish. They would also have been the main habitat of many garden weeds such as silverweed and scentless mayweed before we provided them with even better conditions in our gardens.[3] A rare northern species is the oyster plant which still survives in a few north-east coast shingle shores. I remember finding it growing abundantly in the shingle beach at Annalong, County Down, in the shadow of the Mourne Mountains. The barrier beaches of south Wexford have been well studied by Julian Orford and the late Bill Carter. They found that the shingle here is constantly over-washed by the tides and the sandy 'veneer' is a mobile one.

Shingle beaches in Ireland have been rather overlooked by ecologists to date. Only recently has an inventory been compiled.[4] We now know that many of these beaches hold unique plant assemblages that are scarce in a European context and have been listed for special protection in the EU Habitats Directive. Unfortunately, they are often damaged by coastal constructions of various types. Typically they form the base for roadways along the back of beaches or causeways to islands. The fixing of what are naturally unstable, dynamic habitats cuts off the supply of sediment from the sea and often causes additional erosion problems elsewhere.

Sandy Shores

The typical wide sandy beaches occur in the centre of large bays, such as Dundrum Bay in County Down or Killala Bay in County Mayo, or near the mouths of estuaries, such as Lough Foyle in County Derry or Castlemaine Harbour in County Kerry. In many areas, such as Inner Galway Bay or around Rosslare in County Wexford, the sand accumulates in small coves between rocky outcrops. While the sand itself may vary from coarse to fine, it is often mixed with fragments of shell and pebbles or, as in some parts of Connemara, a coralline alga known as *Lithothamnion*, which forms the famous 'coral strands'.

The animal life of sandy shores has a range of hazards to contend with, especially a constantly shifting substrate with no hard surfaces for attachment. Few seaweeds are present for food or shelter and the surface dries out twice a day at low tide. Not surprisingly, most animals

on a sandy shore are burrowers with special adaptations for moving through the sediment and feeding in it. Typical species include amphipod and isopod crustaceans, with some polychaete worms and bivalve molluscs.

The faunal diversity of sandy shores has been recently reviewed by Jim Wilson and Chris Emblow.[5] The predominantly sandy shores of Dublin Bay have yielded over 70 species of large invertebrates,[6] while seven sandy beaches in County Down produced approximately 50

Mannin Bay, County Galway. Some of the 'coral' beaches here are made up mainly of broken fragments of maerl, a calcareous alga which lives in the shallow water of the bay (Jaimie Blandford).

species.[7] If the microscopic forms are included as well, up to 195 species (including 26 fish) have been recorded from Wexford beaches.[8]

Dublin Bay remains one of the best studied sandy bays due, principally, to the work of Jim Wilson of Trinity College Dublin. He has been monitoring three sites within the bay, at Bull Island, Sandymount and Blackrock. At the latter site the fauna are dominated by the tellin, both in terms of numbers and biomass. The level of recruitment of young shellfish is higher following mild winters, suggesting that cold temperatures may have a negative effect on the populations.

A number of sublittoral species of sandy substrates, such as the heart urchin and the razor clam, may occasionally occur within the lowest parts of the intertidal zone. The heart urchin is encountered usually after death as brittle 'eggshells' cast up on the strandline. I have walked for miles along a sandy beach in Donegal with the white heart urchin 'shells' washed up along the strandline at several hundred per square metre. Its natural habitat is the lower shore of sandy beaches where it lives in a deep (15cm) burrow, thus avoiding the disturbance of the surface layers caused by waves. In life, it is covered with tiny spines, which look like hair. Behind its mouth are spade-like spines, which are modified for digging. Like other echinoderms, it has tiny tube feet, which assist it in moving by stretching out and contracting. Larger tube feet near the mouth collect sand grains, which are cleaned of detritus.

At the top of the beach is the strandline where the high tides deposit the debris of the sea. This is mostly decaying seaweeds but can include large numbers of discarded egg cases of fish or whelks, cuttlefish bones, heart urchin 'shells' and numerous other marine creatures much sought after by experienced beach-combers. The typical strandline inhabitant is the sandhopper, which burrows in the sand by day and emerges only at night. These amphibious crustaceans achieve their explosive hopping by releasing the flexed abdomen very rapidly; this helps to avoid predation by birds. They migrate from the strandline to the lower shore coinciding with the neap and spring tides to ensure both feeding and immersion of their eggs in seawater.

It is a common sight to see foxes scavenging along the strandline in the early morning in the hope of turning up a stranded fish or other morsel. A young, inexperienced fox may try to catch the sandhoppers, but usually has little success. I have even seen a fox digging in sand banks at extreme low tide at the mouth of Inner Dundrum Bay, County Down. Clearly, it was catching and eating adult sand eels that were spawning in the sand at the time.

As the decaying seaweed becomes buried by blown sand, it acts as a fertilizer for the seeds of plants of the strandline. Such typical plants are saltwort, sea rocket, sea sandwort and sea holly. Yellow-horned poppy, with its ridiculously long seed pods, can occur either on sand or shingle and is usually an indicator of lack of disturbance. On remoter beaches there can be an accumulation of large pieces of timber – tree trunks, root masses, boards and boxes – which provide shelter for several specialised invertebrates. Two of these, a large orange and black beetle called *Eurynebria* and an isopod or woodlouse called *Armadilladum* are found only on the south-east coasts. This is probably because they need a minimum amount of warmth and sunshine each year to breed successfully.

Sand Dunes

Few coastal habitats have attracted more attention than sand dunes, whether from recreational, management or scientific viewpoints. Without doubt, they are attractive landscapes and they invariably support a rich diversity of wildlife. I spent five years working and living as a warden on a sand dune nature reserve at Murlough in County Down, so I had ample opportunity to learn about these complex systems. Much has been written about the subject, but among

(Clockwise from top left) The tip of Raven Point, County Wexford is a dynamic area, changing shape with each winter storm (Alyn Walsh); marram grass on a Donegal beach traps blowing sand, forming embryo dunes; the orange berries of sea buckthorn provide a feast for blackbirds and thrushes in winter.

the most useful is a small booklet entitled *A Guide to the Sand Dunes of Ireland*.[9] This contains an inventory, compiled by Tom Curtis, of the sandy coasts of Ireland, including 191 sand dunes, sand hills and machair sites.[10]

Foredunes

The logical starting place to investigate most sand dunes is at the top of the beach, where the first pioneer plants begin to colonise the bare sand. The development of more than embryo dunes is a rather rare phenomenon as most Irish dune systems are eroding along the seaward edge. However, local movements of sand or changes in the position of river mouths can lead to the development of foredunes. An example of this type of foredune is well described for Malahide, County Dublin.[11] On

the north side of Loughros More Bay, in west Donegal, the development of foredunes is associated with changes in the position of a tidal channel. The decaying seaweed on the winter strandline forms the fertiliser base for the seeds of such annual plants as sea rocket and sea sandwort to establish on bare sand. These are usually followed by sand couch grass or lyme grass, which begin to trap small mounds (up to 1 metre high) of blowing sand. The main dune-building species, marram grass, then takes over as it can survive, and indeed often thrives, with burial of up to a metre of sand per year. It sends out extensive rhizomes, or root systems, which not only anchor the plants but also help to bind the mobile sand together.

The importance of marram grass (or bent grass) as a builder of sand dunes is not recent knowledge. A nineteenth-century account of life in Donegal[12] displays a remarkable understanding of the ecology of the species:

Bent is the only kind of vegetation which first takes root in clear white sand and is the only preventative against blowing sand. It is also the only safeguard on such soils for other plants, moss and grass so that after some time the whole surface is coated over, and then the bent itself begins to decay. It can never be overtopped by the sand, no matter what shape or height the sand hills may assume, the bent will always try and overtop it, and where the greatest shifting of sand is going on, there is to be found the longest of the bent.

Between the clumps of marram grass there is still much bare sand but other species, such as sand sedge, sea spurge, sea holly and sea bindweed, are common members of this community. One of the rarest Irish coastal plants, cottonweed, occurs in this type of habitat on the south coast of Wexford. Lyme grass has been planted extensively in attempts to stabilise mobile dune fronts. Also used for this purpose is a thorny shrub called sea buckthorn, which thrives in blowing sand. It was first introduced to Ireland at Murlough, County Down, in the nineteenth century and subsequently was planted widely on the north, east and south coasts. It can form dense thickets, for example at Courtown, County Wexford, which become impenetrable and eventually change the entire vegetation of foredunes.

Fixed Dunes

Once the surface of the dunes has become more or less stabilised it will be colonised by a complete carpet of vegetation. This usually

Bee orchid. The centre of the flower mimics the hind quarters of a bumble bee, attracting these insects in to collect and distribute the pollen.

occurs on the back of the first line of fore dunes, which trap most of the sand blowing off the beach. While marram grass is still present, it is not as vigorous as on the foredunes, and other grasses such as red fescue and bent grasses become common. Various legumes such as bird's foot trefoil and white clover help to trap nitrogen from the atmosphere and fix it into the sand. The increased cover of such plants as wild thyme, lady's bedstraw, lichens and mosses leads to the accumulation of a thin humus layer and the retention of some moisture in the sand.

The fixed dune grassland can be a colourful spectacle in early summer with the yellows of bird's foot trefoil and the reds of thyme and the purples of seaside pansy providing most of the main tints. It is also a wonderful habitat for orchids, with pyramidal orchid, bee orchid and some of the rarer marsh orchids in flower among the grasses. The fixed dunes are often grazed by cattle, especially in the west coast areas, as they provide good dry winter pastures and a mineral-rich sward.

The vegetation is often maintained as an open community by the intense grazing of rabbits. This familiar mammal was introduced to Ireland by the Normans and for centuries local sand dunes were managed as 'warrens' to produce the maximum yield of rabbit meat for sale. This probably included the control of natural predators such as fox and stoat. Even in the early part of the twentieth century, the population of rabbits was much higher than today and many dune systems were more mobile as a result of their intensive grazing and burrowing activities. However, the disease myxomatosis, which was introduced to Ireland in the 1950s, caused a dramatic drop in rabbit numbers and a consequent increase in vegetation cover on many dune systems.

Dune Heath and Scrub

As the dunes become older and further removed from the supply of sand on the beach, rainfall

Fixed dune grassland with yellow variety of the seaside pansy in flower.

leaches the calcareous minerals from the surface layers of sand and acidic conditions can develop. This leads to colonisation by heathers, especially ling and bell heather, and other heathland species such as gorse. However, dune heath is rare in Ireland due to high levels of grazing and one of the few well-developed examples is at Murlough in County Down. On this and a number of northern sand dunes, such as at Portstewart, County Antrim, sea buckthorn has become a dominant feature of the back dunes as well as the foredunes. A more common type of dune scrub, found on the back part of many east coast dune systems, is a mixture of gorse, hawthorn and blackthorn. Where grazing or burning has been a feature in the past, cessation may result in the spread of bracken and burnet rose. Beneath the ground surface, the bracken has a latticework of thick black rhizomes that bind the sand together and make it quite difficult to remove.

Dune slack vegetation is close to the water table and is often rich in orchids (Julie Fossitt).

Dune Slacks

Where a gap in the dune vegetation occurs the wind may open up a 'blow-out' from which sand is scooped out until the bottom of the hollow reaches the water table. At this point some plants that are more typical of wetlands, such as sedges, rushes and even common reed, may cover the floor of the hollow. A characteristic dune slack plant is creeping willow, whose dense, prostrate stems cover the ground surface. Although the bottom of the slack may dry out in summer, the water table never falls below one metre from the surface. Dune slacks are relatively less common in Irish dune systems compared with Britain and continental Europe. One reason for this is that some dunes are perched on top of shingle ridges so that the water table never reaches the surface in winter. Examples of this can be seen at Murlough, County Down and Ballyteigue Burrow in County Wexford. Another reason may be that the more recently built dune systems have not yet been eroded down to the water table.

Dune slacks can also form where new dune ridges develop on the seaward side of a hollow that was once part of the shoreline. Such active dune development often happens at the tip of a dune spit, as in Malahide, County Dublin, where dune slacks are part of the sequence of dune building and erosion. One well-studied dune slack occurs near the tip of the Bull Island in Dublin Bay. This is a large flat area between the dune ridge where the ground water is nearly fresh but with slight salinity. A large part of it is dominated by the saltmarsh rush but it also has a rich orchid flora, including marsh helliborine and a magenta form of the marsh orchid. This slack has also been colonised by alder trees, which has led to its being known as the 'Alder Marsh'.[13]

The Curracloe dunes, north of Wexford Harbour, once had a rich and extensive system of dune slacks. However, these have largely been obliterated due to the development of caravan parks on the northern part and to afforestation on the southern part. A few examples of the dune slack habitat survive among the conifers and these are typically dominated by creeping

(left) A dune slack in Donegal with bulrush growing in the freshwater pools and stoneworts in the foreground; (below) a natterjack toad with its characteristic large front legs. This amphibian is found in only a few sand dunes in Kerry (Eddie Dunne).

willow, with creeping bent grass and silver–weeds being common associates. Wintergreen is a rare plant that occurs in these dune slacks. It may have been introduced here at the time of the forestry plantings but could equally have colonised naturally from one of the known sites across the Irish Sea. The forested area and the unforested tip of the spit are included in a nature reserve where a dune slack restoration plan is being implemented by the National Parks and Wildlife Service.

At Sheskinmore, on the west coast of Donegal, I have seen dune slacks develop in a few years behind a new line of foredunes built up on an accreting beach. The slacks contain fresh water, even though they are close to high water mark, and a wonderful growth of stonewort (*Chara*), which carpets the floor of these hollows. It feels soft to the touch of bare feet but, as the slack dries out in warmer weather, it precipitates a white deposit of calcium, which looks like chalk. The slacks are rich in insect life with numerous beetles and pond skaters in the water, and damselflies hovering above it. In late summer, the ground may be alive with tiny frogs, which have left the ponds,

and provide a feast for all kinds of predators, from foxes to herons.

In parts of County Kerry, some dune slacks are host to a special amphibian called the nat-terjack toad. It is not known if this is a survivor of the last ice age, which hangs on here, or whether it was introduced with a shipload of ballast in historic times. The arguments for and against these theories have been discussed by David Cabot.[14] Either way, the natterjack is a current resident of some dune systems such as that at Castlegregory on the north side of the Dingle peninsula. Walking among the vegetation on the western edge of Lough Gill in late summer, I have come across dozens of young toads walking (they do not hop like frogs) with some purpose to reach the lake. The distinctive yellow line down the spine immediately distinguishes it from other amphibians. Classified as an endangered species, the natterjack has been well studied, with surveys showing that it is restricted to 48 sites in County Kerry and one in County Wexford, to where it was translocated as a conservation measure.

Machair

On the north-western coast between Malin Head, County Donegal and Galway Bay, a type of sandy grassland is found which differs from the other dune systems in the remainder of Ireland. It is known as machair, from the Gaelic word for a flat plain, and it is a habitat type that is unique to Ireland and the west coast of Scotland. It has been formed by a combination

of high winds, which blow the calcareous sands inland to form flat plains, and universal grazing which maintains the vegetation as grassland. These sand plains were extensively cultivated in previous centuries, probably using seaweed as the main fertilizer, but are increasingly being used for recreation today, with sports pitches, caravan parks and other facilities attracted to the flat coastal land.

The machair habitat in Ireland has been well studied and the main characteristics defined.[15] The absence or relatively unimportant role of marram grass is perhaps the most striking feature of these sandy areas. It is thought that most of these systems originally had dune ridges but that heavy grazing, combined with high winds, have eroded the sand down to the water table, producing a level surface. The winds continue to supply fresh sand from the shore, with its calcareous shell fragments, but the heavy grazing prevents marram grass from establishing and thus dune

(right) The flat, windblown sand plain of the machair in Mannin Bay, County Galway; (below) flat machair plains at Doogort on the north side of Achill Island, County Mayo.

Grass of Parnassus growing on a west coast machair plain.

building is inhibited. In some cases, as for example at Lettermacaward, County Donegal, there are typical dune ridges immediately behind the beach. These quickly become deflated to the machair plain, which can extend up onto rocky ground or may end in a coastal lagoon or marsh such as those found at Sheskinmore, County Donegal or Dooachtry, County Mayo.

A thorough botanical survey of the surviving machair sites on the north-west coast was carried out in the summer of 1996.[16] Not all features of machair are present at every site but each place has a unique history and combination of features. All sites covered in this survey have been used for grazing, sometimes intensively. Grazing was regarded as essential for the maintenance of species richness and seasonal

cattle grazing is compatible with conservation interests. Sheep, on the other hand, tend to be detrimental, especially where there is overstocking. Sheep severely cut back the vegetation and their sharp hooves exacerbate erosion in existing blow-outs. Fencing on many sites has increased in recent years in a trend known locally as 'striping' the machair. Fertiliser application is not practical on commonage but as soon as the land is striped some form of land 'improvement' usually follows. This can be detrimental to both plants and birds.

Some of the best and most extensive examples of machair are found in County Mayo, where much of the Mullet Peninsula and neighbouring coastline once carried this habitat type. I remember in the early 1980s walking virtually unhindered here across miles of machair landscapes accompanied by the plaintive calls of breeding lapwing and dunlin. Around this time, I also explored the machair at Sheskinmore, County Donegal where a superb combination of dunes, lake, fen and machair grassland all occur in close proximity. A typical suite of calcareous grassland plants, including red fescue, plantain, daisy, bird's foot trefoil, lady's bedstraw and white clover, is normally found in all machair sites. Where machair marshes occur, such species as grass of Parnassus, common butterwort, the grass *Poa trivialis* and a variety of sedges, become more common. These marshes are often rich in orchids, including rare varieties of the marsh orchid. The machair grasslands are probably a rich habitat for invertebrates, although there is little published information. They do provide suitable habitat for a range of breeding waders and for wintering chough.

It was the breeding waders that attracted me to the machair in 1985. With Ralph Sheppard and several other colleagues, I walked over 50 sites between north Donegal and Galway Bay, mapping and censusing the waders. The richest sites were those that had both dry and wet machair in close proximity. Overall, we found significant numbers of lapwing, ringed plover, dunlin and snipe on these areas, although most of the sites were quite small and fragmented. By the time Brian Madden and colleagues repeated the survey in 1996, the populations had significantly declined, probably due to strip fencing leading to more intensive grazing and other uses of the machair. The 1996 machair survey found that the intensity of grazing was not sustainable and that the rate of sand extraction was a problem during a period of increased natural erosion and sediment depletion.

Birds of Sandy Shores

Waders

The typical wader of sandy shores for me is the sanderling. A tiny bird with brilliant white underside and silver-grey back, it runs about the beach in a frenetic manner, stopping at intervals to feed with rapid probing action. They normally occur in flocks and when they fly they move as one with flashing white and dark in the sunlight. I have seen these birds at both ends of their migratory range, in the tundra of east Greenland and on the long warm beaches of West Africa. Their wintering areas reach as far as South Africa, although my favourite place to see them in action on their long journey south is on the wide, flat expanses of Trá Mór (the big beach) in west Donegal. They seem to prefer long sandy beaches with rough wave action, which suit their special feeding habits. They often chase retreating waves to pick up small prey that are temporarily exposed. Burrowing amphipods and other crustaceans are probably the main food items on migration and during winter.

Another typical bird of sandy beaches is the ringed plover, similar in size to the sanderling, but quite different in behaviour. During the spring and summer, they are usually in pairs and are quite territorial, choosing to nest on sandy or shingly beaches where their speckled eggs are perfectly camouflaged among the pepples

(top) a sanderling follows the edge of the tide as it creeps across a sandy beach; (far left) a flock of turn-stone, dunlin and sanderling forages among the pebbles on a Donegal beach in August; (left) autumn gentian adds a splash of colour to the western dunes in August.

and shell fragments. The nest is usually nothing more than a scrape in the sand where the adults take it in turns to incubate the clutch of four eggs. Within a few hours of hatching, the chicks are mobile and usually move to the cover of vegetation or strandline debris. At this vulnerable time the parents may become quite anxious if a walker enters the territory. They call loudly to the young, to make them freeze, and will even feign injury, using a 'broken wing' display to attract the attention of the intruder away from the chicks. In winter, I have watched ringed plovers in flocks numbering several hundred, tightly packed together at high tide, or scattered around on a beach at low tide. In strong wind conditions, as on the west coast, they prefer to shelter behind seaweed-covered rocks and may stand, apparently motionless, in these favoured positions for many hours.

Oystercatchers are much larger and more boldly coloured waders, which occasionally nest on sand and shingle shores. They are fairly widespread around the country but apparently absent from the south coast, except for the offshore islands. They have a loud piping call when disturbed and will fly around an intruder in wide circles to warn their young to stay hidden. In winter, large numbers of northern nesting oystercatchers move into Ireland and concentrate in the big sandy estuaries and bays such as Dundalk Bay. Others feed around the rocky shores where they specialise in mussels, limpets and periwinkles. At high tide, they form densely packed roosts at the top of the shore, or on rocky islands and headlands.

Little Terns

Of the five species of terns that nest in Ireland, only the little tern is a sandy beach specialist. It can be found from about May to September in sandy estuaries such as Wexford Harbour and on shingle beaches, such as those on the Aran Islands. It can be distinguished from a distance by its dainty fairy-like flight and by the high-pitched call. Close-up, it is the only tern with a yellow bill and legs and a triangular white patch on the forehead. Unlike the other terns, it is not confined to offshore islands but will frequently nest on mainland beaches if the right habitat conditions are present. The largest colony of little terns in Ireland is found on the shingle beach between Kilcoole and Newcastle,

A little tern in its nesting habitat among the cockle shells on a sandy beach (Oscar Merne).

County Wicklow. Here the birds incubate their clutch in a shallow scrape among the pebbles and will rise up calling if disturbed. The colony is protected each summer by a wardening scheme run jointly by BirdWatch Ireland and the NPWS. Unfortunately, the concentration of eggs and chicks on the beach has attracted a variety of predators, from hedgehog and fox to kestrel and peregrine falcon. As a result, the breeding success from this colony is often quite low,[17] but the birds are relatively long-lived and do not need a high reproductive rate to maintain the population. The problem is that their habitat is under some pressure with coastal developments on one hand and marine erosion on the other. The strandline is a precarious habitat at the best of times as high spring tides may even flood the nests.

Harbour Seals

While harbour (or common) seals can turn up on any part of the coast, they favour the more sheltered sandy bays and estuaries for breeding. The harbour seal is the smaller of the two species breeding in Ireland, around 1.5 metres in length and averaging 80 to 100 kg in weight, or about the size of a small man. It has a concave head shape with a short snout, not dissimilar to that of a dog or an otter.

Harbour seal pups sometimes become separated from their mothers by human disturbance on sandy beaches. This girl found a starving pup in Dundrum Bay, County Dublin.

(left) Gweebarra Estuary, County Donegal. The rocks to the right and the sand bars to the left provide harbour seals with alternative haul-out locations; (right) a group of harbour seals hauled out on a weed-covered rock, Bantry Bay, County Cork.

I first became interested in the harbour seals that haul out each summer on the sandy banks in the centre of Dundrum Bay, County Down. Here, the mature females give birth to a single pup in June or July and they lead an apparently easy life basking in the sun and slipping occasionally into the water to catch a passing salmon or flatfish. Using a telescope, I was able to observe the interactions between the different aged seals, to see the closeness of the mother-pup pairs during the short few weeks of their dependence. When startled, the mother will push the pup underwater and swim over it to protect it. Later, I surveyed seals in other parts of Northern Ireland, including Strangford Lough, where they haul out at low tide on seaweed-covered rocks called 'pladdies'. This extremely sheltered inlet seems to be a favoured breeding area as it holds the greatest number of harbour seal pups on any part of the Irish coast. Other traditional haul-out sites for harbour seals in Northern Ireland are on the Ards Peninsula and in Carlingford Lough.[18]

Unfortunately, a very contagious disease known as Phocine Distemper Virus (PDV) was contracted by these seals in 1988, leading to a large number of deaths. A similar outbreak in 2002 was first identified on the Aran Islands and along the west coast. Recent surveys of harbour seals in County Down show that numbers of pups have decreased significantly since 1996.[19] Since the mid-1990s many mother-pup pairs have been leaving the natal sites prematurely and some breeding groups appear to have dispersed to sea within a week of pupping. A hypothesis has been proposed that there are insufficient resources of suitable fish around the pupping sites to sustain the high fat content in the milk of lactating females. This may be linked with the damage caused to the benthic fauna, including fish, in Strangford Lough due to commercial trawling.

I was fortunate to take part in the first comprehensive survey of harbour seals in Ireland in 1978.[20] This was a memorable three weeks of boat work, mainly on the west coast from Donegal to west Cork and it gave me a wonderful opportunity to see the variety of coastal features. There are plenty of places to see harbour seals from the mainland. These include the road along the north of Dungloe Bay, or the south side of Gweebarra Estuary in County Donegal. Inner Donegal Bay and Ballysadare Bay in County Sligo have large groups of harbour seals that haul out on sand banks. The muddy inlets of Achill Sound and the islands

66

in Clew Bay are the best places for harbour seals in County Mayo. In Galway there are groups of harbour seals among the weedy rocks in Kilkieran Bay and in Inner Galway Bay. In Kerry, the main group is on islands in the Kenmare River while Bantry Bay holds the main concentration in County Cork. Special seal-watching trips by boat are available in Donegal town and at Glengarriff, County Cork.

Up to the passing of the Wildlife Act in 1976, seals were regularly hunted and a government bounty was offered for their heads. Some fishermen specialised in the 'control' of seals and particular breeding groups, such as those in Mayo, were subject to repeated culling. Of course, the hunting pressure did not wipe out seals but disturbance on their breeding sites probably influenced the choice of more and more remote locations for pupping. Since the 1970s, with a relaxation of hunting, harbour seals have been spreading to new (or perhaps former) locations such as the Aran Islands, Broadhaven, County Mayo and Wexford Harbour, from where they were previously unknown.

In the summer of 2003, after an interval of 25 years, I was again involved in a national survey of these seals. This time the main census was carried out by air using a high-tech thermal imaging camera, mounted in a helicopter. Recent work in Scotland had shown that the largest number of seals haul out in August during the moult, so no attempt was made to census pups this time. However, with the co-operation of rangers of the National Parks and Wildlife Service, we did census a number of major groups of seals from the ground as a measure of the accuracy of the aerial survey. This ground truth exercise also provided information on the effects of tide and disturbance on the seals.

In June 2003 I spent a long and windy day with a telescope, perched on top of a sand dune in the Gweebarra Estuary, west Donegal. From here I could see all the 50 or so harbour seals in this group as they moved about between rocks and sand banks. Just below me a mother and her new pup emerged from the water, well away from the main group. She positioned herself on the weedy rocks of Illaunawaddyiska and the little pup, barely a few days old, struggled out of the water to lie beside her. Following much tender nose-to-nose contact, she rolled over and the pup began to suckle on her fat-rich milk. Incredibly, this nursing only lasts for four weeks and then the pups are weaned to fend for themselves by catching whatever fish or shellfish they can to survive. Unfortunately, disturbance at the crucial time can separate mother and pup and isolated young animals may turn up starving on beaches.

Beachcombing

Ireland's best-known beachcomber, Michael Viney, who lives on the coast of south-west Mayo, has written a fine account of the various things that can turn up on regular walks along the strandline of a sandy beach.[21] His book, *A Year's Turning*, captures the excitement of a really interesting find on the strandline.

Goose barnacles attach themselves to drifting objects such as timber and plastic, by means of a rubbery black stalk. I once found a large tree trunk on a west Donegal beach with a huge covering of these barnacles, like a glass curtain jangling in the wind. Michael Viney describes another stalked barnacle (*Lepas fascicularis*) that secretes its own raft of frothy bubbles. This ocean traveller can turn up in phenomenal numbers – an estimated 5,000 colonies (perhaps 30,000 individuals were recorded on 2 kilometres of shoreline at Inch, County Kerry in July 1986.[22]

About twenty species of tropical plants have seeds capable of staying afloat in salt water for about fourteen months, the least time it takes for a small object to drift across from the Caribbean Sea to European coasts.[23] Charles Nelson, formerly of the National Botanic Gardens, has made a special study of tropical seeds on Irish

(right) Goose barnacles hang from a piece of driftwood 'like a glass curtain, jangling in the wind'; (below) sea pea — the seeds of this shoreline plant may be carried across the ocean (Faith Wilson).

The sea pea is a rare plant in Ireland, known from a few sandy or shingly beaches. Most of the records are from County Kerry, where they were recorded mainly in the nineteenth century, often growing in abundance on beaches such as Inch and Rossbeigh. More recently a survey of stranded seeds and plants has demonstrated that they are frequently washed ashore on beaches on north, west and south coasts but are virtually absent from the east coast.[25] The small population of growing plants in Ireland would not be able to produce so much seed so it is likely that they originate from the Mediterranean or North America, where the plants are common. The attachment of stalked barnacles to some of these seeds confirms that they have drifted for some time in the ocean.

On summer ramblings along sandy beaches I have often encountered the ephemeral bodies of jellyfish washed up along the shore. Commonest is the moon jelly with the typical four rings of purple markings in the umbrella. Sometimes the larger jellyfish *Rhisostoma*, with long thick trailing tentacles, can be found after

coasts.[24] Coconuts often drift into Irish beaches but, as they remain viable in salt water for no more than 100 days, they are unlikely to produce a coconut palm forest here. The sea bean or sea heart has a tough leather skin that was once used in some coastal communities as a teething ring for babies to chew on.

Shroove lighthouse near Greencastle, County Donegal with stranded kelp on the beach.

storms. The huge Portuguese man-o-war is a really interesting find for an experienced beachcomber. Viney[25] describes how he once found 'this notorious power-pack substantially intact, its glossy gas-filled float shining among the dark rocks like a pink-and-blue party balloon'. The man-o-war, named after the famous wooden battleship of old, packs a powerful punch of stings for anyone unfortunate enough to meet one while swimming. Less daunting, but equally interesting, is the tiny jellyfish quaintly known as by-the-wind sailor. It is usually found on the beach as a small bluish rubbery disc, but when alive it has a small flap of a sail and a fringe of tentacles hanging from the rim. The sail is set diagonally across the oval disc so that it can tack into the wind, in a similar way to a sailing yacht. This carries the species across the ocean with the prevailing winds and they can sometimes turn up on Irish coasts in millions, as happened in the summer of 1992 and again in 2004.[26]

Larger animals are also sometimes stranded, both alive and dead, on sandy beaches. Marine turtles, which are regularly carried into Irish waters from their more familiar tropical habitats, often come ashore, starving and cold, on west-facing shores. Beach strandings are also still one of the principal sources of information about porpoises, dolphins and whales in Irish waters. These are described more fully in Chapter 5 (The Open Sea).

Wandering along a sandy beach after a storm is one of the pleasures of life on the coast. Michael Viney says that he is 'chastened by the overriding role of chance' after 25 years of mooching between the headlands. The finds on the strandline can open up the whole world of the ocean beyond the horizon.

4

Muddy Shores

Malahide Estuary, County Dublin. Vast areas of bare mud and sand are exposed at low tide.

From my office window, I look out on an estuary where the tide ebbs and flows twice each day, bringing an infinite variety of colours, wave patterns and the usual flotsam and jetsam. The animal life is always interesting – it may be a pair of foxes sunning themselves on the shore, a little egret fishing in the shallows or a shoal of grey mullet stirring the muddy bottom. The place where the river meets the sea is also a meeting place of land and marine creatures and a few which specialise in the constant mix of salt and freshwater.

Estuaries

A large number of major estuaries occur around the Irish coast and, so varied are these, that they almost merit a book to themselves.

The principal features that distinguish estuaries are a free connection to the open sea and a significant input of freshwater. The mixing of seawater and freshwater and the constant ebb and flow of the tide lead to continuously variable conditions of salinity and depth with complex habitat patterns. Fundamentally, estuaries are places of deposition when the sediments eroded on more exposed coasts are carried and deposited by the tide. The sediments also arise from the land and are carried into the estuary by rivers. The shallow gradients typically produce very wide 'flats' of sand and mud between high and low water marks, but these are considered in more detail under the sections on mud and muddy sand. The outer parts of large estuaries such as the Shannon/Fergus, Cork Harbour and Lough Foyle are more like the neighbouring areas of seabed except that they are more sheltered and do not suffer the extreme exposure to waves and currents. They often have a sandy substrate and are important nursery areas for fish as well as good habitats for shellfish such as cockles.

The cockle is a typical inhabitant of the outer sandy parts of large estuaries, living buried just below the surface. Like many of the bivalve molluscs, it is a filter feeder, with a pair of tube-like siphons that are used to filter suspended detritus from the water when the tide is in. The outlet siphon is narrower than the inlet, this producing a jet of waste water, which separates it from the intake. The cockle can live from near high water mark to below low water, those lower down being larger because they spend more time each tide feeding. The shell is thickened, which helps it to withstand the pounding of the waves, with distinctive ribs or grooves which assist in anchoring it in the moving sand. To change position, it pushes out the fleshy foot and locks it against an obstacle such as a pebble, then tightens the muscle and pulls the shell along. Empty cockle shells are conspicuous by their whiteness, where they are left by feeding oystercatchers or curlews. They occur in quite high densities and are an important food item for the larger waders, which have bills strong enough to open them.

Cockle, a typical inhabitant of the outer sandy parts of estuaries. It lives buried just below the surface of the sand and feeds by filtering water at high tide.

Muddy Sand Shores

Where mud (the silt/clay fraction) makes up 10-30 per cent of the sediment with fine or medium sand, a distinctive animal community can develop on the extensive flats in the centre of an estuary. This is the typical habitat on Sandymount Strand in Dublin Bay, in parts of Wexford Harbour, Tramore Back Strand in County Waterford, Shannon/Fergus Estuary, Sligo Bay and Lough Foyle. A tell-tale sign of muddy sand is the surface worm casts of the lugworm, which lives in a U-shaped burrow. A depression marks the head where sand is swallowed and organic matter digested. Every 45 minutes the worm slides backwards up the tube and deposits the spent sand on the surface as a cast. This brings it into the depth range of a curlew's bill and many worms may lose part of their body to these waders, although they can regenerate the tail. The body of the worm is rich in haemoglobin in which it can store a large amount of oxygen, thus allowing it to survive in anaerobic conditions. In optimum habitat, these worms can occur at densities of 40 per square metre, especially when they breed, in October. In winter, the population is depleted by feeding fish and birds and does not build up again until the following April.

Sand flats are usually devoid of plant cover, but certain conditions produce a growth of eelgrasses. These are the only flowering plants that can tolerate daily immersion in seawater and they appear just like a thin bed of fine grasses. On the back strand at Inch in County Kerry, I have walked the 5 kilometres or so of eelgrass with a few centimetres of water remaining on the sand at low tide. The eelgrass is soft on the feet and a highly nutritious food for wildfowl in early autumn. One small bed of eelgrass, measuring just over one hectare, grows on Merrion Strand in South Dublin Bay, where it attracts hundreds of brent geese. Micheál O'Briain (UCD) studied the rapid depletion of the eelgrass by grazing brent geese in the months of September to November.[1] The really large beds of intertidal eelgrass occur in four major estuaries – Lough Foyle, Strangford

(left) Lugworm casts on the surface of the mud are a tell-tale sign of the presence of the worms in burrows below; (right) Tralee Bay, County Kerry contains one of the largest beds of eelgrass in the country. It can be seen as a green colour on the mudflats in this aerial view.

Lough, Tralee Bay and Castlemaine Harbour. All of the other eelgrass beds are tiny by comparison. As an intertidal plant, it appears to be absent on the west coast between Tralee Bay and Killala Bay.

Muddy Shores

At the extreme inner part of the estuary, where the degree of shelter is greatest, wave energy has been almost completely dissipated and the very finest sediments are deposited. Walking in such muds is difficult, if not impossible. I have almost lost my boots in soft mudflats at Rossbehy Creek in County Kerry attempting to map the eelgrass bed here. In some of the largest estuaries, soft muds seem to stretch as far as the eye can see. In Strangford Lough some fourteen square kilometres of mudflats are exposed at low tide. In the Fergus Estuary the tidal amplitude is so large that it is difficult to see the water in channels between the mudflats at low tide, so great is the drop in water level.

In such areas, the silt/clay fraction of the sediments exceeds 30 per cent although smaller amounts of sand and gravel may be present in places. An occasional rock forms the only solid attachment for brown seaweeds. Otherwise the only vegetation is green seaweed such as sea lettuce with occasional beds of eelgrass. Again, most animals here are burrowers and the

Muddy shores with hundreds of the tiny laver spire shell Hydrobia *(centre).*

water is often cloudy with silt and organic matter. Drainage through the mud is poor and there are often pools and channels left on the surface at low tide.

The characteristic species in muddy shores are polychaete worms (bristleworms) and certain bivalve molluscs such as the Baltic tellin, peppery furrow shell and cockle. The tiny laver spire shell may live on soft mudflats in densities of tens of thousands per square metre. It may feed on the mud surface or within the sediment. It can also produce a raft of mucus that will carry it on the tide across the mudflats. This tiny shell is quite tolerant of changes in salinity that are found in the upper part of estuaries. Although a dozen of these snails would fit under your fingernail, they are the staple diet of several shorebirds, including the large shelduck.

Another important animal on the mudflats is the amphipod *Corophium volutator*, which can occur in densities of up to 12,000 per square metre. It rises to the surface on an incoming tide, crawling over the mud surface at high tide and burrowing down on a receding tide. It has a very large pair of antennae, used in locomotion. It normally filters detritus from the water while in its burrow, but can also pick up items directly from the surface when walking around at high tide. This crustacean is a favoured food item for many of the

(left) Saltmarsh at Tawin Island, County Galway. Western saltmarshes are almost universally grazed; (below) glasswort is a primary coloniser of bare mud and one of the first plants to appear in a saltmarsh.

waders, especially the redshank, which is a widespread and common winter inhabitant of most estuaries.

The shores of many estuaries can include areas of mixed sediments. For example, parts of the Outer Shannon Estuary have gravel at the high water mark, with sands and muds near the low water mark. The permanent channels that flow down the centre of estuarine flats can be mainly rivers of freshwater at low tide. These are important habitats for many estuarine fish, especially flatfish.

Saltmarshes

In the most sheltered parts of the coast, where fine sediments have accumulated to the extent that they are out of reach of all but the highest spring tides, a special type of vegetation is found. Strictly speaking, saltmarsh is part of the inter-tidal area because it occurs between neap high water and spring high water marks, but it is often treated as a terrestrial habitat because it is dominated by vascular plants. Saltmarsh often occurs near the mouths of large rivers, such as

the Shannon, the Foyle and the Slaney. It can also form in the shelter of sand dunes, as in Dublin Bay, or shingle spits, as at Derrymore Island in Tralee Bay, County Kerry. Patches of fringing saltmarsh may also develop around the edges of lagoons where there is a tidal influence. The substrate on which saltmarsh develops can vary from gravel and sand to mud and peat. The

Clonderlaw Bay, County Clare. Throughout the Shannon Estuary, the introduced cord grass has invaded most of the saltmarshes.

presence of peat on the foreshore shows that sea level was once much lower than at present. The occupation of the coast by early people is proved by the presence of peat cuttings underneath saltmarsh in Loughros More Bay, County Donegal.

The saltmarshes of Ireland have been well documented in a national inventory which highlights the range of substrate types that exist.[2] Just over half of the 250 or so salt-marshes in Ireland are on mud, while in the more exposed north-western coasts of Mayo and Donegal, sand and other coarse sediments predominate. Peat substrates are common on the west coast but are especially prominent in west Galway. Western saltmarshes are almost universally grazed, mainly by cattle. This is because adjacent land is often of poor quality

and the result is a close cropped vegetation on the saltmarsh. The difference between east and west coast saltmarshes was also noted by Micheline Sheehy Skeffington and Eddie Wymer.[3] For example, none of the Galway Bay saltmarshes are associated with sand dunes and may have arisen due to marine flooding of glacial deposits rather than by vegetative colonisation of mudflats.

The vegetation of a number of saltmarshes has been well described. An early study of the Dublin saltmarshes by O'Reilly and Pantin[4] provides a very useful baseline against which to measure change. One of these authors, Helen O'Reilly, with Father John Moore of UCD, went on to describe the vegetation patterns and trends in the saltmarsh at the North Bull Island, Dublin Bay. Here can clearly be seen the process of colonisation of bare mud by vascular plants and the natural succession through a series of zones to higher marsh. The primary coloniser is glasswort, a succulent plant that looks just like a miniature but non-spiney cactus. Where these plants colonise the mud they slow down the tidal currents, causing deposition of fine silt held in suspension. Microscopic algae form a slimy film over the surface of the mud, preventing if from being eroded away. Thus, the surface level of the mud is gradually raised, allowing other saltmarsh plants to colonise. Among the first to arrive are the common saltmarsh grass and sea lavender.

Once a firm surface of the marsh has developed, a series of creeks and channels becomes established by the action of the rising and falling of the tide. The edges of the creek are unstable due to the erosive force of the tide ebb and flow. If a creek becomes blocked, a deep pool or pan may develop and this can hold water long after the tide has receded. Salt concentrations are so high here, due to evaporation of the seawater, that only specialised plants can survive. One of the most successful is sea purslane, which forms bushy growths all along the creeks and pans. It has extensive woody root systems, which grow deep into the substrate and help to stabilise the edge of the marsh. It is very sensitive to grazing and is thus virtually absent on the west coast, but anyway it is near the northern limit of its European range in Ireland and Britain.

Another plant that can transform the saltmarsh is cord grass, which, once established, can spread rapidly and may become dominant. This has happened over large parts of the Shannon/Fergus Estuary, Strangford Lough, Tralee Bay, Baldoyle Estuary, Bannow Bay and many other estuarine areas. It can generally be traced back to the 1920s when a series of deliberate introductions was made to Ireland of a hybrid species first recorded from the south of England. It has since colonised most suitable habitat but, as yet, appears to be absent in parts of the west coast such as Galway Bay and west Donegal.[5]

Cord grass has widely been perceived as a threat to the natural flora and fauna of estuaries and especially to the waders and wildfowl, which concentrate on mudflats in winter. This is because it forms unbroken single species stands of tall grass (looking rather like a cereal crop) in areas that were once either bare mud or colonised by a sparse growth of pioneer species such as glasswort. In some important estuarine areas, such as Strangford Lough, County Down and North Bull Island, County Dublin, cord grass has been the subject of intensive control measures using both physical removal and herbicide treatment. This has largely been shown to be futile as the plants quickly re-establish after treatment is discontinued. A recent review of the issue[6] argues that cord grass is merely a recent introduction colonising a vacant niche in Ireland's flora. The authors point out that if the introduction had taken place 500 years ago cord grass stands would now be regarded as a natural feature of Irish saltmarsh habitats. They believe that cord grass will probably not continue to spread unabated across mudflats but will eventually reach an equilibrium with its competitors and its environment.

In addition to the characteristic plants mentioned here, there are a number of saltmarsh specialists among the animals. To survive in the rapidly changing conditions of salinity and flooding by the tide, few species have been able to adapt to the demanding environment. A small crustacean amphipod called *Gammarus duebeni* lives in the water in saltmarsh creeks, feeding on detritus brought in by the tide. At low water, it burrows under seaweeds to avoid predation. Nearly all the permanent saltmarsh residents are burrowers. This is true not only of worms, bivalves and snails, but also of crabs, shrimps and, to a limited extent, of fish. During a three-year survey of the North Bull Island saltmarsh, Brenda Healy and her associates at

UCD identified a total of 329 species of invertebrates.[7] The juxtaposition of marine, freshwater and terrestrial environments, side by side, makes for a complicated and rich ecological pattern with high productivity.

(Clockwise from left) Lagoon at Loc Con Aortha in Connemara; the outlet of the Salt Lake at Clifden, County Galway; Lady's Island Lake, County Wexford, showing the narrow barrier which separates the lagoon from the sea (Alyn Walsh).

Lagoons and Saline Lakes

Another coastal habitat that has been the subject of a long-term study by Dr Healy is the lagoon at Lady's Island Lake, County Wexford. This is a large natural water body that is separated from the sea only by a barrier of sand and gravel. There is no natural outlet, but seawater percolates through the barrier, which is breached annually by mechanical means in spring in order to prevent flooding of adjacent lands. There are considerable variations in salinity, which is generally described as brackish (part fresh, part salt water). The lagoon has a rich and interesting flora and fauna, with many rare species. It is also of international importance for its nesting tern colonies and wintering waterbirds.

Lagoons have otherwise generally been neglected by biologists in Ireland, so a national survey of this habitat, conducted for the National Parks and Wildlife Service by Dr Healy and associates in 1996, helped to fill a gap in our knowledge. In total 56 sites, each over 0.75 hectares in area, were identified as lagoons or saline lakes. A representative selection of twenty of these sites was chosen for more detailed study. No natural lagoons or saline lakes were found on the east coast north of Wexford. The main concentrations of these habitats are in

County Cork, where many artificial lakes are formed by road embankments, and in Connemara many of the small lakes in the area are influenced by the tide.[8]

The main characteristic that distinguishes lagoons from other coastal waters is the presence of a permanent barrier, with brackish water subject to considerable variation in salinity, both seasonally and in different parts of the lagoon. The barrier may be formed of sand, gravel, cobble or boulders or, more unusually, of peat, rock or glacial deposits. Seawater may enter the lagoon through narrow inlets, by percolation through the barrier or by overtopping in storms. At many sites, artificial outlets have been installed in barriers to prevent flooding of surrounding land. Often these tidal flaps or sluices are old and malfunctioning due to stones or sand being lodged in the mechanism. Although there is a direct influence of the tide, this does not cause lagoons to empty and fill in the way that a normal estuarine mudflat would operate. A number of species of plants and animals are confined to lagoons or are more common in such habitats than they are in other brackish waters, such as estuaries and saltmarsh pools.

The most characteristic plants include tassleweed and the green seaweed *Enteromorpha* at high salinities and pondweed and milfoil at low salinities. Certain stoneworts are characteristic of the habitat, including three species that are rare or threatened in these islands. In total, 248 aquatic animals were recorded, including seventeen species of annelids (worms), 51 crustaceans (shrimps and their allies), 77 insects, 47 molluscs and 21 fish. On the lagoon shores, a range of non-aquatic beetles (and probably many other animal groups) occurs and some fifteen of these were identified as indicator species of lagoons and saline lakes. These habitats are threatened across Europe due to infilling, rising sea level, pollution and general urban development. They have been listed as a priority for conservation in the EU Habitats Directive.

Tidal Rivers

The lower reaches of large rivers, such as the Shannon, the Slaney and the Bann, are influenced by tidal fluctuations and brackish conditions may develop. At the seaward end, the vegetation is often characterised by saltmarsh

Lower tidal reaches of the Gweebarra River, County Donegal.

At high tide, waders such as bar-tailed godwit and curlew (centre) crowd together in roosts on rocks, sand bars and artificial structures, waiting for their feeding areas to be exposed again (Richard T. Mills).

species but, where the freshwater influence is strongest, reed swamps may develop. There are extensive reedbeds along the lower reaches of tidal rivers such as the Slaney, Suir, Barrow and Nore. A number of these south coast locations hold significant numbers of pre-migratory sedge warblers in late summer and autumn, as they fatten up on the abundant reed aphids. Within days, these small songbirds move south through France and Iberia to the west African coast. The reedbeds in the Shannon Airport lagoon, reclaimed from the nearby estuary, have been the site for a large programme of bird ringing, which shows that these tidal rivers are important staging areas for a variety of migratory warblers.

Among the reeds, on the banks of the River Shannon in Limerick city, a very rare plant, triangular club-rush, occurs near low water mark. This species is now virtually extinct in Britain and in Ireland is known only from the Limerick area. Locally abundant here, it is possible that the plant may have been introduced

from the ballast of ships docking in Limerick from the Far East where the species is common. The Upper Shannon Estuary has a huge tidal range (up to 5 metres between spring low water and high water marks). Few other plants could tolerate such extremes and the triangular club-rush appears to thrive in the absence of competition from others.[9]

Birds of Estuaries and Bays

I have always been interested in the constantly changing birdlife of estuaries since living on the shores of Dundrum Bay in County Down. In more recent years I have had the privilege of studying the birds of two contrasting estuaries, Dublin Bay on the east coast and Inner Galway Bay in the west.[10]

High Tide

As well as the daily rhythms of darkness and light, coastal birds must contend with the constant oscillations of the tide. Twice each day

80

their main feeding grounds are covered with water and they must seek out safe refuges where they can rest and preen their plumage. These high tide roosts are often the best places to see large numbers of shorebirds at close range. The locations of roost sites tend to be on relatively inaccessible places such as islands, offshore rocks, sandbars, shingle ridges and the like. Where natural shorelines are largely replaced by artificial structures, as in Dublin Bay, such places as piers, sea walls, jetties and railway embankments are used by certain species. On Sandymount Strand in South Dublin Bay a flock of oystercatchers regularly roosts on the walls of a ruined swimming baths, creating a repeated pattern in their black and white plumage.

However, the height of the tide differs each day depending on the phases of the moon. Spring high tides cover all the shoreline, forcing the birds to move into a few safe roost areas for several hours. On neap tides the birds may remain feeding at the top of the shoreline throughout the high tide period if they are not disturbed. On spring high tides they may find that some of the sandbars on which they generally roost are unavailable and they are forced to use higher features. This movement of shorebirds around a complex of high tide roosts is well illustrated by a series of counts in south Dublin Bay. It is assumed that the birds prefer to roost on any safe sites, which are closest to their low tide feeding ground. By doing so they minimise the amount of energy wasted in flying backwards and forwards between feeding and roosting sites. In Galway Bay there is a large wader roost, with up to 2,000 birds on Mutton Island, alongside a major sewage treatment works. As there is little human disturbance here, the birds continue to use the island even though it is now connected to the mainland by a causeway. The tightly packed flocks include curlew, oystercatcher, bar-tailed godwit, dunlin, redshank, ringed plover and turnstone. These birds feed quite widely along the north shore of Galway Bay but concentrate here at high tide as it is a safe roost. Many times I have stood here, in the shadow of the old lighthouse, as small parties of waders flying across the sea arrive in to the roost amid much calling and jostling for best positions.

In Cork Harbour, I have watched large flocks of waders and gulls move ahead of the advancing tide and concentrate in an artificial lagoon area at Dunkettle, where the tide is held back and eventually overflows the sea wall. On a retreating tide, the reverse situation occurs with shallow water held in the lagoon when the mudflats outside are drying. These shallow pools become a trap for fish and invertebrate life brought in on the tides and a feeding bonanza ensues for grey herons, little egrets, gulls and cormorants.

Some coastal birds manage to continue feeding right through the tidal cycle by moving up the foreshore as the tide rises and then shifting onto coastal grassland, which provides alternative feeding for them during the high tide period. The best examples of this behaviour among the waders are oystercatcher, curlew, black-tailed godwit and redshank, while among the wildfowl both wigeon and brent goose are regularly recorded in such situations. A study of oystercatchers in the Dublin area found that certain individual birds specialise in this inland feeding habit.[11] The behaviour is clearly inherited, as those birds that feed primarily on shellfish on Sandymount Strand have more heavily worn bills from constantly hammering at cockles, mussels and limpets.

Low Tide

As the tide recedes the oystercatchers and other waders spread out across the intertidal mud and sand following the water's edge. This is where the best feeding is to be found because many invertebrates are active and therefore more accessible in the shallows at the tide line. An intensive study of the diet and feeding ecology of common wader species in the

81

lagoons at North Bull Island was carried out by John Grant.[12] This study relied largely on the analysis of remains in regurgitated pellets (containing the indigestible hard parts of invertebrate prey) and direct observation of the prey items as they were being swallowed by the birds. His findings are consistent with similar studies in Britain and other European countries, demonstrating a size preference for certain invertebrate species depending on the bill length and feeding habits of the individual waders. For example, curlew with a very long curved bill was able to feed on ragworms and lugworms, which live deeply buried. By comparison, the tiny dunlin only probes the top one to two centimetres and feeds at a much higher rate of consumption on a greater number of small prey items.

One of the most abundant shellfish in the mudflats is a tiny marine snail known as the laver spire shell (*Hydrobia ulvae*) that forms a staple part of the diet of many shorebirds including the large and colourful shelduck. These attractive ducks feed in the soft mud with a scything action, drawing the bills sideways through the uppermost layers to sieve out the tiny shellfish. In contrast, the ringed plover, grey plover and lapwing appear to stand still on the mudflats for many hours making occasional short walks to peck from the surface food items, which they have located by sight. At Clonakilty Bay on the south coast, a study of black-tailed godwit found that the birds walked, in loose flocks, slowly over the mud picking occasionally to a depth of 10-15 per cent of the bill length. After a few steps the birds would dig deeply into the mud, grasp the prey and roll it up the bill. An alternative strategy involved the birds moving in tight flocks, walking steadily with the bill held slightly open, pecking the surface rapidly and probing occasionally.[13] Little is known about the diet of shorebirds in other intertidal areas of Ireland although Oscar Merne[14] studied the correlation between waders and prey densities in the Shannon/Fergus Estuary. It is clear that the prey spectrum must vary between sheltered muddy estuaries and exposed sandy shores. The latter habitat type is more common in west coast bays such as Galway Bay where such major food items as lugworm are infrequent. In west coast bays and estuaries the nutrient status of the sediments is much lower than on the equivalent east and south coasts, which have greater inputs from agriculture and large towns.

The light-bellied brent goose is an estuarine bird with a very highly specialised feeding behaviour. On arrival from its arctic breeding grounds in September and October the entire population focuses on beds of intertidal eelgrass growing in a number of large estuaries such as Strangford Lough and Lough Foyle.[15] As the beds become exhausted in November, the large flocks begin to disperse in search of other feeding grounds. Geese trickle into all the east coast estuaries and begin to appear in the southwest in places such as Tralee Bay and Castlemaine Harbour. As the eelgrass is depleted or dies back naturally the geese turn to green seaweeds such as *Enteromorpha* and sea lettuce to sustain them over the mid-winter period. Gradually this too becomes exhausted and before the end of winter many of the geese have moved to feed on coastal grassland including golf courses such as those on Bull Island and in St Anne's Park near Dublin Bay. In a few notable cases brent geese have learned to feed on agricultural crops, including winter-sown wheat and barley as it emerges in the spring. This gives them a high protein diet, which is essential to maintain their body condition prior to spring migration to arctic Canada and egg laying in the summer. The numbers and distribution of brent geese were carefully monitored over a decade in the 1980s by Micheál O'Bríain. He showed that the principal concentrations of the geese were directly related to their food resources and his study spanned a period of rapid population growth

(left) Lough Swilly, County Donegal at low tide; (below) Ireland is the main wintering ground for the pale-bellied brent goose which nests in arctic Canada.

in the mid-1980s.[16] Further study of brent geese in Strangford Lough demonstrated a direct relationship between the numbers of geese and the density of their major food plants.[17]

Population size is the primary criterion on which the importance for birds of coastal (and other wetland) sites is rated. The agreed criteria for an internationally important site are that it should hold a regular population of more than 20,000 waterfowl (wildfowl and waders) each winter or that it should hold at least 1 per cent of the individuals in a population of a species or subspecies. Most of the ducks, geese and swans in Ireland belong to the north-west European populations but for the waders we consider the whole of western Europe and north-west Africa, known as the East Atlantic Flyway. I have been fortunate to stand at both ends of this flyway, on the east coast of Greenland and on the West African coast, and see flocks of the same waders, such as whimbrel, sanderling or greenshank, which

pass through Ireland. The increasing knowledge of waterfowl flyway populations has allowed us to calculate the qualifying levels for international and national importance.

Wildfowl counting in Ireland has a long and chequered history. Early efforts in the 1960s were targeted at particular species such as the Greenland white-fronted goose, pale-bellied brent goose and the barnacle goose, which were known to be present in internationally important numbers in Ireland. In the

Clockwise from top: Vast expanses of mud are exposed at low tide in the Shannon Estuary (Richard T. Mills); Sandymount Strand, County Dublin with the Poolbeg power station behind; Black-tailed godwit winter on the south coast of Ireland, returning to their Icelandic breeding grounds in spring (Eddie Dunne).

early 1970s the first comprehensive wildfowl counting was organised by the Irish Wildbird Conservancy and resulted in an important book, *Ireland's Wetlands and Their Birds*.[18] This laid the foundation for further national surveys, which took place in the mid-1980s.[19] In Northern Ireland, waterfowl surveys were much more consistent from the 1970s onwards as they were undertaken as part of the UK national 'Birds of Estuaries Enquiry'.[20] The most consistent effort has been the Irish Wetland Bird Survey (IWeBS), which has covered the entire island and continued into the twenty-first century.[21]

Taken together these extensive surveys have given us an excellent picture of the distribution of wildfowl and waders around the Irish coast. All the counting and recounting has direct value for conservation as we are now in a much better position to define the priority areas for migratory birds and to ensure that these are adequately protected. Some 72 coastal wetlands are either of international or all-Ireland importance.[22] The largest concentration of waders and wildfowl occur, not surprisingly, in some of the biggest estuaries. Principal among these is the massive Shannon/Fergus Estuary, which stretches for some 50 miles (80 kilometres) from Limerick, and from Clarecastle, to the open sea. Here at low tide the mudflats stretch as far as the eye can see and the only truly accurate way to monitor the vast bird populations is from aircraft. Such counts formed the basis for a detailed piece of ecological work by Oscar Merne.[23] He divided the entire intertidal area of the Shannon/Fergus Estuary into a series of sub-sites and in each he sampled the density of the principal prey species of the common shorebirds. Comparison with the aerial counts showed, not surprisingly, that the highest density of birds coincided with the highest density and greatest biomass of their preferred prey items.

The black-tailed godwit is one of the shorebird species which concentrates in the Shannon Estuary in spring, en route to its summer breeding grounds in Iceland. Already in their fine rufous breeding plumage, the godwits make a stunning spectacle on the shoreline. In early winter these waders concentrate in the south coast estuaries from Wexford Harbour to west Cork. A particular flock wintering in Clonakilty Bay was studied over a number of years in the 1970s and 1980s.[24] The peak numbers occur here in October when they are feeding mainly on the mudflats. As the winter progresses the flocks move to supplement their diet by feeding on coastal fields. The gut contents of four birds collected after feeding on pasture consisted of leather jackets or cranefly larvae and the estuarine crustacean *Corophium*.

Certain bays and estuaries have been more closely monitored by small bands of dedicated bird watchers since the 1970s. These include Inner Galway Bay, Cork Harbour, Malahide Estuary and Strangford Lough. The results provide a fascinating picture of long-term changes in certain species. Inner Galway Bay is one such area, where the winter water bird counts, initiated by Tony Whilde[25] in the 1970s, are still carried on today. One of his favourite spots for counting birds through his telescope was at the end of Nimmo's Pier, at the mouth of the Corrib River. Sadly, Tony did not live to realise his vision, but an analysis of twenty years of these data proved the value of a long-term and consistent approach to monitoring.[26] Most of the species counted showed relatively stable numbers but there were declines in some and increases in others. Some of the species' trends mirrored the national or international picture for the population. For example, the marked increase in the wintering numbers of common gull in Inner Galway Bay between the 1980s and 1990s is the reverse of the trend in the breeding population of this species in the west of Ireland, emphasising that the Galway Bay birds are mainly immigrants. Numbers of birds present in one winter can be altered dramatically by a sudden change in food supply. A short-lived sprat fishery in Inner Galway Bay in 1980-81 resulted in extraordinary numbers of gulls and fish-eating species such as cormorant and red-breasted merganser. After the fish were exploited, numbers of birds also returned to more normal levels.

Of particular conservation concern are the changing fortunes of the wigeon, one of the

most numerous winter ducks in Ireland. Several major estuaries, including Strangford Lough, County Down, and Malahide Estuary, County Dublin, show a long-term decline and this has been associated with an increase in recreational use of the foreshore over the same period. In Strangford Lough the activities are many and varied including shore angling, sailing, wild-fowling and bait digging. Despite the presence of several large 'No Shooting Refuges' administered by the National Trust, the wigeon populations have steeply declined as these sensitive birds move out to less disturbed areas. A detailed analysis of a long series of counts suggests that competition with rising numbers of brent geese has not been the major factor in the decline of the wigeon in Strangford Lough.[27] At Malahide Estuary there has also been a rise in recreational use, including windsurfing on the inner part of the estuary. However, there appears to be a direct correlation between the rising population of brent goose and the declining numbers of wigeon. This suggests competition for the food resources, as both species feed together on eel-grasses, green seaweeds and saltmarsh plants.

The Estuarine Wilderness

The rise and fall of the tide in an estuary is one of the factors that makes the coast a place of constantly changing moods and vistas. When I walk out onto the vastness of the intertidal mud or sandflats in a place like Sligo Bay, Lough Foyle or Wexford Harbour, I feel a sense of wilderness, which is quite unlike anything I have experienced inland. Like primitive man, my senses are heightened by the calls of birds, which nest in remote arctic vastnesses, and by the advancing tide, which creeps up unexpectedly through the channels and creeks. Here, I am close to nature and to the sea, which moulds this unique landscape.

5

Open Sea

The open sea is one of the most fascinating, yet poorly understood habitats in Ireland. Sir Alister Hardy, in his classic book, *The Open Sea*,[1] described this environment as a permanent fog bank into which we can only make a momentary plunge. He wrote, 'We find it has life in it as abundant as our own countryside but so different that it might be life from another world'. The open sea begins near the coast but out of reach of the lowest tides. It stretches away to the edge of the continental shelf and beyond.

Life on the Seabed

Normal tides cover an area of the shoreline that, in scientific jargon, is known as the littoral zone. The sublittoral includes those habitats of the seabed, below low water spring tide mark, which are permanently covered with water. This is generally shallow water within 5 kilometres of the coast. The main divisions here are between rocky substrates and those comprised of unconsolidated sediments. The rocky areas are subdivided into those in shallower water where plants dominate and animal communities live among them (infralittoral) and those in deeper water where plants are rare and animals predominate (circalittoral). The lack of light penetration in deep water is the main limiting factor for plant life.

The deeper water rocky areas are typically occupied by soft corals, large sponges and hydroids all encrusting the rock surface. Areas exposed to waves may be characterised by the jewel anemone, cup coral and feather star. More sheltered areas, such as occur in deeper waters, are typically occupied by solitary ascidian species, brachiopods and sponges. In some areas of high current flow, such as off Wickow Head, reefs of honeycomb worm may be built on the seabed. Extensive beds of mussels and brittlestars can also be present in these conditions.

Shallower, rocky areas are often dominated by beds of kelp. The massive fronds or belt-like leaves of these seaweeds can be up to 3 metres in length and en masse they form a veritable forest, waving back and forth with the movement of the waves. I swam with a snorkel among the kelp forest in a sheltered bay on Clare Island, County Mayo. The shafts of bright September sunlight penetrated to the seabed creating a dappled effect, just like the spring sunlight in an oakwood. On the bottom, a dogfish lay curled up among the holdfasts of kelp, apparently asleep, while shoals of silver sand eels darted about in the sunlight. Because of the shelter provided by the kelp forest, a wide diversity of animal life can live here on the abundant food resources. Typical inhabitants

A diver swims among the kelp beds and encrusting fauna on vertical rock faces (Nigel Motyer).

include the edible sea urchin, the common starfish, brittlestars, blue-rayed limpet, topshells and paddle worms. Sea urchins eat the kelp itself and can do a lot of damage to the fronds.

A recent survey of the exploitable seaweed resources off the west coast of Ireland[2] found that they were common or abundant at nearly half of the sites surveyed, with the dominant species being oarweed and the cuvie. The latter has an inflexible stipe (or stalk) which holds the kelp upright, while the oarweed has a flexible stipe allowing it to bend over at low tide and avoid breaking off with wave action. In this way oarweed can live at a higher level on the shore than the cuvie. The west coast seaweed survey investigated a number of locations by diving. At Spiddal, County Galway, for example, the kelp beds occurred in a 100-metre wide belt parallel to low water mark. The kelp was attached to boulders in depths ranging from 1 to 9 metres and at densities up to 10 to 15 plants per square metre. Just as in a forest, the canopy comprises mature plants while young saplings spring from below, especially where there is a gap in the canopy. The average age of the mature plants is estimated at about five years. This is calculated by counting the annual growth rings on a cross-section through the stipe. The sugar kelp or sea belt lives in more sheltered locations or deep rock pools as it is unable to cope with intense wave action.

On parts of the west coast, such as Mannin Bay, County Galway, curious fragments of a branched material replace the usual sand and pebbles on some beaches. These are commonly known as the 'coral strands' and the 'coral' is

really the dead remains of an alga or seaweed known as maerl. Robert Lloyd Praeger included a drawing of one of the commoner maerl species, *Lithothamnion,* in his autobiography *The Way that I Went.*[3] He described it as 'a novel kind of seaweed which, instead of building up a filamentous or leathery body, constructs one of lime derived from the water in which it lives'. He speculated that 'the quantity which is thrown ashore shows what large colonies must exist under the clear waters of western Connemara'. It was not until the late 1990s that a full survey of these maerl beds was undertaken.[4] The term maerl is thought to originate in Brittany as the best European examples are found in north-western France and western Ireland. It generally occurs in transparent, well-lit Atlantic waters at depths ranging from 3 to 20 metres below sea level. Some deposits occur in water depths greater than 30 metres but these have not been confirmed recently. Sizeable deposits of maerl are now known to occur in over 60 locations along the west coast from Cork to Donegal.

The largest single area is in Inner Galway Bay (2000 hectares) while the waters north of Inishmaan (400 hectares) and in Roaringwater Bay (300 hectares) also have large deposits. In more sheltered regions individual deposits may reach several metres in thickness. Collection of maerl was carried out as early as the seventeenth century in Ireland, mainly for use as a fertiliser on lime-poor soils.

Living maerl is a pink colour due to the combination of photosynthetic pigments. The main maerl-forming species of algae in Ireland are *Lithophyllum, Lithothamnion, Phymatolithon* and *Mesophyllum.* The communities of other plants and animals associated with maerl beds indicate a high biodiversity. For example, they harbour over a quarter of all the known species of *gammaridean* amphipods (mainly tiny marine shrimps) known in Irish waters. In fact, over three quarters of the larger benthic animal species associated with maerl beds are crustaceans and the majority of these are amphipods. The algal flora of maerl beds is also

An angler fish disguised on a bed of maerl in a west coast bay (Nigel Motyer).

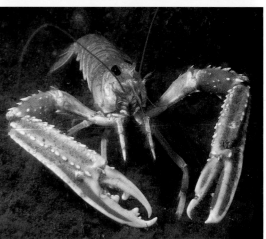

(above) A spiny starfish on a western bed of mearl (Nigel Motyer); (below) the Dublin Bay prawn is found in deep water in the Irish Sea (Nigel Motyer).

extraordinarily rich, with the highest number of species found in the more sheltered parts of the beds.[5]

Where the seabed is made of unconsolidated sand or gravel rather than rock or boulders, a different habitat will develop. Coarse sands and gravels hold a community dominated by bivalve molluscs, anemones, polychaete worms and amphipod crustaceans. A seabed habitat dominated by cobble-size rocks has been found at Aughinish Shoal in Inner Galway Bay. Using a suction sampler, the fauna of this habitat was described by a team from Galway's Martin Ryan Marine Science Institute.[6] The most abundant animals were molluscs, such as the thick-lipped dog whelk, while a total of 47 species of crustaceans was recorded with the porcelain crab *Pisidia longicornis* dominant.

Because of the variety of microhabitats available between the cobbles this is a particularly diverse community.

More sandy seabeds in shallow waters are usually colonised by razor shell and heart urchin, both of which may be washed up on beaches in large numbers after storms. On the east coast, north of Dublin, a fishery for razor shells has developed recently, but this may be damaging the entire community as it involves raking through the top layers of sand and disturbing the habitat. Bottom-dwelling flatfish, such as sole, dabs and plaice, use the soft sediments for concealment and others, such as sand eels, lay eggs in the sand. In stable muddy sediments a variety of anemones, sea pens, polychaete worms and bivalvemolluscs (such as the great scallop) are characteristic. Very muddy areas are difficult for most surface dwelling animals, but burrowing forms such as the Dublin Bay prawn, small molluscs such as *Abra* and small brittlestars (*Amphiura* and *Ophiura*) are common. These animals characterise the deep water sediments of the north-west Irish Sea, north of Lambay Island.

The main bottom-dwelling (benthic) faunal communities of the Irish Sea and Celtic Sea (off the east and south coasts respectively) are now quite well known.[7] The distribution of animal communities is complex, but some clear patterns have emerged. A rocky shelf forms a fringe along much of the south coast. Outside this, there are large areas of muddy/fine sand inhabited by communities dominated by brittlestar *Amphiura* and the striped venus shell.

The Continental Shelf

To the west of Ireland lies a vast area of sea floor, which stretches out to the edge of the continental shelf, at depths of down to 200 metres. At the edge of the shelf the continental slope drops steeply to murky depths of 4,000 metres on the abyssal plain. The shelf itself is not flat but has a series of ridges and valleys with rock formations and sediments, quite similar to those on land. Near the edge of the shelf, to the south west of Ireland, is the Porcupine Seabight, an almost circular basin, covering an area about half the size of the island of Ireland. The water in this vast amphitheatre is stratified so that various water bodies occur at different depths. These water bodies vary in temperature and salinity, with temperature falling steeply from 10°C to 4°C between depths of 600 and

A diver investigates a rich bank of sponges and dead man's fingers, a type of living coral (Nigel Motyer).

1,400 metres. The lack of sunlight at the bottom of the basin, combined with suspended or dissolved particles in the water, due to sea bed erosion by waves and currents, makes this a dark and mysterious world.[8]

In the mid-nineteenth century, it was assumed that no plant or animal life could exist below about 300 fathoms (600 metres) depth. Charles Wyville Thompson, Professor of Geology and Natural History at Queen's College, Belfast, from 1860-1870, set out to disprove this belief through a series of scientific expeditions. In 1869-1870, on board HMS *Porcupine*, he managed to dredge animal life from depths of 2,435 fathoms (4,456 metres), when five days out from Belfast. In the late nineteenth century a series of deep-sea dredging expeditions was sponsored by the Royal Irish Academy. In 1888 Robert Lloyd Praeger was one of a number of early naturalists, led by William Spotswood Green, who took part in an expedition to explore the deep waters off the south-west coast of Ireland. At a depth of 1,080 fathoms (1,976 metres) the sounder came up choked with *Globigerina* ooze, a cream-coloured material made up of the microscopic shells of *foraminifera*, spread across the sea floor. After surviving a gale at night they trawled again the next day at 750 fathoms (1,372 metres) and brought up 'a splendid catch of marvellous creatures'.[9] In the catch were 'great sea-slugs, red, purple and green; beautiful corals, numerous sea urchins with long slender spines; a great variety of starfishes of many shapes and of all colours, including one like a raw beefsteak'. Praeger was fascinated by the amazing colours – purple, scarlet, orange and brilliant green – and, in *The Way that I Went*, he asked the question 'what is the use of colour in absolute darkness?'

In June 1896 a group of the leading Irish naturalists of their time, including W.S. Green, R.M. Barrington, J.A. Harvie-Brown, W.F. de Vismes Kane, H. L. Jameson and R.L. Praeger, set out on board the steamer *Granuaile*, to explore the area around Rockall. This is a small speck of rock in the ocean, 'a tiny cone of granite, like a haycock bent over by the wind'.[10] Unfortunately they ran into a north Atlantic gale and, with the ship 'rolling and pitching heavily', they tried trawling but the gear was torn to pieces. A repeat trip a week later, in calmer weather, proved more successful, with dredging of numerous animals despite some loss of gear. Three sponges new to science were recovered, but more puzzling was the occurrence of dead shells of a number of molluscs, which normally live in shallow waters. This set the Victorian scientists off into speculation about recent changes in sea level.

In the early 1990s exploration scientists first identified and described spectacular underwater mounds on the Porcupine Bank, to the west of Galway. These so-called carbonate mounds were up to 300 metres in height (almost as high as the Eiffel Tower) and 2-3 kilometres in diameter (as big as Lambay Island). Further investigations revealed they were often associated with coldwater corals, principally of the species *Lophelia pertusa* and *Madrepora oculata*. While the existence of these coral reefs off the west coast has been known since they were first discovered by Charles Wyville Thompson in 1869, their full extent and diversity has only become clear in the 1990s with the use of sonar technology and deep sea photography.[11] In 2001 a joint French/Irish research cruise, on board the vessel *Atalante*, using state of the art underwater video cameras, found coral gardens teeming with marine life. On coral reefs in the Porcupine Bank and Rockall Trough, over 900 species have been found associated with the *Lophelia* corals. This species richness is comparable with the more famous shallow-water tropical coral reefs. There is growing concern about the potential damage to these coral reefs from deep-sea trawling for whitefish and from oil and gas exploration. The conservation of coral reefs at depths of around 1,000 metres below sea level is quite a challenge.

The hydroid Neoturris *floats in the plankton* (Nigel Motyer).

Plankton

Plankton is the drifting (often microscopic) plant and animal life of the ocean upon which much of the rest of the marine biodiversity depends. Plankton is collected by trailing a fine net bag behind a moving boat and the catch can then be examined under a microscope. What emerges from this hidden world looks more like something from outer space than from our own marine environment.

The basis of most food chains in the sea is the floating plant life (or phytoplankton). Instead of being composed of large and complex life forms, as are higher terrestrial plants or seaweeds on the shore, the phytoplankton is a mass of tiny single-celled plants, which are mostly only visible under the microscope. One of the benefits of the small size of each member of the plankton is that it has a large surface area in relation to volume thus aiding its ability to stay afloat. Each tiny cell can also gain maximum surface exposure to the sunlight and to the mineral salts in the sea, which are the ingredients for its growth and survival. Although it is difficult to believe there is sufficient volume of this microscopic vegetation to support all the animal life of the sea, it has been estimated that the amount of plant life under a given area of sea may exceed that produced for the same area in a tropical forest.[12] The most significant components of the phytoplankton are the diatoms, single-celled algae that have a hard outer case like a glass box. Some of these diatoms are simple in shape while others have extraordinarily complex shapes with long spikes and some forming long flexible chains. Some are flattened like thin sheets of paper or attached together like a long ribbon. Other important planktonic organisms are the flagellates, all of which possess at least one long whip-like extension that is used like a rudder to stay afloat.

A compass jellyfish pulses through the sea (Nigel Motyer).

Among the flagellates are both plants and animals and some forms that have the characters of both animal and plant in one organism. Many of the flagellates look like stars or sputniks with a variety of spines and surface grooves. One group, the dinoflagellates, can produce a brilliant phosphorescence in the water giving a ghostly glow wherever the water is agitated by waves or in the wash of a ship.

The plant material (phytoplankton) in turn attracts a huge concentration of microscopic animal life (zooplankton). The zooplankton is said to contain a more diverse assemblage of animal life than may be found in any other habitat on earth.[13] Some planktonic animals are the juvenile forms of marine invertebrates and fish. Others live their entire lives as floating microscopic organisms.

The apparently sudden appearance of plankton blooms on the open sea is connected with the upwelling of nutrient-rich waters from the sea floor. Cilian Roden describes this upwelling as being strongest during big spring tides when a large volume of slightly colder nutrient-rich water is stirred up from the bottom and reaches the surface over the underwater escarpment. Here he is referring to an underwater cliff, about 60 metres high, which separates the shallow coastal ledge fringing the mainland and islands of south Connemara from the sea floor. This slopes rapidly to depths of greater than 100 metres. Roden describes this area as holding the largest populations of pollack and coalfish and being one of the best areas to see seabirds such as shearwaters, gannets, petrels and auks, possibly due to the richer feeding. Seamas Mac an Iomaire and the other inhabitatants of *Mainis* (Mweenish Island) were well aware of this rich feeding area above the underwater cliff and they regularly fished on it, but they may not have understood the importance of the plankton to the marine food chain.[14]

It is the boundary zones between mixed and stratified (temperature-separated) water that often produce large concentrations of plankton.[15] There are major tidal fronts in the Irish Sea, between County Down and the Isle of Man and between County Wexford and South Wales. Some biologists think that the meeting of nutrient-rich, well-mixed water and warm well-lit stratified water provide exceptional conditions for growth. Others suspect that the mechanism may be physical accumulation of nutrients. These boundary zones or tidal fronts usually occur in shallow seas over the continental shelf or in locations where there is increased turbulent mixing of seawater near to shore due to the tide being forced between rocks, around headlands or into shallow water. Roden describes the effect as a great stirring up of nutrients fuelling a sudden bloom of plant growth in the sea.

Jellyfish

Most of us are familiar with jellyfish either as a hazard when swimming in summer or as amorphous blobs stranded on the beach. I have often seen countless thousands of the larger forms in the Irish Sea or the Atlantic Ocean in summer from the deck of a yacht. This ancient and primitive group contains many wonderful and varied forms, some of them too small to see except under a microscope. When snorkelling on the west coast of County Mayo

once, I swam into a swarm of tiny sea gooseberries, their transparent bodies pulsing through the sunlit water in a sheltered bay. The jellyfish are mainly siphonophores, that is, they are composite animals, made up of a large number of individuals some of which are polyps, others medusae. Most of the jellyfish drift at the mercy of ocean currents and winds although they can direct their movement by a pulsing action. There are only a few larger species in Irish waters but these can often occur in huge numbers. One of the most abundant is the common moon jellyfish, easily recognised by its four purple oval shapes grouped around the centre of its otherwise transparent umbrella. They feed on planktonic animals which they catch in streams of mucus, 'like catching flies on a sticky fly-paper'.[16] Even more impressive is the large blueish jellyfish *Rhizostoma pulmo*, which has an umbrella or dome up to 60 centimetres in diameter and a dense mass of tentacles beneath. The largest jellyfish known in Irish waters is the lion's mane, which can grow

The moon jellyfish is commonly found stranded on beaches after storms (Nigel Motyer).

Deep water fish include (left) the John Dory and (right) the pogge (Nigel Motyer).

to 75 centimetres across in Atlantic waters but more usually reach 30 to 45 centimetres in diameter. It has a vast number of trailing tentacles, which are loaded with stinging cells to capture passing prey. In the aptly named Portugese man-of-war the tentacles can deliver a sting which can paralyse large fish or any unfortunate swimmers. The swimming bell in this colonial animal is replaced by an enormous float, which can be up to 30 centimetres long. Other members of the jellyfish group are more frequently encountered while beachcombing on the strandline of a sandy beach (see Chapter 3).

Marine Fish

Up to 1998 some 466 species of marine fish had been recorded from Irish territorial waters (that is within the 200 nautical mile fishery zone). While some species occur in both deep and shallow waters, 315 species are known from offshore waters with depths greater than 200 metres, while some 235 species occur in inshore, shallower waters. The fish fauna is composed of a rich mixture of species derived from different origins. Over half of the species are described as indigenous cool-temperate, nearly one third as warm-temperate Mediterranean-Lusitanian, about 7 per cent as cold temperate eastern Boreal and 12 per cent as deep-water species from the upper continental slope.[17]

Some of the shallow water, coastal species are quite familiar to us from the fishmonger's slab. These include such commercially important species as cod and plaice which are bottom dwelling (or demersal), together with species like mackerel and herring which are described as pelagic, ranging widely in the surface layers of the ocean. The Mediterranean–Lusitanian group of species is at the northern limit of its global range in Irish waters. It includes some permanent residents such as the undulate ray or migrants such as Spanish mackerel, which move north as the water temperature rises in summer. The abundance of warm water species in Irish waters has increased significantly in the last four decades. The number of cold water (or Boreal) species has also increased but this is thought to be because a number of smaller fish were previously undetected. Typical of this northern group are some permanent residents with wonderful names such as wolf-fish, snake blenny and jellycat, while migrants such as Greenland halibut are present for only part of the year. In addition to this, the North Atlantic Drift regularly carries several sub-tropical species across the ocean and into Irish waters. Typical members of this group are the wreck-fish and American barrelfish.[18]

More familiar fish occur in the shallower waters of the Irish Sea. Surveys using otter trawls suggest four different fish assemblages, with inshore waters close to the Irish coast holding an abundance of herring and sprat and those close to the British coast dominated by several flatfish, including plaice and dab. The coarser sediments of the central Irish Sea hold an abundance of red gurnard, sharks and rays while Norway pout, witch and long-rough dab are characteristic of the deeper water, west of the Isle of Man. Among the previously unrecorded species, which turned up in these recent surveys, were triggerfish, boarfish, northern rockling and undulate ray. The fish assemblages in the Irish Sea reflect the patterns of benthic (bottom-dwelling) invertebrate communities. For example, the typical witch populations, which are found on the muddy grounds west of the Isle of Man, are associated with the characteristic *Brissopsis* and *Amphiura* communities here. The inshore fish assemblage, dominated by flatfish, occurs primarily on the shallow *Venus* invertebrate community.[19]

Apart from a few commercially exploited species, the population biology and ecology of most of Ireland's marine fish fauna are virtually unknown. This is of particular concern with the deep water species on the upper continental slope, which are increasingly being exploited by commercial trawlers. It is now common-place to find, on the menu of many seafood restaurants, such species as orange roughy, which were virtually unknown a decade ago. Other exotic-sounding species such as blackspot grenadier and black scabbard fish, previously known only from depths greater than 200 metres, have been increasingly recorded in inshore waters. It is thought that the shallower water may be used for breeding and nursery grounds by deep-water species such as rabbit fish and six-gilled shark.

Knowledge of the occurrence and biology of shark species in Irish waters has increased recently with the work of Aaron Henderson of National University of Ireland, Galway.[20] Among the commonest species are the tope, spurdog, smoothhound and lesser spotted dog-fish, regularly caught by shore anglers.s Deep sea anglers often catch blue sharks, but these are mainly returned to the sea, each bearing a tag supplied by the Central Fisheries Board. Indications are that male blue sharks prefer to remain offshore in deeper water while the immature females come closer to the coast, but the reason for this difference remains unclear. The porbeagle is one of the most commer-cially valuable sharks and those caught may be up to 2 metres in length. Examination of the records of porbeagles shows that some of these may be of a very similar looking but rarer species called the mako shark. All sharks grow quite slowly, mature at a late age and produce few young when compared with other fish species. This makes them vulnerable to any commercial fishing pressure and the biology of shark stocks in Irish waters is still poorly understood.

A bull rout
(Nigel Motyer).

Basking shark – the largest fish in the North Atlantic (Richard T. Mills).

Basking Sharks

Imagine if you were sailing in a small boat and a giant shark surfaced beside you with its length overall greater than the boat. Luckily the basking shark is harmless to people as it feeds completely on plankton. The basking shark in Ireland was traditionally called the sunfish (although there is another rare species of this name) because it was most often seen basking on the surface in sunny weather.[21]

Incredibly, the basking shark is the second largest fish on the planet (after the whale shark) and by far the largest fish in the North Atlantic. It can weigh more than an elephant and grow up to 10 metres in length (about the size of a six-berth cruising yacht). However, the most amazing physical feature of the basking shark is its mouth, which has been described as a huge, diamond-shaped hole, looking more like the open cargo doors of a military aircraft than the oral cavity of a fish. With this plankton guzzler wide open, the shark cruises slowly, at a speed of about two knots, capturing the tiny marine creatures on thousands of filters called gill rakers. This feeding method is so efficient that it has been estimated that a single basking shark can filter enough seawater every hour to fill a 50-metre Olympic swimming pool.

The basking shark is widely distributed in cool temperate waters throughout the world. On this side of the North Atlantic, it occurs from Iceland and Norway to the Mediterranean and West Africa. There are a few well-known basking shark hotspots in western Europe including the Irish Sea around the Isle of Man and parts of the west coast of Ireland. The fish move into our waters in spring and summer probably to exploit the upwellings of plankton-rich water which take place at this time along certain fronts (see Chapter 1). After that, they just vanish. One of the great mysteries about the basking shark is where they go in winter. They were once thought to hibernate in deep water, and this is now being investigated by scientists from the Marine Biological Association, using satellite tracking. Special transmitters have been fitted to a small number of basking sharks in the English Channel and off the Firth of Clyde, and these are providing a fascinating insight into the secrets of these amazing animals. Contrary to what was believed for the last 50 years, basking sharks do not hibernate during winter but they undertake extensive horizontal and vertical migrations. Two sharks tagged off Plymouth moved around the south and west of Ireland before heading north to the Outer Hebrides, a distance of about 2,000 kilometres in about two months. Tagged sharks also made some incredible dives, up to 1,000 metres below sea level. Plankton can occur at considerable depths during winter and the fish probably follow this vital food source.

In 1993 a sighting scheme for basking sharks in Irish waters was established using records from fishermen, yachtsmen and other seafarers as well as the general public on land. A total of 425 individual sharks was recorded from around the entire coast but with concentrations off the east, south-west and northern coasts. Sightings peaked in summer and most records were of single animals. Unfortunately, 28 records were of basking sharks entangled in fishing nets or dead fish washed up on the shoreline. The traditional

practice of hunting the basking shark in Irish waters is described in Chapter 7. The sunfish bank, west of Counties Galway and Mayo, was once a favoured hunting ground for fishermen where large numbers of basking sharks were caught. However, none was reported from this area in the 1993 survey.[22]

Turtles

When marine turtles were stranded on western Irish beaches in the past, it was thought that they were, like vagrant birds, unfortunate passengers on ocean currents which had carried them far beyond their native tropical waters. Nowadays, we know that marine turtles move into Irish latitudes every year and that there may be many more around than we realise. I remember the excitment that greeted the arrival at a small pier in west Donegal of a huge marine turtle being towed behind a local fishing boat. The impressive animal, already nearly dead from drowning while entangled in ropes, was hauled out onto the pier where it finally

The leathery turtle migrates annually into Irish waters where it feeds on jellyfish. Unfortunately, many drown when they become entangled in ropes and nets. These large marine reptiles are often treated as curious monsters from the deep.

succumbed to overheating. The reptile was up to 2 metres in length and looked not unlike an upturned boat with a leathery skin stretched across several lengthwise ribs. The leathery turtle, or Luth, is the commonest of the marine turtles encountered in Irish waters and is now known to be a regular part of the summer marine fauna of much of the north-east Atlantic – it belongs here and functions normally in cool Irish waters because it is the only living reptile known to be warm blooded, with a central body temperature of about 25°C.

One leathery turtle captured off County Cork in 1993 had a stomach full of jellyfish, on which it had been feeding. It is thought that the turtles follow swarms of jellyfish in the summer months but little is known about their feeding habits. Tom Doyle of University College Cork is studying this phenomenon in the Irish Sea. The other three turtles known

from Irish waters are much rarer and are usually in poor condition because of hypothermia. The hawksbill turtle is the smallest of those known from Ireland and Kemp's ridley turtle is the rarest with only four known occurrences here. The loggerhead turtle is the most frequent of the three, with most strandings on the west coast. Several of these animals have been rescued alive, rehabilitated in warm water aquaria (particularly at Dingle) and later returned to their native waters by air. The reported strandings of these turtles were listed by Colm O'Riordan[23] of the National Museum of Ireland, while Gabriel King carried out a further review of occurrences in the period 1973–83, mainly by interviewing fishermen whose records add greatly to our knowledge.

Until relatively recently, little detail was known about the migration routes of turtles, but this is now being remedied by the use of satellite tags or recorders mounted on turtle shells. These send information on position, depth and frequency of dives, etc., to a network of satellites. The information can be collected for months or even years and analysed in great detail. Some female leathery turtles that have nested in the Caribbean have been found to follow the Gulf Stream past Newfoundland and out to the mid Atlantic before visiting European waters, then returning to the Caribbean after a journey of thousands of kilometres. From older, more primitive flipper tags (like the ear tags of cattle) it has long been known that baby loggerhead turtles from the Caribbean drift round and round the subtropics and tropics of the Atlantic, passing the Azores, Madeira and Canaries repeatedly en route, growing for perhaps ten to twelve years before returning to the Caribbean to live for the rest of their long lives. It is these drifting turtles that provide the input of loggerheads (and perhaps hawksbills and Kemp's ridleys too) to Irish waters, usually after prolonged south-westerly winds that divert the turtles from their regular paths.

Birds of the Ocean

We are most accustomed to seeing seabirds around their breeding colonies in summer, or scavenging behind fishing trawlers, but we tend to forget that they may be far out at sea for much of the year. The albatross is probably the classic ocean-going bird, cruising for thousands of miles across the open sea with little waste of energy. The seabirds of the northern hemisphere, although smaller and less dramatic, are equally well adapted for life at sea.

The physical characteristics of the coastal seas of Ireland are of primary importance in the distribution and abundance of seabirds at sea. Tidal fronts are areas of high biological activity containing plankton densities several orders of magnitude higher than adjacent waters and floating weed patches or weed lines with

high densities of fish larvae. The birds tend to concentrate where their prey species are most easily found.

Upwelling occurs where cool oceanic water rises to the sea surface. Phytoplankton growth is promoted by the increased light levels acting on nutrient-rich water and this in turn promotes a high concentration of zooplankton and fish, birds, dolphins and whales. Such upwelling occurs in summer off the south-west coast of Ireland supporting phytoplankton densities up to three times higher than those of adjacent waters. Some seabird species (especially petrels and shearwaters) feed directly on the zooplankton, either by pursuit diving or by picking prey from the surface.

Other birds are attracted by the fish shoal that, in turn, is feeding on the zooplankton. Diving birds such as guillemots and razorbills will pursue sand eels and sprat that are shoaling in mid-water or near the surface. Manx

A gannet, with 2-metre wingspan, is ideally suited to long-distance flight and feeding far out to sea (Eddie Dunne).

shearwaters, gannets and kittiwakes concentrate on pelagic fish such as mackerel and sprat, which shoal near the surface. The fishing methods vary, with gannets and terns plunge diving from a height, shearwaters diving from the surface and kittiwakes, which cannot dive, picking the fish off the surface. Sometimes, a big concentration of fish causes a 'feeding frenzy' with numerous birds plunging into the shoal and scavengers such as gulls picking up the discarded fragments.

Many seabirds prefer to feed on fish waste discarded from fishing boats at sea. Simon Berrow has estimated that up to 1,000 tonnes of discarded herring alone may be available to seabirds from boats fishing the Celtic Sea. Fulmars and gulls are especially fond of scavenging in this way but some other species, such as gannets, may compete for these valuable supplies. Unfortunately, when the herring nets are hauled in they often contain the drowned body of a dolphin or a porpoise as well.

Outside the breeding season, some Irish seabirds disperse great distances throughout the oceans. We know from ringing recoveries that Manx shearwaters winter on the east coast of South America, up to 9,000 kilometres from their nesting sites. Gannets hatched at Irish colonies winter on north-west coast of Africa and the western Mediterranean. Guillemots and razorbills spend the winter in the Irish Sea, Bay of Biscay, Celtic Sea and the English Channel. The terns are among the greatest travellers with sandwich terns making annual migrations to western and southern Africa and roseate terns to the Gulf of Guinea. In dispersing across the oceans seabirds are exploiting different fish stocks at different times of year.[24]

Up to the mid-1990s most of the surveys of seabirds at sea in Irish waters were limited to certain parts of the coast or were made from ships carrying out other activities such as fisheries research. Between 1994 and 1997 a series of intensive surveys was made by the Seabirds at Sea Team (SAST) of the Joint Nature Conservation Committee, especially in areas where information was lacking.[25]

Seabirds also use the offshore waters of the continental shelf and a three-year survey of these ocean travellers has just been completed by scientists from the Coastal and Marine Resources Centre (CMRC) in Cork.[26] Ship-based surveys

The roseate tern is a long-distance migrant, wintering off the coast of West Africa (Oscar Merne).

Common dolphins off west Cork (Padraig Whooley).

have now been carried out for a major part of the Irish Atlantic margins including the continental shelf, the shelf edge and the deeper water of the ocean, such as the Rockall Trough. In total, 37 seabird species were recorded during 540 survey days at sea. Overall, numbers were dominated by five common species – fulmar, gannet, kittiwake, guillemot and Manx shearwater. However, rarer species such as sooty and great shearwater, pomarine and long-tailed skuas are now known to move through the Rockall-Hatton region during their annual migrations to and from the arctic breeding grounds. Several seabird species, such as great shearwaters and Wilson's storm petrel, which pass through these remote waters, may act as indicators for climate change.

Whales and Dolphins

The porpoises, dolphins and whales, known collectively by scientists as cetaceans, are among the most highly evolved mammals as they have adapted to a totally aquatic environment. They are highly social animals, mostly living in small groups or pods, and they communicate with a complex sound system, often likened to 'singing'. Those that feed on fish or squid frequently hunt in groups, rounding up or ambushing their prey, just as lions co-operate in hunting antelope on the African plains. Others (the baleen whales) feed by filtering large volumes of water to extract the protein-rich plankton 'soup'. They are all highly intelligent mammals and quite fascinating to watch.

Perhaps the best known cetacean in Ireland is 'Fungie', the bottlenose dolphin which has adopted Dingle Harbour in County Kerry as his long-term home and attracts over 100,000 visitors annually to see a wild dolphin close inshore. Less well known is the fact that a resident population of at least 100 bottlenose dolphins lives throughout the year, just north of Dingle in the Shannon Estuary. Here, they feed on fish running up Ireland's largest river system and calves are born within sight of the coastlines of Kerry and Clare.

A total of 24 species of cetacean has been recorded from Irish waters, either from confirmed sightings, strandings of dead animals or from records of whale hunting (see Chapter 7). Accurate identification at sea is difficult,

(Clockwise from top) Three fin whales surface off the coast of west Cork (Padraig Whooley); *the tail fluke of a humpback whale, now confirmed as an annual visitor to the south coast of Ireland* (Padraig Whooley); *a stranded whale at Magilligan, County Derry in 1907* (R.J. Welch, courtesy of the Ulster Museum).

even in calm sea conditions, as often the only thing visible may be a dorsal fin. However, some marine scientists, especially those at University College Cork and in the Irish Whale and Dolphin Group (IWDG), have developed the technique of photo-recognition and have applied this to identify not only the species but also the individuals among the bottlenose dolphins in the Shannon Estuary. Cetacean biologists usually make their observations on moving boats from which they constantly scan the sea surface with binoculars.

Ship-based surveys have been used to carry out observations on whales, dolphins and porpoises passing through the continental shelf area west of Ireland. Oliver Ó Cadhla and his colleagues from the CMRC have confirmed the importance of this vast area of sea for marine mammals. Using a combination of direct sightings and acoustic equipment, a total of over 1,400 individual records of some 21 species of cetacean was logged. These records included six baleen whale and fifteen toothed whale species. Highly significant records were those of rare, endangered and migratory baleen whales, such as blue whale and northern right whale, the latter of which has less than 300 individuals known on the planet. Some rarely-seen species such as Sowerby's beaked whale, Cuvier's beaked whale and false killer whale were also recorded for the first time as live animals in Irish waters where they had only been known before from strandings of dead animals on the coast.[27]

This ground-breaking research confirms the hypothesis that Ireland's continental margin is one of the richest parts of the North Atlantic for whales and dolphins and that these animals are passing through these waters in significant numbers. New techniques of visual mark-recapture were used by the researchers to derive summer population estimates for the most abundant species, including white-sided and common dolphins. Habitat preferences of some of these mammals for shallow or deep water, warm or cold layers were confirmed, allowing a much more accurate prediction of the regions of the shelf which should receive strict protection under the EU Habitats Directive.

The longest-running record of cetacean sightings in Ireland over the decades has been kept by the naturalists who watch the seas off west Cork from the Cape Clear Bird Observatory. Their systematic sea-watching has produced many records of unusual species passing by this important south-western promontory.[28] However, at best, this can only give a fragment of the story, as the animals are often out of sight, even of a powerful telescope, or are obscured by rough sea conditions. Since 1991 the IWDG has run a Cetacean Sighting Scheme all around the coast and using boat-based observers. A review of the first decade of the scheme contains some useful maps and summaries of the distribution of seventeen species.[29]

Strandings of live or dead whales and dolphins also provide a somewhat biased sample, as the locations are those where the sea has deposited the carcass rather than the areas where the animals would normally live and feed. Nevertheless, stranding records have been kept for centuries and they provide a fascinating list of the species using Irish waters. In the nineteenth and earlier centuries, stranded whales were considered as 'wrecks of the sea' and were much prized either as food or as zoological curiosities. From 1913 the British Museum (Natural History) began to collect systematic records of stranded cetaceans, including those from Ireland, and, most importantly, to publish them in a series of *Reports of Cetacea stranded on the British coasts*. The National Museum of Ireland (in Dublin) co-operated with this scheme and, in 1972, published its own *Provisional list of cetacea and turtles stranded or captured in Irish waters*.[30] This list formed the basis for a summary of strandings published by James Fairley in his classic book *Irish Whales and Whaling*.[31] Since then a more complete analysis has been carried out for the period 1901 to 1995.[32]

I well remember my first encounter with a stranded cetacean. It was on a remote stoney beach at the south end of Gorumna Island in the Connemara Gaeltacht in the summer of 1978. I was taking part, with a team of scientists from Ireland and Britain, in the first ever complete census of breeding harbour seals on the Irish coast. We beached our inflatable boat beside the large carcass, almost 4 metres in length, with skin blotched and peeling from the combined effects of salt water and decomposition. We carefully measured and photographed the unfortunate animal, paying special attention to the teeth. It was the distinctive two groups of four teeth on the lower jaw which suggested that this was a Risso's dolphin. The narrow dorsal fin, bulbous forehead and absence of the 'typical dolphin snout' confirmed the identification. This record, the first for County Galway, was joined the same year by the stranding of a pod (or family group) of nine Risso's dolphins in Blacksod Bay, County Mayo

A friendly dolphin at Fanore, County Clare which allows divers to swim close by (Nigel Motyer).

to the north. I often wonder if this group was part of the herd of twelve to fifteen Risso's dolphins that had surrounded our little boat in June that year in Broadhaven, just north of Blacksod Bay. This is one of their favourite areas, as a number of repeat sightings and strandings have confirmed. Other favoured feeding areas for Risso's dolphin are around Cape Clear Island off west Cork, the Skelligs off County Kerry and the Saltee Islands off County Wexford.

In summer 2003 I was sailing off Wicklow Head when a group of eight to ten dolphins surfaced around the boat. They had all the characteristics of Risso's dolphins. One animal surfaced beside us and then dived beneath the boat. They appeared to be feeding in a small area north of the point, where the tide race may force food to the surface. Risso's dolphins are poorly studied but it is known that they dive to the seabed to hunt squid. Their greyish white skins are often covered with scratches and scrapes which are thought to be caused by teeth-raking disputes among themselves.

Risso's dolphins are regularly recorded inshore from August to February close to the

OPEN SEA

east coast of Wicklow, in St George's Channel off Wexford, in Galway Bay and Clew Bay. In early summer they seem to prefer the continental shelf, with sightings off south-west Ireland and north of Donegal.

The familiar bottlenose dolphins are more frequently sighted between November and May than at other times of year. Offshore they are most often seen in a band along the edge of the continental shelf to the south west of Ireland, where they mix with pilot whales and probably share the same food sources. From June to October they appear to come inshore and are most often seen along the west coast and in St George's Channel. Highest numbers of these dolphins are seen in August. Relatively few bottlenose dolphins have been recorded as strandings, with the majority on the west coast. The mouth of the Shannon Estuary, between Counties Clare and Kerry, is one of the best places in Europe to see wild bottlenose dolphins. Special dolphin-watching tour boats sail throughout the summer from Kilrush and Carrigaholt on the Clare side of the estuary, with at least 15,000 people each year now taking the 'dolphin boats'. The car ferry crossing from Tarbert to Killimer is another good place to see dolphins as this is a narrow neck in the estuary and fish are probably concentrated here. Bottlenose dolphins are also known to breed in the Shannon Estuary, as newly-born calves can be easily recognised from their small size and the conspicuous white vertical lines (neonatal folds) along the length of their body. The sightings of calves in the estuary suggest that the peak birth time here is in the periods June/July and September/October.

Simon Ingram has made a special study of these dolphins and can recognise a large number of individuals from the markings on their fins and backs. He knows that many of the animals either stay in the estuary throughout the year or return here to feed on a regular basis. In May 2001 a lone bottlenose dolphin followed a fishing boat from Carrigaholt in

the Shannon Estuary to west Kerry and then to the Great Blasket Island. For two months this heavily scarred dolphin stayed in the Kerry area where he was regularly photographed and many people watched or swam with him. This friendly dolphin, nicknamed 'Dony', disappeared from Kerry in early July 2001. At the end of March 2002 the same dolphin (recognised by an exact match of his markings) appeared in Dorset in south-west England having been to Brittany, north-west France and the Channel Islands in between. This is the first confirmed record of a wild dolphin moving from the west of Ireland to France and England, but it may be quite normal for this mobile species.

Common (or harbour) porpoise is the most frequently recorded cetacean species around the Irish coast, both from sightings and strandings.[33] The porpoise is known in Irish as *muc mhara*, which means the sea pig. Their regular appearance in summer and apparent preference for herring was mentioned in natural history books as early as the eighteenth century.[34] Strandings of common porpoise have been recorded in all months, with a peak in winter. Sightings from Cape Clear Island, County Cork on the other hand, show a peak in the autumn from August to October. The largest number of porpoises ever seen in a single day, 500 on 25 August 1973, was recorded from Cape Clear. Unlike most cetaceans, some estimates of total numbers have been made for common porpoise. In July 1989 five large strip transects between Galway Bay and west Cork were surveyed by boat and a total of over 19,000 animals was estimated for this area. Even more porpoises (over 36,000) were estimated to occur in the Celtic Sea (between southern Ireland and Wales). Regularly watched headlands such as Howth Head, County Dublin and the Old Head of Kinsale, County Cork, have produced sighting rates of up to one per 90 minute's observation in June.

Despite the evidence that porpoises are among our commonest large mammals, very

(right) Three killer whales in the docks at Cork Harbour in 2001 (Padraig Whooley)*; (below) a stranded pilot whale* (Padraig Whooley)*.*

little is known about their ecology or diet. A total of nineteen animals examined from both strandings and accidental catches (bycatches) showed that whiting and other gadoid fish (cod and its relatives) comprise 80 to 90 per cent of the food remains in the stomachs. Other major items include herring and sprats and a few squid (Cephalopods).[35] Bycatch data suggest that the porpoise also feeds well offshore (up to 200 miles from the coast). It is estimated that between 1,825 and 2,049 porpoises are caught annually in gill nets set for whitefish in British and Irish waters. It is not known how the cetaceans become entangled in the nets in Irish waters, but evidence from elsewhere suggests that they are probably caught on the bottom where their main prey are found. Emer Rogan and Simon Berrow consider that this level of mortality is not sustainable and that some method of preventing these unnecessary deaths is urgently needed.

Porpoises may themselves be regular prey for a related species, the killer whale, which is perhaps the most spectacular cetacean species to be recorded in Irish waters. Their striking black and white markings, tall pointed dorsal fin and their reputation for eating large prey such as seals, make these animals an awesome sight. There have been only ten strandings of killers between 1901 and 1995, including a live stranding of three whales (thought to be a family group) at Dungarvan, County Waterford. Sightings of killer whales in Irish waters are often of small parties, thought to be family groups. At Cape Clear Island, County Cork a school of ten was once seen but the usual number is three or four. These small pods of whales often enter inshore waters and can occasionally be seen in harbours and inlets.

In August 1962, a party of four killers entered 'the Narrows' of Strangford Lough, County Down in full view of the participants of the annual regatta. A very similar observation, of one bull, two cows and a calf killer whale, was made in the same location in May 1975. Sometimes killer whales will swim up an estuary in pursuit of migrating salmon, even pursuing them into freshwater rivers. In November 1977 a celebrated whale surfaced in the River Foyle, between the bridges of Derry city. It was a bull killer whale of about 20 feet (6 metres) in length. After six days of feeding and ignoring all attempts to scare him back to sea, this whale finally moved off to the Lough and into the open sea. Another much publicised whale 'event' was recorded in June 2001 when a party of three killer whales entered the enclosed waters of Cork Harbour, eventually making their way up the estuary of the Lee and upriver of Cork city. The three animals, including an adult bull, an old female and a young animal, were thought to be a family party that had become separated from their school that was feeding off the south coast. Later that month, the female was found dead and post mortem examination revealed that a

serious tooth abscess had made feeding difficult for this whale, probably leading to death from starvation. It may well be that the family party accompanied the sick animal into sheltered waters to assist it in catching slow-moving fish and help it to stay alive. Luckily, the other two returned safely to sea.

Live strandings are a regular, though largely unexplained, occurrence among pilot whales. The reported strandings of this species on Irish coasts include several mass strandings in Donegal, Wexford and Kerry. At least seven pilot whales were stranded on a beautiful remote sandy beach at Lettermacaward, County Donegal in June 1968. In May 1957 a pod of 36 pilot whales came ashore at Fethard, County Wexford. The local press account of their arrival is quite graphic. Having entered the harbour in about 10 feet (3 metres) of water, they lay there, 'like a mighty fleet becalmed' but this soon turned to a frenzy with the whales blowing, milling about and churning up the water. Illustrating how attitudes to whales have changed radically in just a few decades, one of the animals was harpooned by the local garage owner. A rifle and shotgun were used to dispatch some of the whales and others were left to die on the beach whereupon they were cut up by local fishermen and dispatched to a local pet food factory.[36]

The most spectacular mass stranding of pilot whales involved some 66 animals at Brandon, County Kerry, in November 1965. It was reported that the first animal in the herd to be stranded was a large male, which was described as 'the leader'. If this is true, it helps to explain why the rest of the group followed it into the estuary and eventually to their doom. Here again, the local fishermen regarded the stranding as a bonus for the taking and a deal was done with a mink farm nearby which purchased the meat at £5 a ton. Whales still in the water were towed ashore behind currachs and those already on the beach were cut into convenient pieces and loaded on lorries for quick dispatch. Considering the possibility of a health hazard from decomposing whale meat, the Parish Priest gave permission for the work to continue over a Sunday.

Just a few miles away, at Aughacashla beach in Tralee Bay, another mass stranding of pilot whales occurred some 37 years later, in March 2002. Up to 20 whales were successfully refloated by local people but a further seventeen animals died on the shore. The whales were buried within hours, prompted by a rumour that they might carry TB. Over the next 24 hours the surviving whales were closely monitored off the coast and two more females, which had escaped the first incident, became stranded and died. Later the surviving pod of ten to twelve

pilot whales was escorted by the local lifeboat for some seven miles off the coast of Fenit at the north side of the bay. Some lessons were learnt from this event and hopefully, when the next mass stranding occurs, the response rate will be faster allowing more of the animals to be refloated.

This change in attitude to the stranding of whales, over the past century, reflects an evolving view of the sea, from a place to be feared or exploited to a habitat of special value, which needs to be sensitively managed. To understand the role of the coast in the life of Irish people, we need to delve back to the early origins of human settlement here.

6

Living on the Coast

A shell midden and remains of a stone enclosure at Doonloughan, County Galway.

Although, in recent centuries, Ireland has tended to turn her back to the sea, for many thousands of years local communities around the coast have eked out a living from the marine resources close to hand. The sea has provided these communities with a living, often more dependable than that from the land, and traditional boats and sailing craft evolved to cope with the special conditions of the Irish coast. The islands, in particular, supported small and hardy communities, which had to be self sufficient for most of their needs. Many of the islands and remote headlands were also the locations for lighthouses and the homes of the keepers who maintained them. The lights were essential for the safety of shipping and guided seafarers to the safety of ports and harbours.

Prehistoric Coastal Settlements

The earliest known human communities settled in Ireland about 9,000 years ago after the retreat of the last glaciers. These Mesolithic (or Middle Stone Age) people found a progressively

Ceide Fields, County Mayo. Beneath the blanket bog, an extensive network of stone walls is revealed, giving evidence of a Neolithic farmed landscape which is older than the Egyptian pyramids (Alyn Walsh).

wooded landscape, so their settlements were mainly confined to the coast or to river banks. Here they would have had a ready supply of fish, shellfish, birds and small mammals to supplement the diet of wild plants, fruit and nuts in season. The evidence from one of the best known Mesolithic 'basecamps', at Mount Sandel on the Bann Estuary in County Derry, suggests a relatively settled community, living by hunting and gathering before the farming way of life. They caught a variety of fish including migratory salmon and eels together with the typical estuarine species such as mullet and flounder. Sand dunes were favourite places for these early settlers as they provided dry campsites, clear of woodland and often close to a river mouth. The so-called kitchen middens, piles of discarded sea shells, are all that remain today of these nomadic camps. Coastal middens date from a variety of periods from Mesolithic to the Bronze Age. They can be found in sand dunes at Mannin Bay, County Galway, Ballysadare, County Sligo and Dundrum, County Down.

One of the shellfish most prized by these early communities was the dog whelk. It can be found in unusually dense heaps in some of the coastal middens around Connemara. Here the archaeologist Michael Gibbons has suggested that the whelks were collected and processed for the purple dye which they produce.[1] The use of this dye – purpura or Tyrian purple – is believed to have spread out from the eastern Mediterranean and been adopted in Ireland as a result of the trade routes with southern Spain in the Bronze Age. The purple dyes may have had a sacred significance or may have simply been a badge of rank, much like the colour was later used by the emperors of Rome. Whatever its use, the dog whelks in the middens tend to be shattered in contrast to shellfish which were used for food. These concentrations of dog whelks have been found at a number of west coast sites including Ferriters Cove, on the Dingle Peninsula; Inishkea Islands, County Mayo; Dogs Bay near Roundstone, County Galway; and Truska just north of Slyne Head, County Galway. The most recent find was from sand dunes at Culfin, near the mouth of Killary Harbour, County Galway.

On the Knocknarea Peninsula, which juts out between the estuaries of Sligo Harbour and Ballysadare Bay, there is the largest Neolithic cemetery in Europe. Carrowmore contains a remarkable group of stone tombs which were built around 5,800 years ago. These were built by Neolithic farmers who were able to live here, principally because of the rich coastal resources. Nearby, on the northern shores of Ballysadare Bay, a Swedish team of archaeologists uncovered the evidence for a community based mainly on shellfish collection. Kitchen middens up to 100 metres long, 20 metres wide and 5 metres deep consisted almost entirely of oyster and mussel shells. This diet was probably supplemented by fishing and hunting of seals, as Ballysadare Bay supports a large group of harbour seals and part of the bay is known as the Great Seal Bank, indicating the antiquity of these mammals here.

The introduction of domestic cattle and sheep to Ireland in the Neolithic (New Stone Age) period signalled the beginning of the farming way of life. Some of the earliest remains of extensive field boundary systems emerging from beneath the more recent bogs in such coastal locations as north Mayo and Valentia Island, County Kerry suggest a settled community with a mixture of livestock and tillage crops.

A visitor to the north Mayo coast today would see a landscape dominated by blanket bogs stretching almost to the edge of the substantial cliffs that drop into the Atlantic Ocean. However, around 3,500 BC this area would have presented quite a different vista with an organised landscape of small fields and farms divided by a regular pattern of field walls. Within the fields there were dispersed settlement enclosures and megalithic (large rock) tombs. All of this fossilised landscape has been discovered over the last few decades by a painstaking process of probing the overlying bog with long metal rods.[2] The peat of the bog gives little resistance to the archaeologist on the surface but, when the rods hit a line of stones beneath the peat,

a map of the subsurface landscape can be produced. Dating the Neolithic activity at the Céide Fields (as they have become known) was problematic at first but a detailed study of pollen remains from the bog and the dating of ancient pine stumps has demonstrated that the building of the field walls ties in with an intensive period of farming around 3,700 to 3,500 BC.[3] The wall systems (so far discovered) at Céide Fields stretch over an area measuring about 5 kilometres by 4 kilometres and covering at least 1,000 hectares. The fields are draped over low rounded hills with intervening valleys leading down to the coast and these valleys would already have contained small areas of bog.

Similar prehistoric field systems are now known from all along the west coast of Ireland, in places like Inishbofin, County Galway and Mount Brandon, County Kerry. It is suggested that the landscape was farmed by a settled coastal community which, by communal endeavour, produced an organised and planned landscape allowing the better management of cattle grazing. In the warmer climate of the Neolithic, there would have been year-round grass growth to support this grazing practice. The reason for the ending of this farming activity and its replacement with almost unbroken bogland is a question of some debate. It may relate to climatic factors (such as a cooling or an increase in rainfall amounts) or to social or demographic changes (perhaps the farmland was abandoned by the people). Either way, the early farming settlements in these coastal locations are now established beyond doubt.

The materials which Neolithic settlers required for survival included a number of tools such as stone axes and the sources of these special rocks have been traced to several Stone Age quarries on the Irish coast. One of these was on Rathlin Island, off the coast of County Antrim, where an outcrop of porcellanite was excavated from an open gallery and the rock exported thoughout Ireland. On Lambay Island, off the north Dublin coast, a rock known

A promontory fort on the Sky Road, Clifden, County Galway. These locations were chosen for the ease of defending them either from land or sea.

as porphyry was quarried and fashioned into stone axes. The use of island sources of the stone is interesting as it suggests that the quarrying was separate from other everyday activities and it has been speculated that it could have been an integrated part of annual intergroup gatherings, thus these locations acted as sacred places or landmarks.[4]

An interesting feature of the Lambay Neolithic quarries is the discovery of pits on the floor of the valley between the rock outcrops, which contained deliberate deposits of porphyry debris, workings and pottery, sug-

gesting that the people made a ritual offering of materials back to the earth or to their gods. Some other coastal locations, such as the storm beach at Fisherstreet, County Clare, produce sea-worn shale cobbles with flake-like scars on either side, which look like natural versions of the worked stone axe. However, the stone was too soft to produce high quality axes with a good cutting edge, but they could have had some value to Neolithic settlers on the west coast.[5] At Fisherstreet mudstone axes were produced to supply the people on the Aran Islands and in south Connemara.

Iron Age remains on remote parts of the Irish coastline provide further evidence of trading contact between Ireland and the Mediterranean. Among the best known sites are promontory forts - substantial earthworks built on rocky headlands to protect the inhabitants from attack either by land or sea.[6] There are fine examples of these forts at the Old Head of Kinsale, County Cork, at Loughshinny, County Dublin and on the cliffs of Tory Island, County Donegal. Promontary forts are common from Iberia north to the west of Britain – the earliest known use was in the Bronze Age but some were probably occupied up to the medieval period. For example, Dun Kilmore on the west side of Achill Beg, County Mayo has a large promontory fort on top of which is built the Kilmore monastery and a later tower or castle which was probably part of the O'Malley lordship. Other promontory forts were later used as the sites for substantial and dramatic clifftop castles such as those at Dunluce, County Antrim or Black Castle at Wicklow Town. Even the Bailey Lighthouse on Howth Head, Dublin Bay, is built within a promontory fort. Dun Balor on Tory Island was a major fortified settlement with at least twenty fortified roundhouses inside the defensive walls. Promontory forts usually have a combination of earthen banks, stone walls and ditches across the neck of the headland. One of the largest and most impressive coastal promontory forts in Ireland was at Dunmore on the Dingle Peninsula. It covered 80 acres (32ha) and contained well preserved circular huts. It was first established in the sixth Century AD and probably reused over many hundreds of years before it was substantially destroyed by bulldozers in 2004.

Coastal Foragers and Fishermen

The mudflats of the Shannon Estuary were not the most hospitable environment for early coastal settlers. However, recent archaeological work has demonstrated that this area also held a permanent human population from earliest times. Aidan O'Sullivan, working under the Discovery Programme of the Royal Irish Academy, has produced a fine account of the estuary and its inhabitants.[7] Before modern reclamation attempts, the river and its tributaries would have flowed through a complex network of estuarine and freshwater wetlands with mudflats, saltmarsh, reedswamp, fen and bog, giving way further inland to a wet carr woodland. In this environment, the earliest settlers were the Mesolithic hunter-gatherers, who lived in the period 7,000-4,000 BC. They would have fished in the creeks, gathered plant food and hunted for pig, hare and wildfowl in the wetlands and bordering woodlands, in much the same way that primitive tribes do in some equatorial swamps today. In the Neolithic period (4,000-2,500 BC) settled farming communities would have inhabited permanent dwellings all year round. They left behind their stone axes and an interesting concentration of these has been found on the lower River Shannon at Killaloe. By the Bronze Age (2,500-1,600 BC) there was widespread settlement around the estuary, with evidence from bronze axes and similar artefacts. By the late Bronze Age hilltop forts were well established in the region and it is likely that the Shannon Estuary was a base for wider contacts with the Atlantic region of Europe. By the Iron Age (600BC to AD400) the Shannon Estuary was well known as a port and it is notably one of the few rivers marked on the western Irish coastline by the Greek cartographer Ptolemy in the second century AD.

Among the most remarkable features to survive the ravages of time in the Shannon Estuary are the fish traps made from post-and-wattle fences. They were simple devices or V-shaped structures laid out as a wide barrier across a tidal channel. The fish swimming down the shore with the ebbing tide were forced by the fences to swim towards the centre of the trap,

The Early Christians

The early Christian period brought significant advances in agriculture, accelerating population growth, and produced tens of thousands of earth or stone ringforts (or raths) across the Irish countryside. On some of the outlying islands, such as the Skelligs, County Kerry and Inishmurray, County Sligo, there were significant monastic settlements. Few early Christian sites are more inspirational than the cluster of tiny 'beehive' huts that clings to the side of Skellig Micheal some 180 metres above the Atlantic swell. It is difficult to imagine how the monks must have lived here, in splendid isolation about 12 kilometres off the coast of County Kerry, as landing is only feasible in calm weather. The steep flight of steps seems to lead to heaven itself and, indeed, the atmosphere within the walled monastic enclosure between the beehive cells is surprisingly peaceful and calm, even in strong winds. Less well known is the separate monastic settlement on the south summit of Skellig Michael. To reach this the occupants had to climb a steep rocky cliff but, amazingly, it was still being used as a pilgrimage site by local people from Ballinskelligs up to the late nineteenth century. The monks constructed narrow little gardens, fertilised from the steep shore below, on which they would have grown crops to supplement their diet of fish, shellfish, seabirds and their eggs and chicks in the summer. They probably also grazed goats on the steep slopes, as did the lighthouse keepers who came after them. A thousand years ago the 'stone monastery in the sky' was abandoned and became, instead, a place of pilgrimage.

Inishmurray, 6 kilometres off the coast of Sligo, is a complete contrast, being almost flat and subdivided by dry stone walls into fertile fields. Close to the centre of this network is the fortified monastery of St Molaise, founded in the sixth century AD. It consists of a group of stone churches, beehive huts and other remains contained within a massive circular stone wall.

An artist's reconstruction of a medieval fish trap on the Shannon Estuary at Bunratty, County Clare (painting by Simon Dick).

where they were caught in a basket, box or net. These were early historic or medieval in age from between the fifth and fourteenth centuries. Among the best preserved is one on the muddy shore at Bunratty, County Clare, just downstream of the famous Bunratty Castle. The presence of these medieval fishtraps on the mudflats suggests that sea levels then were roughly similar to today.[8] Wood samples taken from a fish trap in the Fergus Estuary, County Clare, were identified as willow, alder, hazel and birch. The tree-ring evidence suggests that the rods were selectively cut for their appropriate size and the closeness in age of the alder and willow rods suggests that they could have been cut from deliberately coppiced woodlands. The prominence of willow and alder confirms the marshy character of the surrounding land at the time. Similar fish traps are known from the Blackwater estuary at Youghal.

In the tidal waters of Strangford Lough a number of stone fish traps have survived the ravages of time and weather. They range from V-shaped to crescent-shaped, each designed to funnel the fish, moving out with the ebbing tide, into a catching device in the centre. Sometimes they were located in the gap between two islands, thus effectively ambushing any fish that tried to swim through on a falling tide.[9]

An ancient pilgrimage route around the perimeter of the island is marked by altars and crosses. Links with other west-coast monastic sites such as those on Inishbofin, County Galway as well as Iona in western Scotland, Lindisfarne on the east coast of England, Orkney and even the Faroe Islands and Iceland, suggest a strong federation of early Christian seafarers all along the eastern Atlantic fringe. The economy was, by now, based on cattle and sophisticated metalwork but fisheries played a big part in supporting these medieval communities.

The medieval and plantation periods brought gradually improving agricultural use of coastal lands and the building of significant ports such as those at Dublin, Waterford, Cork and Galway. The flourishing export trade in Irish-produced cattle fuelled the growth of these ports but cattle also became the primary source of

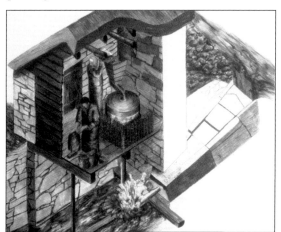

(Clockwise from top left)
An artist's reconstruction of the tidal mill at Nendrum, on Strangford Lough, County Down (painting by James Patience, Environment and Heritage Service, NI.); *monastic site on Inishmurray, County Sligo* (Con Brogan, Department of Environment, Heritage and Local Government); *Little Skellig is framed between two beehive cells of the monastery on Skellig Michael, County Kerry.*

value in the Irish countryside. Regular fairs sprang up, where cattle dealing was the central activity. In the early seventh century AD there was an increase in cereal production, which was accompanied by the construction of corn mills, normally powered by river water.

At the monastic site of Nendrum, on Mahee Island, in Strangford Lough, County Down, there were no freshwater streams so the monks turned to tidal power as an alternative. Recent excavations on the foreshore beside the island have uncovered the remains of a horizontal mill wheelhouse with a specially constructed stone flume (to concentrate the stream of water onto the wheel). This has provided striking evidence for Europe's earliest dated examples of the use of tidal power for milling. The mill is built into a stone embankment, which encloses a large tidal pond. From the oak piles used in its construction it has been possible to date the embankment to around 620 AD. Apart from local stone, a variety of materials including oak, holly, wattle (probably hazel), moss (to aid water-proofing), red marine clay and blue estuarine clay, were used in this sophisticated construction. No doubt, a mill of this elaborate construction would have acted as a focus for the religious and secular community, centred on the monastry.[10]

The Vikings

The traditional view of the Vikings in Ireland is of a bunch of murderers, rapists and thugs from Scandinavia who raided the peaceful Irish settlements, causing mayhem to the early Christian monasteries and plundering their valuables. The archaeologist Michael Gibbons describes the early Viking raiders as coming like the 'Wrath of Hell' out of the northern seas. Even the term 'viking' is derived from the old norse word *Víkingr* meaning a sea robber who lurked in the *Víkr* or fjords of western Norway, from where they raided passing ships. They turned the ports which they established, such as Dublin (or *Dubh Linn*) into slave towns, trading the captured natives overseas.

Most of the Vikings who reached Ireland are

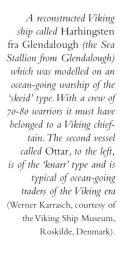

A reconstructed Viking ship called Harhingsten fra Glendalough *(the Sea Stallion from Glendalough) which was modelled on an ocean-going warship of the 'skeid' type. With a crew of 70-80 warriors it must have belonged to a Viking chieftain. The second vessel called* Ottar*, to the left, is of the 'knarr' type and is typical of ocean-going traders of the Viking era* (Werner Karrasch, courtesy of the Viking Ship Museum, Roskilde, Denmark).

thought to have come from rural communities in western Norway, sailing here via the western isles of Scotland. Around the same time they were also colonising the other Atlantic islands of the Faroes, Iceland and Greenland to the north west. It is known that the early Viking excursions to Ireland consisted of a series of hit-and-run raids carried out with a combination of swiftness and surprise. However, after about 830 AD their tactics changed and camps were set up for the raiding parties to spend the winter on the captured sites. The first firm evidence of such bases in Ireland comes from 841 in Dublin and Annagassan, County Louth. Here the annals use the word *longphort*, meaning an enclosure designed to protect ships.[11] The major settlement at Wood Quay in *Duibhlinn*, Dublin, was excavated in the 1970s and produced a rich record of Viking lifestyles. The historical record of Viking *longphorts* is very incomplete but there are examples at Dunrally, County Laois, Athlunkard, County Clare, and Anagassan, County Louth. Each site features a D-shaped enclosure on the banks of a river, but there the similarities end.[12] The remains on Jordan's Island in Limerick are of the only known Viking settlement on the west coast. The Viking settlement at Woodtown, just west of the modern Waterford city, was a base for raiding local communities on the Rivers Suir and Nore. After several centuries, some of the descendants of these Viking invaders eventually settled down as farmers, craftsmen and traders, intermarried with the local people and even converted to Christianity. The Vikings brought new maritime technology such as boat-building techniques, and trading links with the wider world, including a slaving network.

The best evidence for the location of ninth-century Viking settlement in Ireland is provided by the burial sites. With few exceptions these were located on or near the coast, suggesting that the 'foreigners' did not settle far from their ships. The Viking graveyards discovered at Kilmainham and Islandbridge in Dublin would

A surviving tower of the Norman castle at Greencastle, County Donegal.

have been close to the mouth of the Liffey Estuary in the ninth century and just upriver of the major settlement at Wood Quay. These major finds were first recognised in 1836 during gravel quarrying between the Royal Hospital and the River Liffey. Further finds of grave goods such as swords, spearheads, agricultural tools and personal ornaments were found with bodies in the 1840s and 1860s, when the railway lines at Heuston (Kingsbridge) were under construction and again in the 1930s with the laying out of the War Memorial Park at Kilmainham. It was the usual practice of the Vikings to bury their dead in already existing Christian cemeteries. The grave goods found with the Vikings indicate a settled community but the weapons suggest warriors were also living here.[13]

By the mid-ninth century AD it appears that there was a chain of Viking settlements running along the length of the east coast, some of which had a small rural hinterland to support them. The longphorts did not survive for long. The one at Cork was destroyed in 848 AD, bases in Antrim and Down were wiped out in

866 AD and Dublin was abandoned in 902 AD. However, it is likely that the surrounding land was being farmed by the settlers, who were possibly already interrelated with the native people. In the second phase of Viking settlement in the tenth century it seems likely the Scandinavian settlers would have returned to areas where they were likely to find relatives and support. Now the settlers founded a series of urban centres: in Waterford (914 AD), Cork (about 915 AD), Dublin (917 AD), Wexford (about 921 AD) and Limerick (922 AD). The settlement centred in Dublin, then known as *Dyflinarskiri*, was the most extensive, stretching from north county Dublin as far south as Arklow, County Wicklow. Almost all the Scandinavian place-names in this region – Skerries, Lambay, Howth, Dalkey, Wicklow and Arklow – are coastal. Many of the other major coastal harbours of the east coast have Viking origins – Strangford, Carlingford, Wexford and Waterford. The second element of all these names is derived from the Scandinavian word *fjord*. The material remains of this second phase of settlement are not distinct from those of the native peoples, showing that the newcomers were becoming integrated with the native coastal communities.

The Medieval Period

The earliest Norman invaders landed in Wexford in 1169 AD in support of the deposed King of Leinster. By the end of the twelfth Century the Normans had succeeded in taking control of much of Ireland. They came originally from northern France, via England and founded a series of fortified coastal towns such as Sligo, Galway and Dingle. Names such as Ferriter and Fitzgerald, which are common in Dingle, can be traced back to this period. The Normans imposed their feudal system on the areas which they controlled and populated these captured territories with English and Welsh settlers. They took control of many coastal fisheries such as the pilchard industry of the south coast. Fishing weirs were established in a number of river estuaries such as Waterford Harbour. From the end of the twelfth century the Normans began a phase of building substantial military castles, such as those at Greencastle, County Donegal and Carrigfergus, County Antrim.

Among the many changes which the Normans introduced was the rabbit, a mammal previously unknown in Ireland. It was regarded as a useful source of meat and skins and rabbit warrens (or farms) were quickly established on many sand dune sites around the coast. For example, Murlough dunes in Dundrum Bay, County Down was the source of many thousands of rabbit skins exported during the medieval period. Dunes were ideal for the purpose of producing large rabbit populations as they are often isolated from the mainland for defence against poachers and natural predators such fox, stoat and badger could be easily controlled. The dune vegetation was quickly modified by the grazing and burrowing of thousands of rabbits to the extent that many dunes became denuded in the medieval period. This coincided with a period of high winds and many dune systems became quite mobile, with blowing sand inundating neighbouring farmland, houses and, in some cases, whole villages. The impact of the rabbit can be clearly seen in reverse when, in the 1950s, the epidemic of myxomatosis struck Ireland and the rabbit population was virtually wiped out. Within a few years many dunes, which had formerly had large areas of bare sand, become vegetated and eventually covered with scrub and trees.

By the late fourteenth and early fifteenth centuries the Norman lordships were under pressure and the territory under English control was limited to the eastern part of Leinster which was protected by a series of earthworks known as the Pale. Small stone castles, such as that at Carlingford, were built around this time to protect the holdings. The western seaboard

was again ruled by powerful local families such as the O'Driscolls (west Cork), O'Malleys, O'Flahertys (Mayo) and O'Donnells (West Donegal). They established links with Spain and leased out the Irish sea fisheries to Spanish fishermen. This link with Spain is confirmed by the finding of sixteenth-century Spanish pottery at the castle in Ballinskelligs, County Kerry. By the late sixteenth century, the English crown began to regain control of Ireland through military force. The Tudors pushed west and began to establish new 'English' towns in Ireland. During the seventeenth century the ownership of the recaptured territories was transferred to new landlords from England and Scotland while the native Irish remained on as tenants on the land. To consolidate their military control, the English crown built a series of massive star-shaped forts around the coast such as Charles Fort in Kinsale, County Cork. Plantation towns such as Crookhaven and Bantry, County Cork were established and the English took control of the fisheries which had previously been leased to the Spanish. Fish palaces were established to press the oil

from large quantities of herring brought ashore. This period marked a complete change in the local relationship with the sea as the native Irish were forced to convert from fish merchants to subsistence fishermen.

Recent Settlement History

Many of the remoter parts of the Atlantic coast of Ireland were settled between 1700 and 1845 AD as a result of the massive growth in population from three million to eight and a half million people. This human population explosion resulted from the dependence on the potato as a staple crop that could grow in the wet, thin and peaty soils that predominate on the west coast. At first, houses were clustered in small *clachans* and the land holding was communal, mainly among relatives. The *clachan* was surrounded by a permanently cultivated infield or gardens of potatoes and oats which, in coastal regions, were fertilised by seaweed collected from the shoreline. These were separated (usually by stone walls) from the outfield, which comprised of the more

(left) The O'Malley castle on Clare Island, County Mayo; (right) a seaweed kiln at Rosbeg, County Donegal.

Maritime grassland at Rosbeg, County Donegal provides good frost-free grazing throughout the year. The cliffs of Slieve Toohy are visible in the background.

boggy or hilly land used for common grazing of cattle. The availability of seaweed or wrack from the shore allowed coastal *clachans* to grow to a larger size than those inland, and seaweed rights were a prized possession, handed on from generation to generation. As well as using the seaweed for fertiliser, it was also collected, dried and burned in specially built kilns on the coast. The low kelp drying walls, which are dotted along the west coast, date from this period. Iodine was then extracted, providing one of the few saleable products from this essentially subsistence economy. The growth of the fishing industry, especially herring and mackerel for export, also helped to fuel the surge in population in certain coastal areas.

An insight into the living conditions of a coastal population in south-west Donegal in 1821 is provided by a survey conducted by the Reverend John Barrett, Church of Ireland Rector of the Parish of Inishkeel, which covered the area between Portnoo and Ardara.[14]

He wrote:

In the farms bordering on the shores, the usual succession of crops is, first, potatoes followed by barley, then oats or flax. In our very sandy district rye is grown which answers well. Barley and oats are the only descriptions of grain in the parish. From the universal practice of illicit distillation [of whiskey], grain sells much higher in this parish than in many other parts of Ireland. Were it not for the importation of provisions from the province of Connaught, this parish would be frequently in danger of starving. In the districts bordering on the sea shore, sea weed is almost the only manure used, from its producing a greater weight of potatoes on a given surface than any other manure known here. As to lime, it is never used as manure here; why I cannot tell. Very little limestone is raised, as the inhabitants don't raise it as manure and all convenient to the shore prefer the digging of shells of cockles, mussels and oysters, from the superior facility of burning them, to be used in buildings; the lime produced is of a whiteness superior to that from limestone, but requires less sand to constitute mortar. There are only a few small boats. My table is usually supplied with fish taken by a currach, a species of boat composed of wicker work and covered with a horse's skin. Cod and Pollack [are the usual fish]. Not more than 30 people are employed [in fishing] and even that small number are only employed in the summer months when the weather is calm. No fish are cured for distant markets and there is no market to which fresh fish could be sent. I learnt that herring have been, of late years, frequently on this coast but were not taken for want of nets.

Island Resources and People

The islands off the coast of Ireland have a special place in Irish culture. The small communities that they supported a century ago had many of the characteristics that we have come to admire in human society. They were self-reliant yet supported each other in a tough, and often hazardous, lifestyle surrounded by the ocean. They were able to harvest the bounty of the sea and the land in equal measure. In many cases they were among the last strongholds of a dwindling Irish language in the early twentieth century. One of the best books on the inhabited islands was written by a Dublin naturalist and photographer, Thomas H. Mason,[15] who visited many of them in the early twentieth century. More recently, Peter Somerville-Large has produced a fine account

Turf cutting on the inhabited islands removed most of the peat cover, forcing the islanders to import fuel from the mainland.

of the life and legends of many of the larger islands.[16] In this chapter, I have concentrated on the relationship of the islanders with their natural environment, which was often harsh and unforgiving.

Over the centuries, the islands of Ireland have attracted naturalist, geologist, poet and painter alike.[17] They have a special physical and cultural quality that separates them from the mainland and a clear definition that makes them obvious study areas. Robert Lloyd Praeger organised the original Clare Island Survey in 1911 in what is now regarded as one of the finest accounts of an island ecosystem. The New Survey of Clare Island, organised under the auspices of the Royal Irish Academy, is providing a modern equivalent.

Valentia

Frank Mitchell spent ten years of his retirement studying the island of Valentia, County Kerry. The results were published as a seminal account called *Man and Environment in Valentia Island*.[18] Here he laid out the entire history of this 3,000-hectare island from the Ice Age to membership of the European Community. With consummate skill he illustrated the ebb and flow of the environment and its human occupants. In early post-glacial time the soil was probably well drained and covered with woodland. The trees were removed in the early Bronze Age and replaced by well-drained grassland. By the late Bronze Age, perhaps due to soil exhaustion, a worsening of the climate or to burning blanket bog developed and began to creep up the slopes. In the early nineteenth century the island population had risen to over 3,000 and the land-hungry people had covered almost the whole island surface in potatoes. While other parts of Kerry were devastated by the Great Famine of the 1840s, Valentia had a safety valve in the sea which still provided plentiful harvests. In 1837 some 400 people from the island were working in the inshore fishery and a curing station was set

up here during the Famine. However, the slow population decline continued up to the present and grassland again covers the island slopes. The later history of the island is recounted by Daphne Pochin Mould.[19] In the nineteenth century, a stream of English visitors to Valentia included Prince Arthur in 1869 and the Duke and Duchess of York in 1897. The poet Alfred Tennyson, who visited the island in 1856, is said to have got the inspiration here for his famous lines: 'Break, break, break on your cold grey stones o sea.'

The Blaskets

One island group, the Blaskets, is best known for its writers. With the help of some academic yet visionary outsiders, islanders like Tomás Ó Crohán and Peig Sayers were to write accounts of their ordinary day-to-day lives that became classics of the Irish language. The Blaskets form an archipeligo of seven main islands and a number of islets and rocks lying off the western end of the Dingle Peninsula. Because of its long streamlined shape the largest of the islands, the Great Blasket, has often been likened to a whale surrounded by its young. The population of the Blaskets reached a peak of 176 in 1916 but by 1953 there were just over twenty left, for whom there was no alternative but evacuation.

The Great Blasket was the centre of this small community because it provided not only the largest area of farmland but also the safest landing place. The island village is on the eastern end facing the mainland and it is a magical experience to walk among the ruined houses today and imagine the life of the hardy islanders a century ago. Surrounding the houses is a network of small fields in which the islanders grew potatoes, cabbage, turnips, parsnips, corn and wheat together with the hay, which sustained their livestock over the winter. There is also some evidence that flax was grown here for the linen trade. There was originally peat (turf) in the island, which provided some fuel

The island village on Great Blasket with the white strand (An Trá Bán) in the background (David Walsh).

but this was virtually dug out in the early twentieth century and the people were forced to bring in their turf by boat from the mainland.[20]

The sea around the islands provided the Blasket people with their main source of protein and a surplus for sale. Up to the middle of the nineteenth century fishing was mainly done from large boats known as seine boats, which required a sizeable crew, but these were gradually replaced by the smaller *currach* or *naomhóg*. This craft was built on a wooden frame covered with canvas and tarred to make it waterproof. It was also capable of carrying a small sail. The islanders used these boats to catch a variety of fish including mackerel, whiting, pollack, herring, eel and bass but the most lucrative catch was the lobster and crayfish, which were sold at market in Dingle.

Robert Lloyd Praeger 'botanised' on the Great Blasket in the later years of the nineteenth century when the island village held a small population. In *The Way that I Went*,[21] he tells a story about how he and a colleague, A.W. Stelfox, were investigating the molluscs of the island. 'The island children, consumed with curiosity, followed us about and watched with astonishment the collecting of box-snails and slugs. Presently we went home to our usual dinner of one herring and potatoes. When we emerged again, a deputation was waiting for us – half the children of the island, bearing cans, boxes, saucers, cloth caps and what-not all full of crawling molluscs, which they told us, a penny or two might add to our possessions'.

One of the main difficulties for any island community in the nineteenth century was getting stock in and out of the islands. The islanders who lived on the Great Blasket used most of the other outlying islands, Inishtooskert, Inishvicillane, Inishnabro and Beginish, for grazing. With no pier or landing place, the transfer of animals from land to boat could be quite a risky business. Muiris MacConghail[22] describes the islanders climbing down the cliff face of Inishtooskert with sheep on their backs.

Having selected the stock from the herd they brought them to the top of the cliff at Leac na Muice, having first shorn them, a days work in itself, and then tying the horns of the sheep with a special knot, they would pull and jump with the sheep down the cliff edge, almost becoming in the act sheep themselves, until they got to the flagstone at the bottom. Then the problem was to tie the sheep by the feet and get them into the neamhóga *which were bobbing and dipping up and down in the often turbulent sea.*

Apart from driftwood, the only fuel that the islanders had was the turf (peat), which was found at the back of the island at Sliabh Bharra an Dá Ghleann. This provided a hard black sod, which was dried in the wind before stacking for the winter. Many of the islanders carried the turf back to the village (over 6 kilometres) in creels on their own backs but

donkeys were used in later years. Turf-cutting was a ritual activity, which gave the young men and women an opportunity to meet away from the watching eyes of the village elders and it was here that much of the courting was done. But by the early twentieth century, the turf was exhausted and fuel had to be imported by boat from the mainland. This added to the difficulties of island life and was one of the factors that led to the final evacuation in 1953.

Tory

The removal of the turf from Tory, a remote island some 12 kilometres off the north-west coast of Donegal, did not cause these islanders to desert and there is a healthy population there today. The agriculture practiced by the Tory islanders, even in the twentieth century, was a carry over from pre-enclosure times. The village was a cluster of dwellings with fields arranged in strips, each containing some good and bad land. The strips were largely unfenced as the grazing animals were restricted to the outfields.

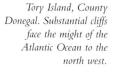

Tory Island, County Donegal. Substantial cliffs face the might of the Atlantic Ocean to the north west.

The hand flail was still used for threshing the oats long after it had died out on the mainland. In the 1930s Thomas Mason visited the island and described the primitive farm implements then in use. Ploughs were made of wood with cutting edge faced with iron from wrecked ships. Harrows were also made of wood with iron bolts from ships. There was no lime on the island so seashells were burnt to spread on the land. Cattle and sheep were the main animals that Mason saw but, when I walked across the island in the summer of 2000, I saw only a few sheep. Even the hay meadows remained uncut as agriculture has now become a secondary form of income compared with that from tourism. The ferry service from Magheraroarty on the mainland is fairly dependable and, in bad weather, there is a helicopter service.[23]

Gola

Less accessible is the small island of Gola, which lies to the west of Bunbeg and just north of Arranmore. The life and last days of this island community were recounted by Fred Aalen and Hugh Brody.[24] When they completed their study, the island population had declined to just twelve people from a high of over 200 in 1926. By the end of the twentieth century the island was effectively deserted although a few of the houses had been maintained as summer holiday homes. When I went there, the ferry from Bunbeg was not planning to continue beyond the summer of 2001 but by 2002 water and electricity were piped out to the island and new houses are now being built. Seasonal migrations were always a part of the life of people living in west Donegal and often included summer periods spent on the islands to exploit the grazing and engage in fishing. Lord George Hill owned the island of Gola and he wrote, in 1841, that the inhabitants 'not having a fixed residence, take no pains to make any one of their habitations at all comfortable'. It is likely that a permanent population only began to settle in the eighteenth century with

pressure for land on the mainland. The practice of 'booleying' or summer grazing on mountain pastures continued into the nineteenth century with many families having houses on the island and the mainland.[25]

Inishkeas

Like many of the islands, the inexorable rise in the mainland population in the eighteenth and early nineteenth centuries led to a steady

Sea Kayakers camped beside the deserted village on Inishkea, County Mayo (David Walsh).

rise in the numbers on the Inishkea Islands off north Mayo.[26] In the 40-year period between 1821 and 1861 the total island population more than doubled to reach 319 people, in spite of the massive fall in population in Ireland during the Great Famine. The two low Atlantic islands were well placed to support a healthy fishing fleet, which exploited the herring and mackerel stocks with salmon and lobster fishing in summer (see Chapter 7).

The sea also provided the islanders with other bounty in the form of passing ships, which often got into trouble in the exposed waters around the islands. In the 1830s and 1840s a form of piracy developed due to the lack of an efficient coastguard and the urgent need for food. Island *currachs* would surround a vessel and shower the deck with stones driving the ship's crew below for shelter, while the attackers robbed what they could. The daring islanders were also known to take advantage

A woman herds cattle on Achill Island about 1900 (courtesy of the National Library of Ireland).

of ships that were abandoned in stormy conditions. In November 1834, a 155-ton ship, *The Mansfield*, was en route from Newfoundland to Ballyshannon, County Donegal when she ran into a gale near north Mayo and was abandoned off the North Inishkea Island. Her crew landed on the mainland where 'the locals stripped them of their few possessions'. The ship was boarded by about twenty people from the south Island who ransacked the cabins, stores and spirits they found.

Inishmurray

Off the coast of Sligo is the heart-shaped island of Inishmurray. Site of an early Christian monastic settlement, it became the home of a hardy group of settlers in the nineteenth century. They eked out a living from the land and sea, through fishing, *poitín*- and butter-making until, in 1948, the island was finally evacuated.[27] Unlike many offshore islands in Ireland, Inishmurray is low-lying and relatively flat, rising to only 21 metres at the western end.

The island soils are peaty and poor with less than a quarter (25 hectares) of the total island being suitable for arable crops. There are no lakes on the island, just three small pools where the turf has been removed. The natural history of the island is interesting as it has both northern and southern elements. The northern element is represented by the eider duck, a species that mainly breeds in the arctic.

Access to the island was always difficult because there is no harbour and boats had to be taken out of the water and stowed safely away from the sea. For this reason, the islanders could only use small boats and crossing the sea to Mullaghmore on the mainland in winter might be impossible for weeks at a time. The isolation of the islanders, however, was beneficial in one way. It allowed them to develop the trade in illegal whiskey (*poitín*) with minimal interference from officers of the law on the mainland. The raw materials used by the islanders were treacle, brown sugar, white sugar, barley and, occasionally, potatoes. Treacle was

preferred because the distillation period was only five days, shortening the period of risk of detection. The 'at risk' period for use of barley was much longer and this ingredient was usually reserved for the winter period when the 'peelers' could not get to the island for many days or weeks at a time.

Saltees

Some islands were too small to support more than a single family. The farming lifestyle on the Saltee Islands, off County Wexford, was mentioned by visiting naturalists who came to study the flora or the seabirds of the islands.[28] The botanist H.C. Hart, who visited Great Saltee in 1883, wrote: 'On this island, which is partly cultivated, there is a resident family. The Lesser Saltee is used as pasturage and contains but one cabin for the use of herd boys.'

The family in question was called Parle and, although their life was a spartan one, it was full and diverse. The crops they grew included wheat, oats, barley, beans, mangolds, turnips, cabbage and potatoes. Even today one can still see the stone platforms in the old farmyard on Great Saltee. These were used to store the sheaves of corn off the ground and they had an overhanging lip to prevent rats from eating the grain. There was plenty of grazing on the islands for sheep and cattle and cows were kept for fresh milk while hens, ducks and geese provided fresh eggs and meat. This near self-sufficiency was supplemented by sale of produce to the markets on the mainland. The head of the family, John Parle, lived on the Great Saltee until his death aged 87. In his prime, he was said to have been a powerful man. He was reputedly able to lift two full-grown sheep, one under each arm, and could carry two twenty-stone sacks of meal in the same way. A major difficulty was the winter storms that could cut off the island inhabitants for weeks at a time.

But it was another factor that forced the evacuation of the islands in the end. The local priests were concerned about the spiritual well-being of the islanders who were frequently unable to attend mass on the mainland due to rough seas. It seems that the family left the island around 1905 as the naturalist Robert Lloyd Praeger wrote after his visit in 1913: 'Up till ten years ago, the island was inhabited. Some 80 acres were under tillage and cattle and sheep grazed all over the higher, rocky grounds at either end.'

When Praeger returned in 1934, he mentioned that the island farm had been 'derelict for twenty years' and that 'the flora of the large island was still in the process of re-organisation after tillage'. However, it was not left to nature for long as, in the late 1930s, it was bought by Claud Francis, who burned the bramble and bracken thickets on the old fields to expose the soil for ploughing again. Wheat and early potatoes were grown, the latter being ready before most other crops in Ireland, due to the favourable, frost-free climate. Barley was also grown here, mainly as a food for horses and cattle. However, family ill-health forced Francis to abandon Great Saltee in the mid 1940s and it has not been farmed since. A few years later, in 1950, the Saltee Bird Observatory was set up

A lichen-covered farm wall on Great Saltee, County Wexford.

in the old farmhouse by Major R.F. Ruttledge and John Weaving. Half a century later, this historic site is still in use as a bird observatory and ringing station, although it is privately owned.

Irish Lighthouses and their Keepers

(below) The modern lighthouse on Arranmore Island, County Donegal; (right) the Fastnet lighthouse, County Cork, under construction 1900 (courtesy of the National Library of Ireland).

The first attempts at using lights as navigational aids to shipping were probably beacons lit on hilltops near the coast. These proved unreliable and in the early nineteenth century the British Government gave control of all lighthouses in Britain and Ireland to Trinity House. Later, the control of those in Ireland was devolved to the

Commissioners of Irish Lights. The oldest lighthouse in Britain or Ireland is on the long, flat, limestone point of Hook Head in County Wexford. It was first established as a light in the fifth century, when a monastery was founded here by St Dubhán. The present massive tower was built in about 1172 and was maintained by the monks of nearby Churchtown. After a period of abandonment, the lighthouse was restored in the 1660s. In the early nineteenth century, the lantern was lit with twelve oil lamps, but by 1871 this was replaced by coal-gas which was manufactured beside the lighthouse. Vaporised paraffin was the fuel used from 1911 and this, in turn, was replaced by electricity in 1972. The 1970s also saw the end of permanent keepers and their families living at the lighthouse.[29]

One of the most dramatic of Irish lighthouses is the Fastnet, which lies 7 km off the

The Old Fastnet lighthouse County Cork, c. 1900 (courtesy of the National Library of Ireland).

south coast of Cork and was often the last part of Europe seen by emigrants departing to America in the nineteenth century. The building of the present tower in 1900 to 1904 is captured in a wonderful series of images in the collection of the Commissioners of Irish Lights.[30] The tower's masonery work comprised 89 courses or layers of cut stone made up of 2,074 blocks. The Commissioners made annual tours of inspection of the lighthouses and these were carefully recorded on photographic glass plates by Sir Robert Ball, scientific advisor

Disused lighthouse on Mutton Island, Galway Bay. Sea campion grows on the shingle bank in the foreground.

to the Commission. These pictures provide an insight into the technology of the time but also into the lives of the keepers and their families in the late nineteenth and early twentieth century.

Up to the end of the nineteenth century it was normal practice for the families of keepers to live with them, even on remote islands and rocks like the Skellig, Inishtearaght, Eagle Island and Tuskar Rock. Hardship for these men, women and children must have been very great, especially during periods of prolonged bad weather in winter when they were cut off from the mainland and essential supplies. In December 1894 a massive storm hit Eagle Island off the north-west coast of Mayo. Some of the dwellings were damaged beyond repair and the terrified women and children took

refuge in the lighthouse tower itself. Even here the sea broke the lantern glass and water showered down the inside of the tower.

Despite such severe conditions, it was felt that keepers were more contented and likely to behave better on shore leave when their families lived with them. The Commissioners encouraged the keeping of goats on these remote rocks, as recorded in a memo sent in 1918 from Head Office to all lightkeepers. It read:

In view of the difficulty experienced at many lighthouse stations in obtaining supplies of fresh milk for young children, the Commissioners desire to draw the attention of their lightkeepers to the desirability of keeping goats wherever practicable.

Good milking breeds of goat were recommended, but it was noted that these 'are by no means as hardy as the ordinary goat, and that they require reasonable care and shelter from cold winds and rain during the winter months especially'. On the larger islands and mainland light stations it was normal for the keepers and their families to maintain small gardens around the tower for growing fresh vegetables. Seaweed collected from the rocks was the main fertiliser and, over the decades, a rich fertile soil was built up inside the garden walls. At Mutton Island in Galway Bay, as at many other sites, these gardens, now disused, have been colonised by rabbits that honeycomb the soil with burrows. At Rockabill, County Dublin, the gardens now have a dense 'forest' of sea mallow, which acts as a refuge for nesting roseate terns, among the rarest birds in Europe.

Mutton Island has also been an important tern colony at times, but today it is the location for the main sewage treatment works for Galway city. Although only a mile from the mainland shore, this lighthouse could often be cut off by bad weather. In 1923 the keeper received permission to keep a small boat at the lighthouse to take his children to school. However, as high winds and rough seas could isolate them for days, the children were later educated as boarders in Galway with the aid of an allowance to the keeper.

In 1900 the families of the keepers on both Skellig and Inishtearaght off County Kerry were re-housed in a terrace of eight, two-storey houses on Valentia Island. This was the period when most of the more remote lighthouses became 'relieving stations', with keepers working six weeks in every eight. At Valentia, the little community of keepers and their families became well established and the profession was often passed on from father to son through the generations. At Scattery Island in County Clare, the light was tended by three generations of the McMahons. The last of these was Patricia McMahon who was born on the island and had been assistant to her father all her working life. She retired in 1993 when the light was abandoned.

The automation programme for all the lighthouses, which was completed in the 1990s, brought the service into the computer age, but also marked the end of an era when the lighthouse keepers were not only the guardians of the lights but an unofficial coastwatch service.

(left) Semaphore party at Greencastle, County Down c. 1900. In the foreground a complete set of signal flags are folded ready for action (courtesy of the National Library of Ireland); (right) the lighthouse buildings on Clare Island, County Mayo have been reconstructed as a private dwelling (Alyn Walsh).

A log boat is excavated from the tidal area of Greyabbey Bay, Strangford Lough, County Down. This method of transport was probably used in sheltered waters in the Neolithic (Wes Forsythe, Centre for Maritime Archaeology, University of Ulster).

The sadness and finality of the evacuation of these famous lighthouse buildings, which were locked up for the last time, brought a ground-swell of sympathy from the Irish public. Although regularly visited by workmen and technicians for maintenance purposes, the light-houses had lost their 'lived in' feeling and were largely left to the seabirds and seals once again.[31]

Traditional Boats

Ireland appears to be a cultural meeting place or crossroads between major boat-building traditions, occupying a midway position on the Atlantic seaboard of Europe. Some of these vernacular craft have survived in remote areas. It is even possible to see traditional boats fishing in the Liffey Estuary in Dublin city and in waters around Cork city. Other boat types are effectively extinct and are only known from drawings, documentary records or from surviving wrecks.

Uncovering the details of extinct boat types requires painstaking historical detective work. For example, a design of the extinct Kinsale Hooker, from west Cork, was assembled using local records from a nineteenth-century Washington report and from a model in the National Museum of Ireland. A set of constructional drawings was then produced based on a survey of the closest related type, the Rathcourcy Hookers of east Cork. A collaborative project between Irish institutions and a French publisher has been set up to create an archive of Irish boats, fishing techniques and maritime folklore. During the course of the project some replicas have been built of traditional boats, including two Long Island-type mackerel boats from west Cork.

Log Boats

It is widely believed that dug-out canoes, such as the magnificent example on display in the National Museum of Ireland, were the earliest form of boat in Ireland. However, such a design

would be quite unstable in open seas and most of the log boats recovered by archaeologists have been found on lakes and rivers, often at narrow crossings where the boats would have been used as ferries. Several logboats have been found in the sheltered tidal waters of Strangford Lough, County Down. One of these, discovered in Greyabbey Bay, has been radiocarbon dated to the Neolithic Period. It is suggested that log boats would have been a convenient method of moving about in sheltered waters but not on the open sea.[32] In the summer of 2002, an exciting discovery was made on the seabed less than a mile off the coast of Gormanstown, County Meath. Archaeologists, monitoring a dredging operation for a new gas pipeline, spotted a large piece of timber which, when recovered, proved to be a hollowed tree trunk, originally measuring up to 7 metres in length. The boat is made from a hard wood and may possibly have been washed out to sea from the nearby Boyne Estuary.

Basket Currachs

The estuary of the Boyne also has a special place in Irish maritime history. It was the last known location of the skin-covered coracle (or *currach*). Like its Welsh counterparts, it was a circular basketwork construction with a skin made of a tanned ox hide. Since the netting of salmon in fresh water became illegal in 1948, the currach was restricted to the tidal part of the Boyne. The Boyne *currach* was in reality an oval shape measuring about 6 feet by 4 feet (2 metres by 1.5 metres) or large enough only for a single fisherman. Its design evolved because of the lightness and ease of handling the boat in a shallow restricted waterway. Two men would crew the *currach* with the paddler kneeling in the deep bow and drawing the boat along with alternate left and right strokes. The second crewman sat facing the rear and payed out the net, the other end of which was held by a third man on the shore. Having reached the far side of the estuary, the paddler raced downstream and back across the current to close the net in a large circle, thus trapping any salmon resting below the weir. This traditional method of fishing probably continued unbroken here since the Middle Ages as the monks of Mellifont Abbey operated a weir here and a similar boat was examined in the 1950s by the geographer Estyn Evans.[33] The coracle is structurally similar to the rowing *currach* of the west coast and both probably had a common ancestry. Thomas Mason, who visited most of the inhabited islands in the 1930s, believed that the Tory Island canoe was the next stage in the evolution of boats from the round coracle. This now-extinct vessel had a rounded bow, was propelled by paddles

rather than oars and could easily be carried by one man. When fishing, one man sat in the stern with the line and another worked the paddle, kneeling on a pad of heather in the prow.

Boyne Canoe and Suir Prong

Yet another traditional boat design still survives on the Boyne Estuary. This is a wooden clinker-built boat with a keelless hull and a distinctive truncated bow. Two versions of the boat are found on the Boyne – one used for salmon netting and the other for mussel fishing. The salmon boats are shorter - from *c.* 4.25 metres to 4.85 metres (14 to 16 feet) long as opposed to 5.8 metres to 6.4 metres (19 to 21 feet) long in the case of the mussel boat. The salmon boats are rowed in the conventional way but the mussel boats are propelled by a single scull, working through a semi-circular cut in the transom. The mussels are raked up from the bed of the estuary using a 5-metre long rake. However, recent dredging activity for the port of Drogheda caused the mussel fishery to be closed. A very similar design of boat called the Prong survives in the estuary of the Suir in County Waterford. It has the keelless hull and truncated bow but is carvel rather than clinker-built. Both designs resemble the Pram boats that are found in parts of Scandinavia and northern Germany. It is possible that they may have been introduced here by Vikings who settled on the east and south-east coasts of Ireland as early as the ninth century AD. They have survived on these estuaries because they suit the local environmental conditions and are cheap to build.[34]

West Coast Currach

The high-pointed bow, long sleek lines and lightweight construction of the *currach* made it ideal for use on the big seas of the Atlantic coasts. The rowing *currach* of the west coast is still in use today from Donegal to Kerry.[35] The frame is built up of wooden laths, which are

(right) Currachs near the Aran Islands, County Galway (R.J. Welch, courtesy of the Ulster Museum). *(below) Currachs on the slip at Dunquin, near Dingle, County Kerry.*

covered with tarred canvas. This can be repaired by the rather dramatic technique of setting the tar alight and, when is has become liquid, sticking a new piece of fabric over the damaged part.

The oars of the *currach* are so long that the looms (the ends in the boat) overlap and the oarsman pulls cross handed. They are balanced by a heavy wooden counterweight, called the bool, near the oarsman's hands and the blade is generally narrow to slice through the water. Unlike the oar of a normal rowing boat, which sits in a horseshoe-shaped rowlock, the oar of the *currach* is pivoted by means of a round hole in the bull, which sits on a wooden peg driven into the gunwale. A *currach* can be rowed by two, three or four men and the largest is reputed to have a carrying capacity of two tons. The *currachs* of the west coast have been put to a variety of practical uses including the setting of lobster pots, inshore net fishing, gathering seaweed and ferrying passengers, livestock and freight, especially between the islands and the mainland. They were even used for hunting the basking shark in years gone by.

It was often said by disapproving visitors that the Irish would not go out to fish but would wait for the fish to come inshore. However, this type of inshore fishing was well suited to a crofter economy, which involved the husbandry of both land and sea. A coastal-dwelling farmer would always have a net handy and would watch for the signs of shoals moving close to the coast. There were traditional watching points on cliffs overlooking small bays and from these points the watchers would direct the seine fishing boats to surround the shoals of pilchard, herring and mackerel when they came inshore.

Estuary Cots

A cluster of traditional flat-bottomed wooden boats, known as cots, developed in the estuaries of south-east Ireland such as those of the rivers Blackwater, Suir, Nore, Barrow, Bann and Slaney and more remotely, in the estuaries of north Derry. All of these were originally developed from river craft and evolved to cope with the shallow conditions of large estuaries where the tide can move in or out rapidly over vast expanses of intertidal mud or sand. An exception to this was the Rosslare cot, which evolved into a successful sea-going craft. It is thought that the historical contacts between Somerset and Wexford fishermen were responsible for the strong similarities between the design of the Somerset 'flatner' and the Rosslare cot. Its clinker-built planking may even date from the boat-building methods of the Vikings who settled in Wexford. Before 1926, the largest Rosslare cots were between 30 and 40 feet (9-12 metres) long and ranged over the Irish Sea. During the 1920s, as many as 46 large cots were fishing regularly out of Rosslare. More recently, cots were built under 20 feet (6 metres) in length and were suitable only for inshore fishing when the weather was good. A large cot was crewed by four men. It was double ended with the stem and stern posts being slightly raked. There was no keel and the bottom was essentially flat for use on rollers up or down the beach. In suitable weather it was not unusual for Rosslare fishermen to row the cot to Tuskar Rock (a distance of 10 miles in the open sea) where the line fishing was good.[36]

The Galway Hookers

There are few more inspiring sights in Irish waters than a fleet of Galway Hookers in full sail with the landscape of Connemara behind. Unlike many other traditional craft, this fishing and cargo boat survived into the twentieth century and is alive and well today. With its trademark dark red sails and wide-beamed hull, the Hooker is now almost a symbol of the west. Its

A converted Gleoiteog, *named* Widgeon, *under sail in Connemara. The wooden cabin is a later addition to the traditional open boat.*

Hookers and Pucáns *at the annual sailing festival* Cruinniú na mBád *(meeting of the boats) at Kinvara, County Galway. This harbour was the destination for generations of turf boats from Connemara.*

origins probably go back to the medieval period, but one school of thought suggests a Dutch design which may have developed as a result of Galway's export trade of herring.[37]

Often known collectively as Galway or Connemara Hookers, the boats are found in several shapes and a decreasing size range as follows:

> *Bád Mór* (big boat)
> *Leath Bhád* (half boat)
> *Gleoiteog*
> *Púcán*

The largest of these, the *Bád Mór*, has an overall length of 40 feet (12 metres) and can carry 12 to 15 tons of cargo. The Hooker has a gaff rig, which means that the main sail runs up an extension of the mast which is carried at about 45 degrees to the vertical. The sail area would be about 900 square feet (90 square metres) of heavy calico. Other distinctive features of the Hooker include the wide belly of the hull, designed for carrying bulky cargo such as turf, and the steeply raked transom at the back of the boat.

The *Gleoiteog* is similar in shape and rigging to the Hooker but her overall length is only 24-28 feet (7-8 metres). Some of these boats have a short foredeck as in the Hooker and some are completely open. In the nineteenth century the *Gleoiteog* was the general work boat of Connemara, used for fishing and carrying

small cargoes, as most boatmen could not afford the cost of the larger Hooker.

The *Púcán* is the last of the Hooker family, similar in hull form and size to the *Gleoiteog* but with a different sail rig involving a lug sail and a small jib set on a running bowsprit. The last working *Púcáns* plied the waters around Kilkieran gathering seaweed for the local Arramara factory where it was dried and exported for the alginate industry.

The Slaney Gabard

Slaney *Gabards* were sailing cargo boats which were designed for use on tidal stretches of the River Slaney and Wexford Harbour.[38] They were up to 55 feet (17 metres) in length, with a 12 to 14 foot (3.5-4 metres) beam and flat bottomed to manage in the very shallow waters of the harbour. The boats had a small working deck between the forward bulkhead and the bow on which a bowman stood with a long pole, which he used to help the boat go about through the wind. The bowman also had the job of poling the boat forward against the tide by walking the length of the catwalk along the side. The *Gabard* had a single sail, which could be easily lowered to pass beneath the bridges on the river. These working boats would carry cargo, livestock and even passengers throughout the tidal waterways of the Slaney. About 1730, *Gabards* transported the surplus stone from the demolition of Wexford Castle for use in the building of a Protestant church at Killinick. At the beginning of the twentieth century, they delivered the sand and gravel needed for the construction of the Rosslare-Waterford railway.

The Drontheim – Yawl of the North Coast

Up to the mid-twentieth century, there was remarkable traditional craft on the north coast between Donegal Bay and Rathlin Island, which could trace its origins back to the Viking ships of the eighth and ninth centuries.[39] Often referred to by locals simply as a 'yawl' or a 'skiff', its real name was the *Drontheim* boat from its

original port of Trondheim, on the west coast of Norway. The *Drontheim* was a distinctive open boat, up to 26 or 28 feet (8-8.5 metres) in length, with pointed bow and stern and could be used either as a rowing boat or a sailboat. Often built in Norway and imported complete on the decks of timber ships from Scandinavia, the boats were 'clinker-built', with planks overlapping down the sides. They could carry either one or two masts and had a distinctive 'sprit' sail rig. The keel of the boat was light but strong and the *Drontheim* had a sharp narrow bow and stern which enabled it to cut cleanly through the big waves, which are typical of the north Irish coast. The wholesale depletion of Irish native timber by the eighteenth century was one of the factors which prompted the importation of these boats, but the cultural links between the coastal communities of the north Irish coast, the Scottish islands and Scandinavia were also an important element. At the end of the summer salmon-fishing season, the *Drontheims* were often rigged for racing regattas. The enormous canvas sails

(above) Racing Drontheims at Portstewart, County Derry, 1930s; (below) a Glengad Drontheim at Greencastle regatta August 1951 (photographs courtesy of Donal McPolin).

(right) Hansard's yacht in Waterford Harbour; (below) a yachting party in Cork Harbour. The yacht was possibly the 'Leander' a 20 ton cutter (courtesy of the National Library of Ireland).

produced a fast race but required skilful handling in a strong wind. Regattas were held up to the 1950s at Moville in Lough Foyle, and Portrush, County Antrim.

The Early Sport of Sailing

Cruising the oceans from a base in Ireland can be traced at least as far back as St Brendan and St Columcille in the sixth century AD. The history of cruising in Ireland has been chronicled by W.M. Nixon for the Irish Cruising Club.[40] The world's first yacht club was established in 1720 with the foundation of the Water Club of the Harbour of Cork. The present Royal Cork Yacht Club claims direct line of descent with this early group of sailing enthusiasts. The formation of the original Water Club was the result of a period of affluence in the Cork area when trading increased and the more affluent merchants acquired their own sailing vessels to improve communications across this natural harbour. The style of the yachts was based on the Dutch vessels of the previous century and sailing for pleasure was a natural extension of their use for trade. The coast of west Cork is still regarded as one of the finest cruising waters in Europe.

In 1830 the Royal Northern Yacht Club was established in Belfast Lough and the Royal Western Yacht Club in the Shannon Estuary. These were outposts of the Royal Yacht Squadron, based in the south of England. The first recorded event was a regatta at Kilrush in 1832 with eight yachts taking part. The opening of the new harbour at Dun Laoghaire on the south side of Dublin Bay in the 1830s provided an ideal deep-water mooring for larger yachts close to the capital. It was quickly followed by the foundation of the Royal St. George Yacht Club and the Royal Irish Yacht Club, both based in the new harbour. Most of the yachts involved in this period were large and were sailed almost entirely by professional crews. But it was also the start of the ocean-cruising tradition, which lives on today in the Irish Cruising Club. Pioneering cruises were made

from Ireland to Iceland and on to Norway. The summer of 1860 saw the first offshore yacht race from Dublin to Cork.

Ireland's most important contribution to the development of cruiser racing has been the development of five classes of inshore keelboats that improved the racing skills of Ireland's sailors. The oldest is the Cork Harbour One Design, which first raced as a class in 1896. These were sizeable keelboats at 30 feet (9 metres) overall length and were originally open without a deck. Next to start racing as a class were the Howth 17s with their distinctive topsails. Although only 17 feet (5 metres) overall, some were used for cruising in the Irish Sea. The larger Dublin Bay 21s and the Fairy Class of the Royal North of Ireland, both made their debuts in 1902-03. The latter had a hull length of 22 feet (6.6 metres) and a distinctive bowsprit. The International Dragon, originally designed in 1926, is still a significant racing class in Dublin today.[41]

Dinghy Sailing

Although sailing cruisers have been racing in Ireland for many centuries, Dublin Bay has been the centre of dinghy racing since at least

Dinghies racing in Dun Laoghaire Harbour, County Dublin in the 1960s. The boats include Dublin Bay 12, an IDRA 14 and the Coote (white hull in centre), a sundry class boat. The Irish Lights tender is moored in he background (courtesy of the National Library of Ireland).

Groomsport Harbour, Bangor, County Down with Belfast Lough 25 footers rigging their sails for a race (courtesy of the National Library of Ireland).

the 1880s. The formal beginning of Dublin Bay Sailing Club began with a notice in the press in July 1884, which read,

> *In order to provide as much sport as possible, with a minimum of expense, the races are to be strictly limited to open-sea boats, with a light draught of water, such as can be easily rowed and beached if necessary.*

The starting line for the first races was a former gun emplacement known as 'The Battery' at Sandycove Point, just south of Dun Laoghaire. The first boats were open sea boats with a maximum length of 6 metres 18 feet (5.5 metres). After a while, bigger faster boats were attracted

to the regular Saturday afternoon racing and the fleet was divided into A and B classes. Thomas Middleton, who lived near the beach at Shankill, south County Dublin, had the idea that yacht racing should be carried out in boats of identical shape, size and sail area so that the race should be a contest of sailing skills not boat design. By 1888 a third class, the Water Wags, was included in the racing and these classic boats are still racing today under the flag of DBSC.[42] In 1899, with the introduction of the Twenty-five Footers, the club abandoned the Battery and the races were started at the mouth of what was then Kingstown (now Dun Laoghaire) Harbour.

7

Harvesting the Sea

Fishing has always been important to coastal communities in Ireland from earliest times when Stone Age people collected the shellfish and trapped the salmon at river mouths, to the modern super trawler which is like a small industry in itself. But the harvest of the sea has not been limited to fish. Whales, seals, seabirds and seaweeds have also been used as key resources in certain parts of the Irish coast over the centuries.

Old Sea Fishing Methods

One of the earliest types of sea fishing in Ireland would have been the catching of eels in places such as the mouth of the River Bann, by Mesolithic hunter-gatherers.[1] In April or May the young elvers arrive from the ocean and enter the rivers, often leaving the water to wriggle over damp stones where they could be caught by hand. In the rivers they could be caught with simple hand nets and spears or even by turning over the stones, beneath which they hide. In autumn, as the eels migrate back to the sea, they were caught is specially designed traps made of woven rods of hazel which were placed in the water.

In Viking Dublin, cod and ling bones have been found in the excavations, so these settlers must have fished off the coast.[2] By medieval times there were major sea fisheries in progress in Irish coastal waters.[3] Herring were caught in the Irish Sea and off the west and south-west coasts throughout the fourteenth, fifteenth and sixteenth centuries, and in the latter period, a herring fishery also developed off Donegal. Other sea fish landed in those days included cod, ling, hake and haddock, so today's sea fisheries have a long history.

In the nineteenth century there were considerable efforts to improve Irish sea fisheries. By 1829 the number of men engaged in Irish sea fisheries had reached over 64,000 and there is some indication that coastal communities fared

Islander long-line fishing from the cliffs on Inishmore, Aran Islands, County Galway (courtesy of the National Museum of Ireland).

suggested that for the Irish, 'with such a complete menu, varied in some places by the abundance of salmon, sea-fishing was an unnecessary employment, and could not have been attractive to a population, mainly pastoral'. As part of his investigations Green visited America and one outcome of this was the establishment of a major export trade in salted mackerel from Ireland to the USA. Green also introduced the technique of fish smoking to Ireland. The period from 1900 to 1914 was one of the most productive for fisheries research under the direction of Green as Chief Inspector. He established a team of fisheries scientists and, between them they produced a huge amount of published work on the marine fauna of Ireland, in the first decade of the new century.

The ways of an ordinary fisherman in Connemara in the early twentieth century are beautifully recounted by Séamas Mac an Iomaire in his book, recently translated from Irish by Padraic de Bhaldraithe as *The Shores of Connemara*.[5] Mac an Iomaire was a fisherman-naturalist but he would have been typical of his people, except in so far as he wrote down and published the knowledge he gained in a lifetime of fishing and exploring the rich coastline of south Connemara. The first edition of the book, written in the 1920s, provides an account of fishing from Connemara a century earlier – in the early 1800s. In those days there were few sailing boats due to extreme poverty (several decades before the Great Famine).

Most people had báid iomartha (rowing boats or currachs) and they fished mainly with hand lines, except that the odd person had a piece or two of netting. The women would clean and repair the nets in those days. The boats would head out to the fishing banks to set their nets for the night. They usually made a fixed cast at that time – that is to set the nets on the fishing ground with a big four-cornered stone which would have a groove cut around it so the rope would

Mweenish Island, County Galway, home of the fisherman-naturalist Seamas Mac an Iomaire.

better in the Great Famine of the 1840s than those inland. The hunting of the basking shark off the west coast was one of the pursuits which continued during this time. Estuarine fisheries in the nineteenth century mainly concentrated on salmon and eel. Salmon were caught using stake nets and other permanent structures described as 'fixed engines'. In some of the larger estuaries such as Waterford Harbour, there were sprat or white-fish weirs, which also caught a great variety of small fish.[4]

In 1887 the Royal Dublin Society (RDS) commissioned William Spotswood Green to carry out a survey of fisheries in south-west Ireland and to suggest how the industry in Ireland could be developed. In 1890 Green undertook an important boat-based survey of Irish fisheries, with a number of eminent colleagues, and in his report he commented that, 'at the time of the survey there were practically no fisheries of importance on the west coast'. Green, who later became a Government Inspector of Fisheries, wrote an interesting account of Irish Sea Fisheries in 1902. He

fit into it. There were about 30 fathoms of strong rope from the net stone with other end attached to the clew of the net. The boats would head for home then and leave their nets there until the following morning when they would come to lift them, hoping to have a haul of mackerel or herring. They often had. Other times they would have nothing after all their hardship rowing throughout the night. Fishing was hard, stressful, cold work at that time.

By the early years of the twentieth century things had changed somewhat as most of the serious fishing was done using the traditional wooden sailing boats – the *Púcan, Bád Mór* or Nobby. The catch was made with nets, long lines or trammels. With the herring or mackerel net, the top rope was kept afloat by a line of corks and the bottom of the net was weighted down with stones. To prevent the nets rotting too quickly, the threads were covered in tar and stained to prevent them absorbing water.

The boats sailed out from Connemara into the Atlantic Ocean to search for mackerel west of the Aran Islands. They sailed in the afternoon and reached the fishing grounds as the sun was setting. Here they would shoot the nets in a single line of corks, 'as far as you can see'. As soon as the nets were set, they would drop the mast into the boat to cut down the area of windage and limit the amount of drifting. One man would keep watch by the light of an oil lamp (probably using whale oil) until the nets were hauled in the middle of the night and the boat set sail for port to land its catch either in Roundstone (on the mainland of Connemara) or Kilronan (on Inishmore) in the Aran Islands.

One of the best fishing areas on the west coast was known as Bofin Bank, off the Galway island of Inishbofin. Even in the time of the legendary Grace O'Malley it attracted fishermen from continental Europe, from whom the local Irish families, the O'Malleys and the O'Flahertys, extracted fishing dues. The herring were caught by net in winter while the mackerel were a summer catch. Fleets of local Hookers from the Claddagh in Galway city, from Westport and from harbours all along the west coast, would sail to the Bofin bank. In 1873, Inishbofin alone had a fleet of 52 boats including nobbies, *Púcáns,* and *currachs.*[6]

In the 1880s the Congested Districts Board (CDB), swept in on a tide of Victorian social reform, set about improving the lot of the most impoverished areas on the west coast of Ireland. The Board funded the building of new piers and harbours, many of which still remain today, albeit in a poor condition. It also paid for the purchase of new fishing boats and established twenty fish-curing stations down the west coast. It changed whole coastal landscape by encouraging the development of dispersed settlement where once only the *clachan* or cluster of dwelling houses had dominated.

By 1923 when the CDB was dissolved, fishing was already in decline on the west coast. In those days fishing took place mainly at night

A disused stone pier in Connemara, County Galway. Hundreds of such piers were built in the late nineteenth century by the Congested Districts Board.

(right) Women work at cleaning the herring catch for curing at Ardglass, County Down (R.J.Welch, courtesy of the Ulster Museum); *(below) fisherwomen with their wares at the Claddagh, Galway city* (courtesy of the National Library of Ireland).

in open boats, each with a crew of four or six men. On the night of 27 October 1927 a terrible storm blew up hitting the boats between Cleggan and Inishbofin and a total of 28 men were drowned, nine of them from Inishbofin. Many were reluctant to release their valuable nets thus causing the boats to capsize. This decimated the local fishing community and threatened the complete desertion of the islands. The night of 27 October 1927 also saw the decimation of the population of the Inishkea islands off County Mayo. A total of 24 *currachs* had set out that night from the Dock area between the two islands. When the big wind hit them the boats were shattered on the rocks like matchsticks. Nine island men died that night and the effect of the loss of so many young men was a disaster from which the island community never recovered.

Richard Murphy[7] has described the terror of a gale at sea in his epic poem, the 'Cleggan Disaster', which was based on the storm of 1927:

A storm began to march, the shrill wind piping,
And thunder exploding, while the
lightning flaked
In willow cascades, and the bayonets of hail
Flashed over craters and hillocks of water.
All the boats were trapped.
None had reached the pier.
The target of the gale was the mainland rocks.

Other fishing was done in those days in Connemara among the weedy shallow water around rocks. The long line was commonly used with hooks bated with sand eel or pieces of mackerel. The head stone was used to sink the line and a buoy at the surface of the sea marked the site. After a couple of hours waiting, the line was pulled into the boat and one man removed the fish while another settled the line in a basket, carefully fixing the hooks on the rim. The haul could include a whole range of bottom-dwelling fish such as eel, ray, skate, flatfish, turbot, halibut, ling, cod, hake, haddock, dogfish and others.

The trammels were set on the weedy areas and on the bare flat rocks. Here lead weights were used to keep the trammels on the sea bed and corks to keep the head rope at the surface. In these nets the Connemara men caught common rock fish like wrasse and pollack as well as migrating sea trout. But Mac an Iomaire was clearly not enthusiastic about this method. 'You would often be fishing all day long without catching anything', he complained, going on to define the best and worst type of weath-

er for sea fishing. 'Like everything else', he believed, 'the fish is happy in the sea on a fine day, unlike the cold un-natural day that would put numbness in your fingers if you weren't working hard'.

Salmon fishing was of great importance to many of the coastal communities down the west coast but it was a very short season. Near Gola Island in west Donegal the dense runs of salmon along the coast took place in June and July.[8] The small open boats, usually with a crew of four men, would leave for the fishing grounds in the evening, reaching the target area, between 5 and 6 miles (8-10 kilometres) out to sea, at about sunset. John McClune, a retired fisherman living in Rosbeg, west Donegal, told me they would often row the open boats for many hours in rough sea conditions. He was born in the 1920s and remembers the fishermen of Gola and Arranmore coming to Loughrosmore Bay for the salmon season. As the light was fading, up to 4,000 yards (3,500 metres) of drift net was laid in a long line perpendicular to the coast. In this way the path of the salmon, returning along the coast

Fishing boats on the slip at Ballycastle, County Antrim. Most are the double ended Drontheim *but the* currach *in the foreground is from Donegal. Some nets, lobster pots and the fish catch are visible in the foreground, 1935* (R.J. Welch, courtesy of the Ulster Museum).

Lobster in its rocky shore habitat. These crustaceans provided subsistence fishermen with a cash bonus to their normal catch (Nigel Motyer).

to their natal rivers, was intercepted. The net was hauled at dawn and the fishermen returned to their homes between five and six in the morning. The net, although immensely long, was only about 30 meshes deep, as the salmon run close to the sea surface. After the end of July the salmon runs came to an end and the fishermen turned their attention to lobsters and crayfish.

Lobster fishing provided these subsistence fishermen with a 'cash crop' which in the early twentieth century was a special bonus to their normal hard-won netting. The fishermen made their own lobster pots from hazel or sally (willow) rods cut inland in winter. From this naturally pliable wood were made baskets of various shapes but with certain standard features. A flat bottom, weighted down with stones, was essential to make the pot sit firmly on the sea bed. In the top was a hole 'that your hand could go through'. The bait was placed in the basket which was then lowered into the seaweed-covered bottom, especially near rocks

where the lobsters hid by day. Incredibly, in these days of depleted lobster populations, Mac an Iomaire often had more than one of these giant crustaceans in a pot along with eels and edible crabs. 'Certainly, if there are more than a couple of lobsters in a pot the third is finished.' He writes that they all 'flay each other bloodily and often one of the lobsters is killed'. He knew that, 'the lobsters come in from the deep sea in shoals like every other fish, and it's said there are large numbers of them together'.

The lobster fishermen of the Inishkeas would travel considerable distances to set their pots. They preferred such deserted areas as the north side of Achill Island, where they built shelters or 'booley huts' for themselves. They also travelled north to the neighbouring flat island of Inishglora, where they lived in primitive stone huts for six to eight weeks at a time. The lobsters were sold for about five shillings a dozen in Belmullet, and sent by cart to Ballina and thence to England. At the time of the Congested

148

Districts Board, the lobster fishing fleet in north-west Mayo consisted of about 50 boats and 100 fishermen.[9] Lobsters were also important in the economy of Inishmurray off County Sligo. The short lobster fishing season was the most remunerative, although the islanders here only earned about the same price in the 1930s as did the Inishkea fishermen several decades earlier. At this price it is not surprising that lobster was sometimes used as bait when fishing for *balláin* (wrasse).

Whaling

The Inishkea Islands were also the location for Ireland's first whaling station and the history of this venture has been thoroughly researched by James Fairley in *Irish Whales and Whaling*.[10] The capture of slow-moving great whales may have been carried out in Ireland from ancient times but the first recorded whaling operations were off Donegal in the eighteenth century. Two brothers, Thomas and Andrew Nesbitt, from Killybegs, County Donegal, caught an average of two to three whales each season using the first known harpoon gun. By the

mid-nineteenth century stocks of both right whales and sperm whales in the North Atlantic had already been reduced by over-exploitation. The larger and faster-swimming whales, however, were beyond the reach of early whaling boats, until the introduction of the swivel harpoon gun. By 1896 there were 47 steam-powered whaling boats working off Norway and Iceland, taking about 2,000 whales per season.

In the early 1900s Norwegians were looking for a suitable site for a whaling station in north-west Ireland, and enquiries centred first on Gola Island and then Arranmore off County Donegal. A site for the station was even bought on Arranmore Island but there was considerable opposition to the scheme from local fishermen in both Donegal and Derry. An enquiry was held in February 1908 and the proposal was rejected but within two weeks it was announced that the same company would build a whaling station on the island of South Inishkea. Both of the Inishkea Islands were, by now, owned by the Congested Districts Board, a member of which was the enigmatic W.S. Green, also Inspector of Fisheries for the government. He had persuaded the board to sell the site at

Captured whales at the mooring bouy at Inishkea Island, County Mayo in 1911 (photo courtesy of James Fairley).

A whale is towed to the bottom of the slipway by rowing boat at Rusheen, Inishkea Islands, County Mayo (photo courtesy of James Fairley).

1912. Fin whales were the most frequently caught (with a total of 218 between 1908-1913) but the catch included blue (66), sei (61), sperm (25), right (14) and humpback whales (3). During this period, opposition to whaling in Ireland was growing. The Whale Fisheries Act of 1908 brought in a licencing system, a closed season and a prohibition on whaling within three miles (5 km) of the coast. After the poor year of 1912 (possibly due to competition from the Blacksod station, but also to overfishing of the stock near the Irish coast), the company was put into liquidation and in 1913 it closed, with the station being dismantled in 1914.

The Blacksod station was slightly more successful than that on Inishkea. A total of 296 whales was landed here in the period 1910 to 1914. The outbreak of the Great War brought a halt to whaling in Ireland and prevented the machinery from the, now abandoned, Inishkea station being sold immediately. After the war whaling resumed at the Blacksod station only and a total of 202 whales was brought ashore in the period 1920-1922. Again fin whales (157) made up the majority but there were also blue (27), sperm (15) and sei whales (3). However, falling prices for whale oil and a mysterious fire in 1923, which burnt a large part of the station, put an end to whaling in Ireland for good. Under the Whale Fisheries Act of 1937, whaling was forbidden in Irish territorial waters and in 1991 the Irish government declared Irish waters a Whale and Dolphin Sanctuary.

Very occasionally, local fishing communities would hunt whales and dolphins, but they were usually too fast for the small open boats. Tomás Ó Crohán, in his famous book *The Islandman*,[11] describes one such encounter off the Blasket Islands, in the 1860s, when he was eight years old. Although they were described as porpoises, they were more likely to have been pilot whales from the description of the fins and the animals' behaviour:

Inishkea to the Norwegians, believing it would bring employment to this impoverished area.

The islands at this time had a resident population of about 290 people, mainly engaged in fishing. In March 1908 the whaling station was built, from a shipload of imported timber, on the islet of Rusheen, just off the east side of Inishkea South. A slipway and flensing stage (for cutting the meat) were built and three powerful steam winches were installed to haul up the whale carcasses from the sea. I can remember walking around the island during a brief visit in the 1970s and finding the rusting remains of this ironwork still there on the shoreline.

The station buildings were still incomplete when whaling began in the summer of 1908. The principal whaler, Lorentz Bruun, left the island in 1909 and set up his own whaling station on the mainland in Blacksod Bay. The catch of whales at the Inishkea station varied from 102 in the best year, 1909, to only 26 in

1910

Eely Bay whaling [illegible] Belmullet Mayo

Maura cast an eye along the strand and saw a
school of porpoises rounding the Gob from the
south … with their great fins sticking up out
of the water, all of them close together like any
shoal of fish. When we got home my mother
cried out that the boats were coming and that
some of them were making a ring around the
porpoises, trying to drive them ashore. At last
one of the porpoises went high and dry up on
the strand. One able fellow drew his blood and
when the rest of the porpoises smelt the blood,
they came ashore, helter-skelter, to join the
other high and dry on the strand.

At least ten large boats were involved in rounding up the whales, seven of these from Dunquin
on the mainland. When the mainland fishermen
saw the stranded cetaceans, they tried to come
ashore and take 'boatloads of them home' but
the islanders treated the catch as their own and
drove the Dunquin men down the strand covered in cuts and wounds 'till the men there
were as bloody as the porpoises'. It must have
been a mass killing of whales as all the islanders
took part. Ó Crohán recalls how he was 'jeer-
ing at the old woman when she would come
along with a creel full of porpoise meat balanced on her rump. You might imagine that
she came out of one of the porpoises herself
with her creel, she was so thickly smeared
with blood'. This first-hand account is quite
reminiscent of more recent records of beached
schools of pilot whales in west Kerry (see
Chapter 5).

*A fin whale on the flensing
deck at Blacksod, County
Mayo in 1910. In the
background is the boiler
house with its two elevators
(photo courtesy of
James Fairley).*

*A basking shark caught
by net fishermen at
Achill Island in 1984*
(Erwan Quéméré;
Le Chasse-Maree).

Shark Fishing

Tomás Ó Crohán[12] also described the accidental capture of a basking shark in the nets just off the White Strand of the Great Blasket Island. 'It dragged the nets and the boat for about a mile and came near to drowning us at that effort, only there were twenty fathoms of rope tied to the end of the net, and I had to pay all that out down to the last bit that I held in my hand'. After finally capturing the shark, Ó Crohán, recalls how, 'the liver in him provided the whole island with light for five years'.

The appearance in Irish coastal waters each summer of the enormous, slow moving basking sharks must have been a huge temptation to coastal fishermen. These are the largest fish in the North Atlantic and, unlike most sharks, feed entirely on plankton (see Chapter 5). It was well known for centuries that the sharks congregated in summer on an area about 30 miles (48 km) west of Inishbofin, County Galway, which was known as the 'sun fish bank'. Here the sharks were slaughtered for at least two centuries but, as the population declined, fishermen

began to wait for the remaining fish to come closer inshore before they killed them.

One favoured location was Keem Bay on the western end of Achill Island. A long net was set with one end attached to the shoreline and the other attached to a boat while a sharp-eyed lad was sent to keep watch on the cliffs surrounding the inlet. When a shark was spotted feeding near the surface the net was slowly hauled around it to capture the fish and a harpoon was thrust into the unfortunate victim as it struggled to free itself. There were dangers associated with the 'sunfish hunt'. As early as 1767 an account in the *Faulkner's Dublin Journal* recounts how 'one experienced fisherman received so violent a stroke on the small of his back from the tail of the fish, as totally to sever his backbone and kill him on the spot'.[13]

The main attraction of the basking shark was its liver, which when rendered down, could produce nearly 200 kilograms of oil per fish. This was a valuable commodity in the early twentieth century. In the immediate aftermath of the Second World War, mineral oils were again in short supply and liver oil fetched as much as £140 per ton. Between 1947 and

1975 over 12,300 basking sharks were killed at Achill and, even discounting those additional sharks killed at sea by Norwegian whaling vessels, this level of exploitation was too much for the population of these long-lived animals, which produce very few young. The numbers of basking sharks coming into western waters declined dramatically and the Achill fishery, that had peaked at 1,800 sharks per year, closed altogether in the mid-1980s.[14] Between the 1970s and the 1990s there were spasmodic attempts to hunt basking shark off the south coast but numbers here were not large and the fishery has not survived. Today, basking sharks are relatively scarce in Irish waters, but it is a poorly studied species, and the interaction of natural changes with the heavy fishing pressure in the mid-twentieth century is not well understood.

Hunting Seabirds

On the Aran Islands off County Galway, as on many other Atlantic islands, seabirds were once a staple part of the diet for the local people. The sheer cliffs, which are formed of horizontal beds of limestone and shale, provide numerous ledges for nesting guillemots, razorbills,

kittiwakes and shags. The softer shale has been etched out by the weather to create 'paths' just wide enough for a man to walk. The cliffman's kingdom has been graphically described by Tim Robinson in *Stones of Aran: Pilgrimage*.[15]

This savage place was like one of the island's fields, cropped every year, and perhaps has been so since the Stone Age. Its ledges, wet with ground-water flowing out of the shale bands, its slimy rock-slabs the waves explode over and the low-roofed caverns they surge into along the foot of its walls, were all ways to a livelihood for the cliffman, who prowled them alone and at night … The men would walk across to the cliffs at dusk with the rope which was oftena communal investment. One end of it would be tied around the cliffman's waist and between his legs, and the other made fast to an iron bar driven into a crevice or wedged in a cairn on the clifftop … The cliffman would carry a stick to keep himself clear of the cliff face while swinging on the rope and wedges to help him around awkward corners of his climbs. Having reached the chosen ledge, the cliffman would remain crouched in it until darkness came. When all the birds had flown in from the sea and settled down to roost, he would begin to crawl along and would silently murder the first bird he came to. Then he would move on, pushing the dead bird before him until it was up against the next victim, which thus would not feel his hands until it was too late. At dawn, the cliffman would be hauled up again, bent and rigid with cold and cramp.

Seabirds were also hunted on the Blasket Islands up to the early twentieth century. Here the islanders spent the months of April, May and June harvesting the cliff-breeding seabirds and at the beginning of August, they turned their attention to the puffins. The reason for this is that the kittiwakes, guillemots and razorbills have mainly left the cliffs by August and taken to the sea, while the single puffin chick is still being fed in its underground burrow by the adults and is already quite fat. It is possible that the puffin referred to here may include the bird now known as the Manx shearwater (*Puffinus puffinus*), another burrow nester, which has a much longer nesting season than the common puffin (*Fratercula arctica*). Both puffins and shearwaters nest in old rabbit burrows and they are both common on the Blasket islands. This account is given by Seán Ó Crohán (son of the author Tomás Ó Crohán who wrote *The Islandman*).[16]

They say there is no nicer bird to eat than the puffin, it is so appetising. When the puffin season came around, the steward, Bess Rice always arrived with her salt and her firkins to kill them for her. She would dispatch one man from each house to the Tearaght, a sea rock which teemed with those puffins. The islanders were always prepared for the day of the puffin's arrival, and if the puffins wreaked havoc among the rabbits they themselves suffered the same fate at the hands of the islanders who would spend two days and a night killing them so that when the men arrived home laden with birds the women's fingers had plenty to do plucking them, storing the feathers, cutting them up and curing them. Such houses weren't short of tasty food.

Seán Ó Crohán believed that the wiping out of large predators, such as the eagles and ravens, had allowed the seabirds to increase until 'the islands were chock-full of them'. He also comments on how the seabirds kept the islanders alive during the Great Famine. 'That was the time when many people in other places had no appetising food but it was a time of tasty food and fare on the Island. Then the islanders, both young and old, had grease to their ears from eating sea-birds, which were full of oil and fat.' The seabird harvest was even used to pay the rent and the Blasket Islanders would go as far as the Skelligs to harvest young gannets in late summer, resulting in much fighting among local communities over this valuable resource. Tomás Ó Crohán tells in *The Islandman*[17] of one such expedition (probably in the late nineteenth century):

A boat with a crew of twelve men used to be guarding the rock, well paid by the man who owned it. This time a boat set sail from Dunquin, my father among them, and they never rested till they got to the rock at daybreak. They sprang up it and fell to gathering the birds into the boat at full speed; and

Little Skellig, County Kerry. Every available ledge is covered with nesting gannets. The Blasket Islanders would sail to the rock to harvest young gannets in late summer throughout the nineteenth century.

it was easy to collect a load of them, for every single one of those young birds was as heavy as a fat goose.

The Dunquin boat was intercepted by the guard boat and a fierce fight ensued leaving two of the guards dead and the others unable to row. The Dunquin men set the sail of the guard boat to bring her back to shore and got their own boat back to their harbour, 'its crew cut and gashed and mangled, their boat full of fat young gannets and they themselves not too easy in their minds'. Des Lavelle[18] records that as late as 1869, the Little Skellig was rented annually for the taking of feathers and young gannets and at that time gannets were each fetching 1s 8d to 2s 6d each (or about 10 to 15 cent). This was clearly a price worth fighting for.

Hunting Seals

Hunting of seals was commonplace in the nineteenth century and earlier. Seal skins made excellent coats and waistcoats and they were also in demand for making floats for fishing nets and for covering boats. In the Rosses of west Donegal there is an account of funeral processions to the island of Arranmore which comprised as many as 60 or 80 *currachs* covered with seal skins.[19] On the Blasket Islands seal meat was considered superior to pork. The hunting was dangerous and difficult as this account by Tomás Ó Crohán[20] indicates.

The cave was in the western end of the Great Island. It was a very dangerous place, for there was always a strong swell round it and it's a long swim into it, and you have to swim sidelong, for the cleft in the rock has only just room for a seal ... The swimmer went in first, carrying the end of the rope in his mouth, the slaughtering stick under his oxter, a candle and matches in his cap and the cap on his head ... They kindled a light and when they reached the end of the cave, there was a beach full of seals there – big and little, male and female ... The two inside made themselves ready for the great enterprise

A grey seal pup lies on a breeding beach for up to three weeks when it is weaned and begins to feed for itself. During this vulnerable period, these animals were hunted by the islanders on the Blasket Islands, County Kerry (Oliver Ó Cadhla).

before them. Each of them had a club and they aimed a blow at every one of the seals … When they had finished the slaughter and all the seals there were killed, they had more trouble in front of them … They dragged every one of eight seals down to the water, and by the time they had done, the swell burst into the cave, and the two of us who were on the bridge had to grip the rock wall high up.

Seals were an important part of the Blasket Island economy and must have been readily available for hunting by the islanders. Their blubber was rendered down for oil to light the lamps. Tomás Ó Crohán in his book *Island Cross-Talk*[21] gives this first hand account from his diary, dated September 1922.

When I came home in the evening after the travels of the day, it reached my ears that there were two currachs *in the harbour full of seals … There were seven full-grown seals and five young in one* currach. *A bull seal in one cur-rach was ten feet long and in the other were two bulls eight feet long. They would hardly have been lifted out of the* currach *yet for all the willing hands that were gathered around.*

From the date given, this took place during the pupping season when the bulls were probably defending their breeding beaches. The number of animals taken was clearly unusual for that time but may have been a typical catch for the islanders in the late nineteenth century, as this passage suggests.

The young people were astonished to see them. The old women were eager to see again this sight that belonged to the old days.

Seal hunting was clearly a speciality of some coastal communities but not part of the lives of others. Seamas Mac an Iomaire, a fisherman-naturalist who lived on the Connemara island of Mweenish in the early twentieth century, made no mention of seals in *The Shores of Connemara*.[22] However, the hunting of seals features extensively in folklore and story-telling. David Thomson recounts many tales in his book, *The People of the Sea*.[23] One story came from a village on the northern coast of Erris (County Mayo). 'It was the practice of the fisherfolk of that place to be catching and killing the seals for their skins and for making seal oil.' Two men went seal-hunting one day and with them they took a young baby because its mother was absent on that day. But a storm blew up and the baby was lost in the mouth of the cave where the men intended to hunt the seal. Two days later the men returned to find a seal suckling the young baby, which was unharmed. Such legends have led to a belief among many coastal communities that seal-hunting would bring bad luck to the hunter.

Shellfish Collecting

There is no doubt that shellfish were an important food resource for the earliest inhabitants of Ireland as the remains are found widely in archaeological sites.[24] Several times, I have come across the so-called 'shell middens' in the sand hills near Slyne Head in County Galway. Standing here with the ocean on one side, the lowland bogs inland and the Connemara hills in the background, it is easy to imagine an encampment of Stone Age people. The huge piles of discarded periwinkle and limpet shells show how important such food was to them.

The edible periwinkle *(Littorina littorea)* is relatively common and widespread around the

coasts of Ireland, typically found on rocky shores and mainly in semi-exposed to sheltered situations. In many parts of the coast, the local inhabitants still collect periwinkles by hand among the rocks and seaweed, in much the same way as was done in the Mesolithic era. However, now they are bagged and exported to France. An extensive survey of the periwinkle in the late 1990s[25] found that there was a noticible trend in density of the shellfish between the east, south and west coasts. Lowest densities on harvestable shores were found around Galway Bay where the granite shore-lines provide few suitable crevices. Some of the highest densities were found on the shores of east Cork and Waterford, especially where gravel in small gullies provides ideal settlement conditions for the larvae.

Most periwinkle 'pickers' are active on spring tides because this period gives the greatest number of hours of exposure and the greatest area of shoreline at low tide. The Christmas period is one of the busiest collection times as extra demand from France drives up the prices and the financial return is higher for the effort of collecting the shellfish, often in cold and wet conditions. Winkle picking is essentially a

Evening light at the Blasket Islands, County Kerry.

(left) Collecting mussels at low tide among the rocks; (right) periwinkles cluster together on the rocks at low tide.

'free for all' situation, although some families have traditionally harvested the same stretch of shoreline. There may be about 500 part-time winkle pickers active in the country although this is very difficult to estimate as many sell direct to French or Belgian buyers. The majority are men over the age of 40 years, who mainly use this as an income supplement during the winter months when fishing and farming activities are at a seasonal low.

In the nineteenth century the situation was somewhat different as food shortages forced families to collect the shellfish at all times of year. An early government fisheries report[26] indicated between 300 and 400 people engaged in winkle picking in the early 1900s in the Belmullet area of County Mayo alone. By 1998 only two or three individuals were thought to be active in this area.

Other shellfish are quite easily collected if you know where and when to look. The edible mussel grows attached to rocks near the low water mark but is often hidden by curtains of brown seaweed. One of my favourite places to collect mussels is the mouth of the Gweebarra estuary in west Donegal where, on the low spring tides, I walk for a mile or two across rippled sand flats to reach the mussel rocks. Watched by a group of curious seals, which shares these rocks, I have often collected a bucket of large blue mussels in a few minutes. These bivalve molluscs are filter feeders so they grow best where there is a fast flow of water, such as in the tide race between two rocks. They also have a tendancy to concentrate any pollutants in the water in their flesh, which is why one should never eat mussels growing near a sewage outlet or other discharge.

A number of shellfish live buried in clean sand in estuaries. These include the cockle, made famous by the traditional Dublin song *Cockles and Mussels,* about Molly Malone.

> *She wheels her wheelbarrow*
> *Through streets broad and narrow,*
> *Crying cockles and mussels, alive, alive-O.*

The collection of these shellfish was once a common practice among coastal communities in Ireland, but has now almost died out. Towards the end of the nineteenth century landings of some 4,000 tonnes of cockles were recorded annually in Ireland by local coast-guards, up to 500 people made a living from collecting them and there was a substantial export trade.[27] But even this is a gross under-estimation, as the vast bulk of the collection was taken by local people for home consumption. In Dublin hundreds of individuals collected the cockles on Malahide, Portmarnock, Baldoyle, Clontarf and Sandymount strands at low tide and sold them on the city streets up to the early years of the twentieth century. In 1904, it was estimated that 80 tonnes of cockles were eaten in the city, three-quarters of them in a raw state. After 1908, the consumption of cockles dropped dramatically and there is circumstantial evidence to suggest this was due to the association between the shellfish and a major outbreak of enteric fever. The Dublin cockle beds were grossly polluted with sewage from the city and the high incidence of typhoid was also attributed to eating the shellfish.

The razorshell, the otter shell, and the sand gaper each require different techniques to extract them from their burrows. None of these

Whelks caught in Wicklow Bay using baited pots.

is collected today, although a short-lived razor clam fishery in the 1990s involved suction-dredging of the seabed off north Dublin and Meath coasts.

Oyster Beds and Mariculture

In prehistoric times the native oyster was abundant in shallow, sheltered waters all around the Irish coast. Inner Galway Bay is one such place where the clean Atlantic waters are warmed on the extensive banks and shoals before they carry their rich plankton soup into the intricate bays and inlets all around the east and south side of the bay. To judge by the frequency with which archaeologists encounter oyster shells in their excavations, early inhabitants of this island must have collected these shellfish in abundance. In the nineteenth century it was said of the oyster: 'It can make the sick well, render the healthy stouter, prolong

the shortening days of senility and impact an additional charm to youth and beauty.' Such tributes to the native oyster are not uncommon in literature, but its popularity and the ease with which it was harvested, have been its undoing.[28]

The oysters grew in traditional 'beds' or 'banks' which were uncovered at low tide. In the nineteenth century, the collecting of oysters in Galway Bay was normally women's work. About 35 or 40 women, of all ages, wearing red petticoats, formed a line, shoulder to shoulder. They traversed each bank slowly, advancing as the tide receded and then retreating as it rose again. Each had a small stick in her hand with which she winkled the oysters from the ground, throwing the larger ones into a basket on her hip. The best area for 'fattening' the oyster was around Clarinbridge on the east side of the bay, where the mixing of freshwater and seawater was thought to be

A disused pier in Oranmore Bay, County Galway was used to land oysters from the beds in Inner Galway Bay.

necessary for good oyster quality. In the nineteenth century there were oyster beds in most of the inlets from Oranmore Bay in the north east to the Burren in the south. Here, the oyster spat (or young larvae) were laid out to grow in the tide. Some of these beds were regarded as private property – Lord Wallscourt's bed, Red Bank Private Bed – while some were treated as public beds. The people of Croshooa always regarded the Kinvara Public Oyster bed as their own property and even paid extra rent for them in addition to their land rent. Around 1900 the bed produced about 100,000 good-quality oysters annually but by 1971 landings had declined to about 30,000. Ultimately, this bed suffered the same fate as all others in the twentieth century, and it is no longer harvested.[29]

The massive overfishing of the native oyster in the late nineteenth century has been likened to the clearance of the oak forests on land by Cilian Roden, a coastal ecologist based in Galway. He finds coastal ecosystems intensely disturbed and he lays at least some of the blame on the removal of this important shellfish from many areas of sheltered waters. He recently told a marine workshop, 'we have eradicated a once extensive marine community whose grazing and filtering activities largely determined species composition, the flow of nutrients, biomass and even inorganic sediments in many inshore waters'.

The Galway beds relied on regular restocking from the natural beds of Mayo and Connemara, which, by the early twentieth century, had become largely worked out. In 1901 an Inspector of Fisheries, Ernest Holt, began a series of experiments involving the transplanting of large numbers of oysters to Galway Bay from numerous exotic sources such as the south of England, Holland and Auray and Arcachon in France. By 1903 he was experimenting with spat introduced into a seawater pond or 'saleen' in front of Ardfry House. However, climatic conditions in Ireland are not the best for oyster spawning and the

Aerial view of tanks in Cork Harbour, used for the cultivation of Pacific oysters (Richard T. Mills).

experiments were not very successful. Noel Wilkins asks the obvious question as to how native oysters ever managed to grow and reproduce in the wild in Ireland without human intervention. The answer is that stocks increase very slowly on their own and, if left alone or only lightly harvested, the beds become large and self-sustaining over time. However, the rate of exploitation of native oysters in the nineteenth century was unsustainable and almost all the native oyster beds disappeared. Oysters, like most filter feeding shellfish, are very sensitive to water quality. So in certain bays, like Cork Harbour, there have been repeated problems with oyster mortality due to pollution. Elsewhere, as in Bantry Bay, there have been difficulties with algal blooms which produce a toxin, making the shellfish unsaleable.

The remarkable development of aquaculture in Victorian Ireland is recounted by Noel Wilkins in his book, *Ponds, Passes and Parcs*.[30] Early attempts to farm salmon included the building of a hatchery by E.J. Cooper in 1856 at Ballysadare Bay, County Sligo. About this time there was also an attempt to rear salmon in a sea cage in Kingstown (Dun Laoghaire) Harbour but the experiment failed as the food supply for the fish was inadequate.

Seaweeds

The typical rocky shore of the Atlantic coast of Ireland is draped in a curtain of slithery, slippy brown seaweeds. Below the low tide line a virtual forest of kelp sways to and fro in the underwater currents. Just like native forests on land these kelp beds are rich and varied habitats for a multitude of animal species from barnacles to grey seals. They have also provided a valuable source of fertiliser and other products for coastal people, probably since the first farming of coastal lands. The geographer Estyn Evans described the seaweed harvest in his book *Irish Folk Ways*:[31]

> *The great bulk of the wrack taken all round the coast for manure was driftweed thrown up during storms, but the supply was often supplemented by cutting or pulling weed from the rocks, and in some places there were complicated methods of regulating and distributing*

(above) Brown seaweeds blanket the rocky shores on the Irish coast; (right) harvesting seaweed on the west coast, about 1900 (courtesy of the National Library of Ireland).

the harvest. The weed had to be carried away among the slippery boulders in back-creels and hand-barrows and stacked on the beach ready for the carts and creel-asses.

The importance of the seaweed as a fertiliser for coastal farmland cannot be underestimated. In rocky places, such as the Aran Islands, where soil was scarce, the very fields themselves were created over generations by dragging seaweed from the shore. The playwright J.M Synge lived here in the early years of the twentieth century and, in a lyrical account of life in *The Aran Islands*,[32] he wrote:

At the south-west corner of the island I came upon a number of people gathering the seaweed that is now thick on the rocks. It was raked from the surf by the men and then carried up to the brow of the cliff by a party of young girls. In addition to their ordinary clothing these girls wore a raw sheepskin on their shoulders, to catch the oozing seawater, and they looked strangely wild and seal-like with the salt caked upon their lips and wreaths of seaweed in their hair.

Estyn Evans[33] recounted the importance of the seaweed in fertiliser production. The most profitable way of exploiting seaweed down to recent times was for the burning of kelp, which became a considerable business among shore-dwellers in the eighteenth century as the growth of industry stimulated the production of soap, bleaching materials and glass. More recently kelp was chiefly in demand for the preparation of iodine. Kelp was made by burning the thick stems of tangle (*Laminaria*) or other coarse weeds – to which, as well as the ashes, the name kelp is applied. These were thrown up in the winter storms or cut at low tide. The weeds were dried on low stone walls and ricked and thatched until ready for the kiln on summer days.

The practice of making the kelp on the island of Inishmurray, off County Sligo, is well

The old stone tower on Tory Island with seaweed drying on rocks at its base, 1910 (R.J. Welch, courtesy of the Ulster Museum).

described by a former islander, Patrick Heraughty,[34] who left the island at the age of twelve in the 1930s.

Sea rods were gathered in winter and dried on low stone walls. Wrack was collected in May and dried somewhat as hay by spreading it out to dry – 'lapping' – and finally building it into cocks. The collection of the wrack was well organised. There were two traditional stewards, who divided the block of wrack between the claimants and who, for their trouble, got an extra 'half share' each. Towards the end of June the kelp was burned. First a rectangular stone hearth about 2.5 metres long by one metre wide was built. Turf was placed on this hearth and lit. Once it was burning well, the dried wrack was laid over it. And when this in turn had been lit, the sea rods were laid on top and replenished as necessary. This process produced an immense volume of thick black smoke and, as it was almost always done on the common beside the school, the lunch-time game of running through the smoke, despite its effect on clothes and faces, was enormously popular with the 'school let-out'.

There is a spot I know at Rosbeg in west Donegal where, among ancient stone walls above a small storm beach, there still stands a perfect circular wall of flagstones alongside the remains of a kiln, with its characteristic corbelled fireplace. In the early decades of the century the dense oily smoke from the kilns drifting far inland was a familiar sight, each kiln burning for many hours and consuming several tons of weed, which was fed in a little at a time. Fisherman John McClune, born here in 1924, remembers working on the kelp as a child. He told me that the weed was collected from the beach after the storms and dried on the walls until it was suitable for burning. It would then smoulder in the kilns for several days before the final product, like hard black

toffee, was broken up and carried off by donkey and cart.

On the islands, any seaweed washed ashore was especially valuable as fertiliser, as the Blasket Islander, Tomás Ó Crohán recounted:[35]

One morning, I remember, I set my face to the shore. It was the season when we were getting seaweed for manure. I was bright and early and had a fine, new fork with me for gathering any handful of weed that should come my way. When I came to the cliff above the strand, I leant with my breast against a little round-topped fence, but there wasn't light enough to see anything from the top, and, that being so, I made my best speed down till I came to the pebbles. There was a little weed lying high and dry all along the line of the high tide, and I heaped it together with my fine new fork. I was by way of being rather set up with myself to think that I had done that much work while the rest were asleep, but I fancy that kind of conceit never lasts a man long — and that's how it was with me too.

Tim Robinson, in *Stones of Aran*,[36] described the practice of seaweed harvesting in the Aran Islands in recent times. Gathering searods here was an intermittent occupation for a few Aran farmers in the winter when little could be done on the land. 'It puts the time by', one or two of them told him, and indeed a superfluity of time is one of the rigours of the season. A man might expect to gather one or two tons of searods, or even more, in the course of a winter. The lump of cash comes in handy, and buys a calf when the grass is greening to feed it. In the 1970s the island was producing about 30 tons a year; Inis Oírr was producing twice that, alternative employment being scarcer there, while Inis Meáin contributed much less as comparatively few searods came ashore there.

Just like the stone walls, which subdivide

A circular kelp-drying wall near the shore in Rosbeg, County Donegal with a kiln to the left which was used for burning the weed.

A kelp grid in Strangford Lough, County Down, with rows of large stones laid out for attachment of seaweed, which was harvested by the local inhabitants (Thomas McErlean, Centre for Maritime Archaeology, University of Ulster).

the holdings on land, there are clear divisions of the shoreline, which Tim Robinson[37] discovered:

> *Two boreens come down to An Gleannachán, the one from Eoghanacht already mentioned, and another from the next village to the east, Sruthán. The boundary between the two villages is the west wall of the latter boreen, and the boulders lying in the shallows of the bay are the continuation of this boundary towards the low tide mark. Thus the Sruthán people could gather seaweed off the eastern half of the bay and the coast around the headland to the middle of the next bay, Port Chonnla. Within this division by villages subdivision by households was equally clearly established. These long-standing regulations of the shore have not always prevented disputes. On the north shore of Inis Meáin, for instance, the name* Cladach an tSiúite, *the shore of the quarrelling, is said to derive from the fact that the weed always seemed to drift ashore there exactly on the boundary of the two townlands.*

The gathering of seaweed was an important economic activity for some communities. Estyn Evans[38] surveyed the tradition thoughout Ireland. 'In the Rosses of west Donegal around 1750 the rents were paid in kelp: any surplus was bartered for the "two luxuries, spirits and tobacco, enjoyed by men and women alike". For the lesser weeds growing in shallow water ordinary sickles were employed when the tide was low, but these species made inferior kelp. In the sheltered waters of Strangford Lough, County Down, seaweed was such a valuable commodity in the eighteenth century that it was cultivated by placing lines of boulders across the sand or mud flats. The brown seaweeds will readily colonise a fixed rock with their holdfasts and these kelp grids were laid out with about 60 centimetre spacing between the stones.[39] Old seaweed beds may also be seen in Lough Swilly, Clew Bay, Achill Sound

and probably elsewhere. Today the most remarkable area of cultivated weed is near the mouth of Carlingford Lough in County Down, where at low tide a wide stretch of mud and sand is exposed in Mill Bay. Through the second half of the nineteenth century some 1,000 beds, covering well over a square mile (2.5 km²), in area, were maintained in Mill Bay, and it was not until the depression between the two world wars that they began to be neglected.'

The health-giving properties of seaweeds have long been known by coastal communities.

The seaweed baths at Enniscrone, County Sligo have provided thallasotheraphy and relaxation to generations of customers.

One establishment, in Enniscrone, County Sligo has been using seaweed for health reasons since the 1930s. For several generations the Kilcullen family have run their seaweed baths using the brown *Fucus* seaweeds harvested from the surrounding shorelines. At Celtic Seaweed Baths in Strandhill, County Sligo, patrons have the luxury of private rooms, each with a Victorian cast iron bath filled to the brim with hot water and seaweed. When I took the plunge recently, I was astonished at how relaxed and refreshed I felt after an hour of lounging in hot, silky, aromatic water. The benefits of immersion in seaweed and saltwater include relief from aches, rheumatism, arthritis, dry skin conditions, stress and even wrinkles.

Modern biologists are realising that the seaweeds offer one of the most valuable resources on the Irish coast. The Marine Institute has encouraged the collection of data on seaweed resources and has published accurate maps of the distribution of various species. This has assisted the development of a purpose-built seaweed processing plant in County Kerry and of a related project on the drying of seaweed for human consumption, mainly to supply the Japanese market. Other possible future uses of seaweed, currently being investigated, include its application in bio-purification processes. It may also be possible to use aquaculture techniques such as long-line cultivation and hatcheries to rear seaweed spores and plantlets for ongrowing at sea.

8

Respecting the Coast

There is no doubt that previous generations of Irish people viewed the coast and the sea as an abundant and sustainable source of food and useful materials. However, their exploitation was limited by the technology of the time – wooden boats powered by the wind and by human muscle, home-made nets made of thread, lobster pots made of willow or hazel rods, and the use of marram or bent grass for thatching. Most of all, they respected the power of the sea and knew that human efforts were often overwhelmed by the more powerful forces of wind, tide and waves. The preceding chapters describe the natural features of the coast and the history of human settlement and use of its bounty. This chapter brings the two together and looks at how we care for the natural environment of the coast. The critical question is whether humans can again find their place in harmony with nature so that the beauty and diversity of the coastline will survive in future.

Threats to Coastal Habitats

Over the centuries, Irish people had varied success in managing coastal habitats in a sustainable way. Some coastal plants, such as seakale, were harvested for food and are now rare.

The depletion of fish and shellfish stocks is well known. Among the worst cases were the wholesale overfishing of native oyster beds in the late nineteenth century and the slaughter of large numbers of basking sharks off the west coast. Harvesting of seaweed on rocky shores was extensive and an important part of the local economy on many coasts, over a number of centuries (see Chapter 7) but there is little

Plastic refuse litters many remote stoney beaches around the Irish coast.

(Clockwise from left) Sewage pollution on the shore at Merrion Strand, Dublin, before the new Poolbeg treatment works was opened; car dump on a western island; golf links developments have been the cause of damage to a number of significant dune systems.

evidence that this caused any long-term ecological damage. The effects of overgrazing and other disturbance on coastal dunes are well recorded and, in some cases, had dramatic effects.

Most of the larger offshore islands were inhabited in the nineteenth and early twentieth centuries so that their habitats and species were as intensively used as the mainland in the period leading to the Great Famine (see Chapter 6). The exploitation for fuel of all the turf (peat) on islands such as the Great Blasket, the Aran Islands, Inishbofin and Tory Island are well documented. This must have had a devastating effect on the islands' ecology. Robert Lloyd Praeger recorded how the sheep on Achill Island in the nineteenth century became lost on the mountain slopes, such was the luxurious growth of the heather. Today the same area has been grazed to a short sward of boggy grassland. Our knowledge of the present state of coastal habitats is quite limited but there are certainly indications of continuing problems for conservation.

A partial survey, carried out in the mid 1990s by Jenny Neff on behalf of the Heritage Council, considered the impacts on legally protected areas on the coast. In 114 Natural Heritage Areas (NHAs), for which information was available, she found that almost half were subject to grazing on a level that is detrimental to the habitat.[1] After agriculture, dumping was the most significant type of damage with domestic rubbish, home appliances, cars, farm machinery and farm refuse as the commonest things left in NHAs. In Donegal, for example, illegal dumping was listed as a damaging operation in all but one of the sites for which information was available. Recreational activities, such as camping and caravanning, were the damaging activities in the majority of legally protected areas.

A detailed botanical survey of the unique machair sites of north-west coasts in 1996 found that most of the sandy grasslands were severely overgrazed exacerbating the damage by wind and marine erosion.[2] This appears to have significantly reduced the number of breeding waders, especially the lapwing and dunlin, on these fragile habitats.[3]

Karin Dubsky of Coastwatch Ireland has decades of experience in monitoring the impact of human activities on the Irish coast. Their annual survey of coastal habitats shows we have not learnt much about care of the coastal zone. Dumping, littering, and unsuitable discharges to beaches are among the most obvious causes of damage. However, more invidious effects, such as disturbance due to recreational pressure, are more difficult to record and measure.

Have the recent designations of numerous coastal sites under EU Habitats and Birds directives led to any more enlightened habitat management? It is probably too early to judge but the indications are that, at least, the problems of overgrazing are being addressed. Whether the recreational uses of coastal dunes

and other areas for golf links, caravan parks and the like, are sustainable remains to be seen. Unfortunately, these permanent features tend to artificially stabilise the dynamic beach-dune interface leading to erosion and consequent effects elsewhere.

Coastal Erosion

Erosion is one of those terms which, like war and famine, is usually regarded as bad and damaging. However, coastal erosion is a natural process, which is simply the reverse of accretion and is usually part of a dynamic balance in coastal cells. A beach may be eroding at one time and accreting a decade later. It is the human interference in these beach-dune processes, which most often causes problems.

The importance of marram (or bent) grass in sand dune building was well known in nineteenth-century Ireland.[4] From the mid-1780s the erosion of dunes on the north coast of Donegal had caused extensive areas of arable land to be covered by sand. By 1806, Rosapenna House, a mansion built by Lord Boyne about 1700, was almost completely covered by sand and had to be abandoned. The Ordnance Survey letters record the movement of large sheets of sand in the area around Dunfanaghy and Horn Head. Large-scale movements of sand continued throughout the 1830s and various townlands in north Donegal were inundated. The Earls of Leitrim spent significant sums of money planting marram grass to arrest the problem.

However, during the 1914-1918 World War, the landlord on the Stewart estate at Horn Head cut large areas of marram grass and shipped it abroad as fodder and bedding for cavalry horses. As a result the dunes became mobile again and Horn Head House was inundated and eventually abandoned in 1931. An auction was held from the roof with the auctioneer sitting on the slates, which he then sold from under himself. In the 1930s the inundation

'Reconstruction' of a sand dune system at Portnoo, County Donegal for the extension of a golf links.

of more houses and roads by moving sand forced the Irish Land Commission to take control and, by 1937, planting with marram grass had succeeded in stabilising the dunes. In 1938 an order was made under the Land Act, 1936, prohibiting the cutting of marram grass in this area and in the 1940s trees were planted to complete the stabilisation.[5]

In the nineteenth century marram grass was considered an important resource on the coast of Donegal: 'This species of grass is used for thatching houses and making ropes, and is far superior to the best straw.'[6]

In the 1970s I visited the mobile dunes at Magheroarty in north Donegal and saw local farmers still cutting the marram grass for thatching of their houses. During the nineteenth and twentieth centuries many misguided efforts have been made using boulders, timber and other hard materials to attempt to stabilise the coast. In effect, these attempts usually interrupt the beach-dune processes leading to sand loss, beach lowering and erosion of adjacent

coasts, indirectly caused by these 'hard engineering' techniques.

The precision of the early editions of the Ordnance Survey maps of the 1830s–1840s offers an important baseline for coastline changes over the last century and a half. This is well illustrated by a study of the Inch beach and dunes in Dingle Bay, County Kerry.[7] This massive beach is a wonderful area to escape from the noise and hassle of modern living, with just the sound of the waves and the wind for company. Behind the beach is the largest, relatively undamaged sand dune system in the country at over 12,000 hectares. The shoreline here has changed significantly over recent centuries, especially in the southern 3 kilometres of the beach with a maximum horizontal change of 300 metres. The truncation of the 'nose' of the spit has happened at least three times – around 1840, 1900 and 1960. Andrew Cooper has examined the annual record of storms but there was no annual increase in storminess around these periods. However, three extreme storm events did occur around the time of these cutbacks in the Inch dunes. These were the 'Big Wind' of 1839, a severe storm in 1903 and the Hurricane 'Debbie' which stuck Ireland in 1961, with wind speeds up to 45 metres per second. Such storms can lead to the deepening of the foreshore slope, allowing large storm waves to break much closer inshore. Modelling of the 1961 storm shows breaking waves of 6 to 7 metres high (the height of a two-storey house) on the beach at Inch. Such waves would be sufficient to erode and move a substantial amount of sand.

In the nineteenth century there were major attempts throughout Ireland to reclaim land from estuaries. Dutch engineers were often employed to design schemes which entailed the building of bunds or sea walls with the pumping of water out of the impounded intertidal areas. Similar developments took place in Lough Foyle, Strangford Lough, Wexford Harbour, Cork Harbour, and the Shannon Estuary. Famine relief schemes in the mid-nineteenth century further accelerated the works, such that

in a period of 30-40 years there were few estuaries which did not suffer some loss of intertidal area. Many of these schemes subsequently collapsed, either because they were poorly planned, through lack of maintenance or due to lack of understanding of estuarine processes.

(above) A farmer cutting marram grass for thatching on sand dunes at Magheroarty, County Donegal, 1975; (left) increased storminess in Irish latitudes over the next few decades will lead to greater erosion pressures on the coast.

Wexford Harbour is a classic example of how human interference in coastal areas can have unforeseen consequences generations later. This shallow natural harbour at the mouth of the River Slaney lost nearly half of its tidal area in less than a decade (1847-54). The reclamation started in 1814 when two brothers named Thomas built a bank to enclose 800 acres on the south side of the estuary. However, in 1816, a high tide caused a breach in the bank and the sea reclaimed the area. In 1840 a Scottish syndicate began an ambitious project to claim both north and south wings of the estuary from the sea. The project was prompted by an Act passed by the British Parliament providing government aid for the reclamation of 'waste land' in Ireland. Despite considerable local opposition, the scheme went ahead in 1847 with the construction of the bank enclosing the North Slob. Hundreds of labourers worked with spades, shovels and picks to create an embankment which was eight feet wide (12.4 metres) at the top and mostly faced with stone. This

enclosed a tidal area of more than 2,400 acres. In 1850-51 the entire area was ploughed into ridges and a series of canals and drains were created leading to the principal outlet where sluices and a pumping station were built to discharge water to the remainder of the harbour. In 1854 work began on the South Slob and, on its completion, a total of 4,600 acres of polder land had replaced the equivalent area of intertidal sands and muds.[8]

By the 1920s erosion of the sand spit of Rosslare was becoming noticeable as the dynamics of the mouth of Wexford Harbour began to change. Consequential retreat of the shoreline at Rosslare Strand continued from the late nineteenth century despite coastal protection measures such as the building of groynes. The blame for this was attributed to the building of Rosslare Harbour, but in fact the problems began not long after the building of the North and South Slobs. This had the effect of reducing the southerly drift of sediment past the mouth of Wexford Harbour

Blackwater Head, County Wexford. Erosion of soft glacial cliffs along the Irish Sea coast threatens properties such as this farmhouse.

and starving Rosslare Point of sand. The inevitable consequence of this was the retreat and breakdown of the dunes at Rosslare Point, which finally breached in 1924-25 more than a century after the enclosure of the inner estuary.[9] In the 1970s, I remember rowing out across Wexford Harbour to a small sandy island that had a wonderful seabird breeding colony with all five species of terns. Tern Island was also a temporary feature resulting from the movement of sand from Rosslare Point and it too was destroyed by a storm in about 1975.

The extent and severity of coastal erosion around the coast in 1989 was considered important enough for the establishment of a National Coastal Erosion Committee. Made up largely of City and County Engineers, it set out to quantify the scale of the 'problem'. A needs study was carried out by the state science and technology agency, Eolas,[10] which found that out of a total coastline of 5,800 kilometres (in the Republic of Ireland) over 1,500 kilometres was at risk and some 490 kilometres required immediate attention. This figure included repairs to minor piers and harbours, under the control of local authorities, but excluded major harbours. Over 500 small harbours and piers were identified in the study. These were generally built in the nineteenth century and, although important for local fishermen and for tourism and leisure activities, many were found to be in a serious state of disrepair. The cost estimates for remedial action were largely based on traditional 'hard' structural solutions but, for the first time, there were signs that 'soft' ecological techniques were being considered, perhaps for reasons of cost if nothing else.

Fortunately, some alternative strategies in beach and dune management have been pioneered by the University of Ulster, in collaboration with Donegal County Council. A recent project, involving the local communities, and funded by the EU LIFE programme, in beach-dune sites around County Donegal,

Lahinch, County Clare. rock armouring has been used here to protect the town and sand dunes from marine erosion. However, it has also separated the beach and dunes, thereby reducing the supply of sand to the beach (Julie Fossitt).

has produced some valuable results. It has prepared beach and dune management plans for seven sites from Culdaff on the Inishowen peninsula to Rossnowlagh in Donegal Bay. Effective management must be based on accurate scientific information such as sediment type, wave processes and knowledge on the historical trends in coastlines as derived from early maps and air photographs.

Brittas Bay, County Wicklow, is one of the most popular east coast beaches, being about 40 kilometres from Dublin city and largely in public ownership. The beach and a significant dune system here were the subject of a major study in the 1960s by An Foras Forbartha (The Physical Planning Institute).[11] This found that there were serious problems arising from the uncontrolled use of the dunes by vehicles and some parts of the dunes were devoid of vegetation. In 1996 and 2004 my colleagues and I repeated the vegetation survey here. Significant changes were noted as a result of concentration of car parking into two main public car parks at the back of the dunes. Vegetation cover had increased in most areas, with the exception of several heavily eroded paths and exits near the car parks. Despite annual trimming of the dune front by winter high tides, it was shown that the same sand regularly moves back onto the beach and dunes in the summer, restoring the beach-dune profile.

This example shows that engineering solutions to marine erosion processes are quite inappropriate and can even be counter-pro-ductive by interfering with the natural cycling of sand from beach to dunes and back. A much better approach is to concentrate on proper management of human pressures on the dunes and prevent the concentration of people and vehicles in sensitive locations. The processes of short-term erosion are often balanced by accre-tion elsewhere and the whole coast is subject to much greater forces such as sea level and climate change, on which we can have little influence.

Climate Change

The issue of 'global warming' has moved from a dull scientific discussion to headline news as the impacts on human activities start to be accepted. The facts are plain to all. Globally, the 1990s was the warmest decade since wide-spread instrumental measurement of weather conditions began in the 1860s. Considering the longer term changes in climate of the northern hemisphere, the twentieth century was the warmest of the last 1,000 years. In mountain areas, glaciers have been melting and the fre-quency of serious floods has become greater. In Ireland we have had a run of mild winters with snow and ice becoming a rarity.

At the end of the last Ice Age, about 10,000 years ago, freshwater from the melting of polar ice disrupted the normal marine currents of the North Atlantic, bringing arctic water to Irish coasts. If this were to happen again, as a result of global warming, there could be serious implications for the North Atlantic Drift (or Gulf Stream), the current from the Caribbean, which keeps Irish shores warm in winter. There are already indications of a change in the way in which the Gulf Stream recycles warm water as it reaches northern latitudes. It is widely pre-dicted that what some scientists call a 'climate flip' will happen, switching off the warming effect and cooling Irish winter temperatures by as much as 30°C. Such changes are possible in the next 30 to 50 years so the implications for Irish coasts are significant.[12]

Among the other changes likely to occur as a result of global warming is a significant rise in sea level with melting of polar icecaps. Estimates of the scale of change have been consistently revised downwards to a level of about 49 cm by the year 2100. In Ireland the effects of this must be placed alongside the continuing readjustment of land and sea levels which is known to be taking place as a result of the melting of the last ice sheet in the Pleistocene era. This has resulted in sea level rising by about 1-2mm per year over the last century. This readjustment is uneven in its effects as the northern part of the island is ris-ing and the southern part sinking relative to modern sea level. The evidence for this is clear from the classic raised beaches around the northern coast and the drowned peatlands around the south-west coast. Thus the most significant effects of a new rise in sea level are likely to be in the southern part of the country.[13]

The most obvious effects will be seen in terms of an increase in the frequency of storm surges, resulting in increased coastal erosion, estuarine infilling, coastal flooding, changes in dune-beach systems and saltwater intrusion of coastal aquifers. At present it is estimated that about 130-160 hectares of coastal land are lost each year from about 300 localities around Ireland, mostly from the east coast.[14] Rates of recession average about 0.2 to 0.5m per year but in places, up to 2m per year may be lost to the sea.[15] Classic examples are the glacial cliffs at Greystones, County Wicklow and Blackwater Head, County Wexford. In some places, the natural processes of erosion are exacerbated by dredging, beach sand removal and inappropri-ate coastal protection measures. The present loss-es in these areas will almost certainly increase as storm surges take more sediments from the land.

Coastal flooding can occur occasionally when a high spring tide coincides with onshore winds and high rainfall. The most graphic examples of this were during the aftermath of Hurricane Charlie in August 1986. Significant

(Clockwise from top) Rinavella Bay, County Clare, where a drowned forest on the shoreline provides visible evidence of sea level rise (Eugene O'Kelly); *recent marine erosion on the popular coastal walk of the Murrough, County Wicklow; coastal flooding inland of the railway line at Kilcoole, County Wicklow following Hurricane Charlie in August 1986* (courtesy of *The Irish Times*).

areas of low-lying land on the east coast, especially in Dublin, Bray and Arklow were flooded. This was a forewarning of things to come. The late Bill Carter, of the University of Ulster, carried out a survey of the entire Irish coast and produced a series of 64 maps which delineated and measured the areas at risk of flooding as a result of sea-level rise.[16]

The combination of greater rates of erosion, coastal flooding and more rigid coastal protection leads to a phenomenon known as the 'intertidal squeeze' as the area between high and low water mark is reduced to the minimum possible. Good examples of this may be seen in all the major ports such as Dublin, Belfast and Cork where reclamation and port development have removed most of the natural shoreline and threat of erosion is a constant problem.

The predicted global climate change will alter the environment of typical coastal animals such as the cockle through a rise in sea level, which will reduce the intertidal area available to the shellfish population. Additionally, rises in water temperature, while unlikely to directly kill the cockles, may promote instability in the populations with cycles of scarcity and abundance. Other possible effects could include increased predation and changes in competition for food between shellfish but these impacts are much more difficult to predict.[17] Changes in the area of intertidal habitat and in the invertebrate populations will, almost certainly, have negative impacts on bird populations, especially some of the waders, such as sanderling, dunlin and ringed plover, which do not use inland habitats.

Minor changes in sea water temperature may have knock-on effects on seabird populations through effects on their prey. For example, sand eels are quite sensitive to water temperature changes and they form a staple diet for such birds as roseate tern and razorbill, which currently nest in internationally important numbers in Ireland. Overall, the effects of climate change on flora and fauna represent mere speculation as we cannot predict accurately how these organisms will respond to the changes.

Energy from the Sea

Anyone who has ever watched the power of Atlantic rollers breaking on a rock or a beach will appreciate the energy which the sea possesses. Waves, currents, tides and wind all generate natural and renewable energy. Harnessing this energy for useful purposes has long exercised the human ingenuity.

Wind

Perhaps the earliest sailing boats represented the first human attempts to capture wind power. The principle is a simple one. The wind strikes the sail and drives it to the side but the keel (or centreboard projecting downwards from the hull) prevents the boat slipping sideways through the water and movement is at an

angle to the wind. The direction of movement of the boat can be varied by moving the position of the sail relative to the wind. The only direction a yacht cannot sail is directly into the wind. Variations on this simple theme are almost infinite, from the traditional Galway Hookers to the modern, highly tuned fibreglass racing yachts. There is something wonderful about the silent, yet powerful, thrust of a yacht through the water using only wind energy that is unquenchable and free.

Coastal lands, especially those facing the Atlantic Ocean, are very windy places. This wind was used as a source of power for windmills from earliest times. One of the finest restored examples is the windmill at Blennerville in County Kerry. The sails of this prominent structure were among the last landmarks seen by emigrants sailing to America in the nineteenth century. The power from this windmill was used to pump water from the nearby canal, thus keeping the low-lying land behind the sea wall free from flooding.

Modern wind energy projects have been concentrated in western coastal counties from Donegal to Kerry where the wind speed across the land is highest. One of the main constraints is the visual effect of placing large numbers of modern turbines in highly scenic coastal landscapes. However, 'beauty is in the eye of the beholder' and opinions on the appearance of wind farms vary from complete acceptance to total opposition. Recent attention has focused on the use of offshore banks, such as the Codling, Arklow and Blackwater banks off the east coast to site huge clusters of wind turbines. At distances of up to 15 kilometres from the coast, these wind farms would have only a minor impact when viewed from the land. However, seafarers may have a different view, as a forest of steel structures in inshore waters is not a sight with which they are familiar. Other issues surround possible interference with traditional fishing grounds, hazard to seabirds and cetaceans and the more difficult

New wind turbines dominate the seascape at the Arklow Bank, off County Wicklow (Jaimie Blandford).

question of the artificial stabilising of naturally dynamic features. The role of these offshore banks in beach erosion on neighbouring coasts is poorly understood at present.

Waves

Waves represent the transfer of energy through the water, just as sound waves pass through the air. This transfer can take place over vast distances as well, which moves across the ocean from the site of a storm to the nearest coast. The Irish coast, particularly the Atlantic region from Malin Head, County Donegal to Mizen Head, County Cork, has some of the highest sustainable wave power levels in the world. It has been estimated that a thirteen-mile (21 km) long line of wave energy devices could provide up to 10 per cent of the national generating capacity.[18] Until the 1970s the only commercial use of use of wave energy in Ireland was the powering of small navigational aids such as lights and whistles. Serious wave power research in Ireland began in 1975 with the invention in Belfast of a self-rectifying air turbine. Theoretical work on using the resonant properties of harbour waves has been carried out at University College Cork. A natural 'blow-hole' on the remote island of Bull Rock

Wave energy. It has been estimated that a 21-kilometre long line of wave energy devices in the Atlantic could provide up to 10 per cent of the national generating capacity, but this potent form of renewable energy is still at the research and development stage.

off County Cork, was the location for a full feasibility study to use wave energy here to power the lighthouse on the island. In practical terms, wave energy in Ireland has been poorly addressed as a source of power, except by surfers who ride the rollers for pleasure.

Tides

The inexorable movements of the tides around the coast have been a fascination for people since the earliest times. The gravitational pull of the moon around the earth causes the alternate rise and fall of the oceans, and the rotation of the globe forces the ocean's water to 'pile up' against the continents, with two high tides and two low tides within each 24-hour day. In fact it takes about 24 hours and 52 minutes (or one lunar day) to complete two full tidal sequences.

At the early Christian monastic site of Nendrum, in Strangford Lough, County Down, recent excavations have revealed one of Europe's earliest dated examples of the use of tidal power for milling. The mill is built into a stone embankment, which encloses a large

tidal pond, thus harnessing the energy of the falling tide as it is forced through a restricted exit (see Chapter 6). On a larger scale, it is easy to see how impoundments such as Dunkettle Intake in Cork Harbour could have turbines installed to generate electricity from the power of the tide as it surges through the gaps in the sea wall.

Tidal energy has not been harnessed in modern times in Ireland but one could envisage floating (or even submerged) turbines located in key places such as the tide races between islands and the mainland and where tides move around headlands. These would have the advantage that they would be no more visible than, for example, modern salmon farms, but the hazard to shipping may be a significant drawback.

Coastal Zone Management

The term Coastal Zone Management (or CZM) has become quite a 'buzzword' in recent times. In simple terms, it means managing the coast in an integrated way so that the land and sea are viewed as interdependent rather than isolated components. In practice, there are so many administrative and stakeholder divisions on the coast that getting any kind of consistent approach to management is difficult if not impossible for a whole country. For example, local authorities have no juristiction over planning below high water mark, while central government controls developments in the intertidal area and inshore waters. In harbour areas, such as Dublin Port, the port authority controls most development. In the mid-1990s a Draft Policy for CZM in Ireland was drawn up, on behalf of the Irish Government, with a similar statement in Northern Ireland. Stripped down to its bare essentials, this is about government reorganisation. A decade later, despite much posturing and paperwork, there is little change in the situation.[19]

In a few places, however, there are examples of how integrated management of the coast might be made to work effectively. Strangford Lough in County Down, is one of the largest and most biologically diverse sea loughs in Europe. It is covered by numerous statutory designations and much of the coast and islands are managed by the National Trust, a voluntary body funded by membership subscriptions. It faces serious problems such as disturbance to wildfowl from shooting, overfishing of certain shellfish and increased recreational

pressure in certain areas. The response of the authorities has been somewhat piecemeal, but at least all the stakeholders have been galvanised to joint action to meet some of these problems, through the Strangford Lough Management Committee.

Bantry Bay, County Cork, was the subject of a major marine disaster with a shipping fire and oil spill at the Whiddy oil terminal in the 1970s. It is also one of the most important mariculture locations in the country, with extensive mussel cultivation. In the 1990s it was the location for the Bantry Bay Charter, an agreement between local authority and local communities, with support of national agencies. However, several years later, the government withdrew support from the Charter, minimising its impact.

Conclusion

Managing the coast is a difficult and complicated process. We should use the common sense and hard-won knowledge of past generations who survived hardship and isolation. Good management requires scientific knowledge of the natural resources and processes at work. It needs an integrated approach, which views the land and sea as interdependent and it needs environmentally sensitive solutions, tailored to each individual section of the coast. A sensitive, ecologically-based attitude to the coast implies

(from left) Mussel rafts in Killary Harbour, County Galway; salmon cages in Lough Swilly, County Donegal; sign prohibiting removal of stones from a storm beach at Bloody Foreland, County Donegal.

that we do not try to dominate or defeat the coastal forces, but that we design our developments to accommodate change and that we heed the abundant warnings from history about overexploitation of coastal resources. Most of all, coastal management requires the involvement of all the occupants and users of the coast in a concerted effort to protect one of our finest and most vulnerable resources for the long term.

Haymaking near Malin Head, County Donegal, with the Garvan Isles on the horizon.

9

Enjoying the Coast

In Ireland's long and varied coastline, there are many places, like the Cliffs of Moher, Giant's Causeway or Dublin Bay, which are well known attractions, but there are also many little-known spots – the hidden coast. This chapter brings together information about places to visit, whether for water sports, sea angling, watching wildlife or simply rambling on beaches or cliffs. The maps are intended only as a guide and should be read in conjunction with the specialist literature on each leisure activity.

We have all enjoyed the coast at some time in our lives. From the ageless pleasure of a sandy beach, to the fun of a boat trip, to the satisfaction of a good seafood restaurant, there are numerous ways to enjoy the coast and the

Brittas Bay, County Wicklow. A popular holiday beach-dune system may become eroded due to visitor pressure.

Map showing holiday beaches and surfing beaches in Ireland.

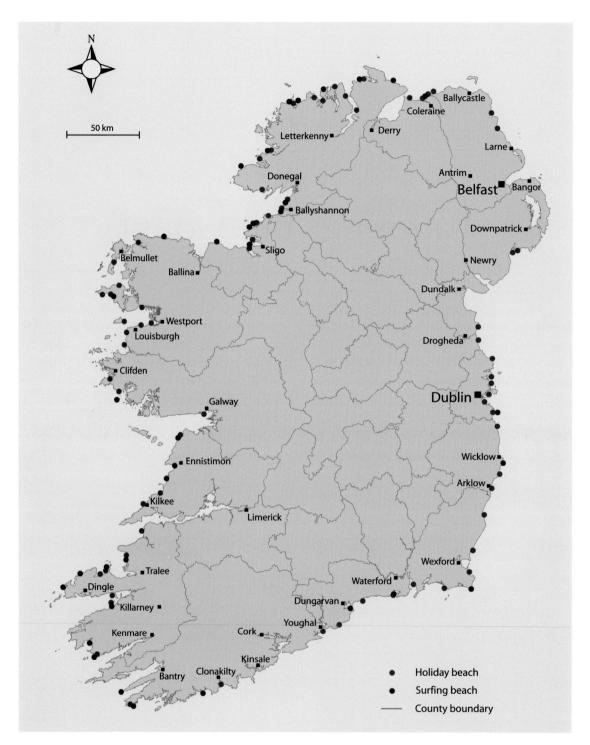

N

50 km

Ballycastle
Coleraine
Larne
Letterkenny
Derry
Antrim
Belfast
Bangor
Donegal
Downpatrick
Ballyshannon
Newry
Sligo
Dundalk
Belmullet
Ballina
Drogheda
Westport
Louisburgh
Dublin
Clifden
Galway
Wicklow
Ennistimon
Arklow
Kilkee
Limerick
Wexford
Tralee
Waterford
Dingle
Dungarvan
Killarney
Youghal
Kenmare
Cork
Kinsale
Bantry
Clonakilty

● Holiday beach
● Surfing beach
— County boundary

seas. The coastline is a major attraction for tourists as well as domestic holiday-makers. Just compare the location of holiday resorts with the distribution of sandy beaches. The coast is a significant resource for all kinds of water-based activities which, between them, contribute a large annual sum to the national income through tourism. This chapter reviews some of these activities and the places where they are enjoyed. For further details of particular regions, the reader is referred to local tourist offices.

Holiday Beaches

Mayo has by far the greatest length of soft coastline, with over 800 kilometres, followed by Cork, Kerry, Donegal and Wexford, each with a significant length of sandy beaches. There are many places in the west where you may be the only person on miles of coastline, even in mid-summer. The sandy beaches nearer the cities, and especially on the east coast, tend to be more crowded. European Blue Flags are awarded each year to those bathing beaches that meet a set of exacting criteria for good water quality, litter collection and other facilities.

Surfing

The west coast of Ireland is fast becoming a major destination for surfing, with Atlantic rollers to rival the best in Europe. Most of the information is transferred by word of mouth between the surfers but the latest news can be found on websites such as www.isasurf.ie and www.surfingireland.net or magazines such as *Fins* (see www.finsmag.com). For specialists involved in the new sport of kite-surfing check out www.kitesurfing.ie. Many of the best Irish surfing locations have only been discovered recently as surfers seek out more and more exciting breaks. Weather conditions are vital in this sport because the height and direction of the biggest waves depends on storms at sea. On the Atlantic coast, where the fetch (distance across open water) stretches to America, a distant storm may produce a big swell on the Irish coast for days afterwards. In the Irish Sea this is rare and only in south-easterly gales will the wave height rise sufficiently to produce a surfable break. East coast surf declines rapidly after a gale as there is a small fetch to the British coast. Some of the best locations are given overleaf.

Surfing on the west coast is among the best in Europe.

COUNTY	LOCATION	COMMENTS
Wicklow	Magharamore	Works well in a strong south-easterly but typically short-lived.
Waterford	Tramore	Beach break with surf shops and changing facilities. Best on a south-westerly.
Kerry	Ballinskelligs	Beach break which works on south to west swell.
	Rossbeigh	Beach break is open to the west.
	Castlegregory	Beach break open to the south west and west.
	Banna Strand	10 km of beach break
Clare	Spanish Point	Beach and reef break which requires respect in a big swell.
	Lahinch	One of the pioneer locations – surf shop.
	Fanore	Beach break – can be subject to strong long-shore rip.
Mayo	Carrownisky	Miles of beach break.
	Achill Island	Good beach break at Keel.
Sligo	Easky	Not for the beginner – a fabled reef break.
	Strandhill	Beach break on a north west – can be strong rips.
	Streedagh	Beach break with access to the south end only.
Donegal	Bundoran	The Point. Rates in the top ten European sites. Not for the beginner! Surf shop.
	Rossnowlagh	Mile of beach break in another 'where it all began' location.
	Dooey	Beach break.
	Falcarragh	Works in a north-westerly swell
Antrim	Portrush	Requires a north west to north-east swell.

Cruiser sailing at Wicklow Head, the starting point of the biannual Round-Ireland Yacht Race.

Sailing

Ireland offers unrivalled sailing from the sheltered inlets and estuaries of the east coast to the wild remote islands and bays of the west coast. The Irish Sailing Association is both the regulator and the representative body for the sports of sailing and boardsailing. See the ISA website www.sailing.ie for all the latest news and racing events calendar.

Long-distance cruising has been greatly enhanced by the development of marinas in many harbours and bays. One of the most popular areas for cruising is the coast of west Cork, which has many attractive harbours and islands. The Irish Cruising Club publishes *Sailing*

Directions for the East and North Coasts of Ireland and *Sailing Directions for the South and West Coasts of Ireland.* These indispensable handbooks should be on board all sailing cruisers as they provide up-to-date information on harbours, lights, anchorages, tides and general hazards.

Cruiser racing is almost exclusively a summer activity and takes place most weekends between May and October. The premier ocean race is the biannual *Round-Ireland Yacht Race* which starts in Wicklow and takes a clockwise course around the entire island.

Map showing the main coastal sailing clubs and marinas in Ireland.

Cork Week is the most popular regatta and is based at Crosshaven in Cork Harbour.

Dinghy sailing is usually confined to the more sheltered areas and is especially popular in Cork Harbour, west Cork, Dublin Bay, Strangford Lough and a number of smaller east coast harbours. Most dinghy sailing takes place between May and September but some hardy souls continue racing throughout the winter in the so-called 'frostbite series'.

Board sailing (or windsurfing) has become a very popular sport in recent years because it is exciting and relatively cheap and easy to undertake. Popular locations are Malahide Estuary, Dun Laoghaire Harbour and Lady's Island Lake, County Wexford. The world windsurfing championships have been held at Castlegregory, County Kerry. Many of the beach break sites listed under surfing offer great potential for short-board enthusiasts.

Sailing schools are well established in some areas. The largest is the Glenans sailing school, which has its headquarters in France but outposts at Baltimore, County Cork and Clew Bay, County Mayo. It offers tuition and sailing holidays in both dinghies and keelboats and through several languages. In Dun Laoghaire, County Dublin, the Irish National Sailing School runs continuous courses for both beginners and more advance sailors. There are also a number of outdoor pursuits centres, such as the Kilrush Creek Activity Centre, County Clare, or the Little Killary Adventure Centre, County Mayo, which offer sailing activities among their courses.

Scuba Diving

Ireland's coastline has some of the clearest waters in Europe. Combine this with the rich and fascinating underwater marine life and you have the essential ingredients of good sport diving conditions. For a detailed guide to Irish

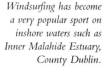

Windsurfing has become a very popular sport on inshore waters such as Inner Malahide Estuary, County Dublin.

dive sites see *Underwater Ireland* edited by John Hailes[1] or the website of the Irish Underwater Council www.scubaireland.com. This includes a section on Dive Centres and a detailed inventory of good diving locations. Also included in this guide are the locations of wrecks on the sea bed, which make interesting dives. The best dive sites are summarised below.

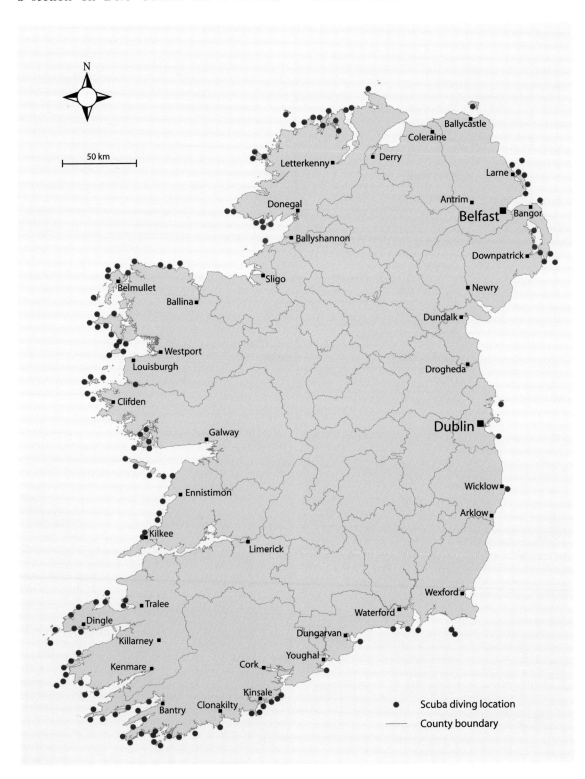

Map showing the best scuba diving locations in Ireland, including off-shore wreck sites, as listed in Underwater Ireland.

COUNTY	DIVE SITE	COUNTY	DIVE SITE
Dublin	Lambay Island	Galway	Aran Islands
	Dalkey Island and Muglins		South Connemara
Wicklow	Wicklow Head		North-west Connemara
Wexford	Hook Head		Killary Harbour
	Saltee Islands		Inishbofin
Waterford	Helvick Head	Mayo	Clare Island
Cork	Knockadoon, Ballycotton		Achill Island
	Kinsale, Galley Head		Belmullet
	Roaringwater Bay		North Mayo
	Mizen Head	Sligo	Mullaghmore
	Dunmanus Bay	Donegal	St Johns Point
	Bantry Bay		Malinbeg
Kerry	Derrynane		Aranmore
	Skelligs		Tory Island
	St Finan's Bay		Malin Head
	Valentia Island	Antrim	Rathlin Island
	Dingle and the Blaskets		Antrim's Wrecks
	The Magharees	Down	Strangford Lough
Clare	Kilkee		Annalong
	North Clare		

(left) Sea kayaks on the beach at Inishkea Islands, County Mayo (David Walsh)*; (right) kayak beneath the Cliffs of Moher, County Clare* (Sean Pierce).

Sea Kayaking

The sport of sea kayaking is relatively recent. The Irish Sea Kayaking Association is a voluntary group with the aim of developing and promoting the sport of sea kayaking in Irish waters, in harmony with the environment, the local people and landowners. The ISKA encourages the responsible enjoyment of our marine heritage and low-impact recreation. This includes sea paddling, exploration of and camping on deserted islands, education and safety. A strong emphasis is placed on training and education, in order that the sport can be enjoyed with minimal risk to the participants

Check out the association website www.irishseakayakingassociation.com and the top-quality photographs on the website www.oilean.org which have now been published in a book entitled *Oileain*.[2]

Sea and Shore Angling

Ireland is near the divide between cold northern waters and warmer waters from the North Atlantic Drift and as a result over 80 fish species may be caught around the Irish coast. Deepsea fishing is generally done from charter boats which are located in a number of traditional centres such as Westport, Fenit and Kinsale. These boats provide the opportunity to fish for blue shark off the south and west coast and for conger eel, ling, pollack, coalfish and cod from sunken wrecks or tope and flatfish over sandy ground. Fishing tackle can usually be hired in the main angling centres and the boat skippers provide most other requirements.

The Central Fisheries Board website www.cfb.ie has much useful information. A detailed guide is given in the book *Sea Angling*.[3]

Inshore fishing from small boats, especially in the months of May to September, provides an ideal way of exploiting the places which are inaccessible to either the commercial fishing

boat or the shore angler. Light spinning tackle is used for mackerel or pollack. Bottom fishing for ray or tope is possible in places such as the Shannon Estuary, perhaps using a whole mackerel as bait.

Shore angling in Ireland is a special experience, especially on a west coast beach when a big surf is running. Ray, flounder and dogfish are plentiful on these shores while sea bass, once a common shore fish, are now in recovery. The shingle beaches of Wicklow and Cork produce codling in winter while the beaches of north Wexford offer smoothound and ray fishing in spring. Tope may be caught on west coast beaches of Clare, Galway and Mayo, providing vigorous sport. By contrast, mullet are delicate fish which inhabit sheltered estuaries and harbours where they can be caught with a light freshwater rod and float tackle. Rocky shore fishing offers pollack and wrasse and plenty of seaweed on the hooks. There is good rocky shore angling all around the coast but especially in Kerry, Clare, Galway and Donegal.

Sea angling on a fresh winters day at Wicklow Harbour on the east coast.

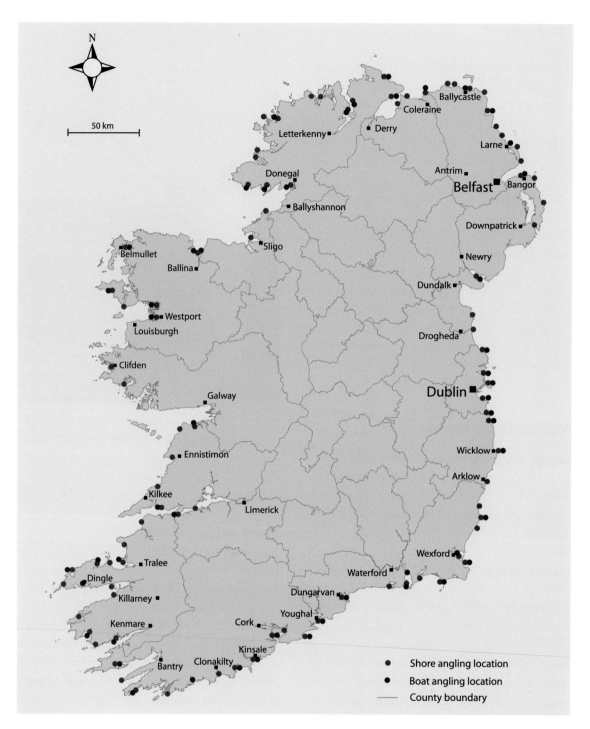

Map showing best shore angling marks and boat angling centres in Ireland.

●	Shore angling location
●	Boat angling location
—	County boundary

Birdwatching

A high proportion of the best birdwatching places in Ireland are along the coast. This includes the seabird colonies at their best in summer, coastal lakes and estuaries filled with wintering wildfowl and waders, and good sea-watching locations and migration staging points like Cape Clear Island. For detailed accounts of birdwatching locations see *Where to Watch Birds in Ireland* by Clive Hutchinson.[4] A good general account of *Birdwatching on Estuaries, Coast and Sea* is given by Lloyd.[5] For more up to date information see the website of BirdWatch

Sea-watching on Cape Clear Island, County Cork.

Ireland www.birdwatchireland.ie. For all the latest news of rare birds in Ireland see www.birdsireland.com and www.irishbirding.com.

Seabirds: The best time to visit a seabird colony is in early summer (May-June) when the birds are clamouring for nesting space and the first of the chicks have hatched. Many colonies are in quite remote locations, especially off-shore islands where they are largely free of ground predators. However, some mainland colonies are more accessible. They include Horn Head, County Donegal; Cliffs of Moher, County Clare; Old Head of Kinsale, County Cork; Dunmore East, County Waterford, Wicklow Head, County Wicklow; Howth Head, County Dublin. The typical cliff-breeding species are fulmar, shag, guillemot, razorbill, kittiwake and the larger gulls. In a few locations, you may see gannet, cormorant, puffin and black guillemot.

Less likely to be seen are the nocturnal seabirds such as Manx shearwater and storm petrel, which prefer remote islands, such as the Blaskets and the Skelligs in County Kerry.

Terns: The terns have quite different tastes in nesting habitat. They prefer low islands, either offshore or in sheltered inlets and coastal lakes. Typical nesting colonies of the Sandwich, common and arctic tern can be seen on islands in Strangford Lough, County Down; Lady's Island Lake, County Wexford; Magharee Islands, County Kerry; Dungloe Bay, County Donegal. The rare roseate tern is confined to a few key locations, notably, Rockabill Island, County Dublin. The little tern, in contrast, nests on mainland or island beaches, which provide the right combination of shallow water and nesting shingle. Typical examples include Kilcoole, County Wicklow;

Seabirds like razorbills are easily seen on many coastal headlands in summer.

Raven Point, County Wexford; Aran Islands, County Galway.

Seawatching: Seawatching for migrating seabirds is most rewarding from late August to mid-October. On some coasts, heavy passage can also be observed in spring from March to early May. During mid-summer, most movements are local feeding trips to and from the colonies. Identification of birds at sea is difficult, especially in stormy conditions, and requires a telescope or powerful binoculars. The best conditions for watching from land are usually during onshore winds when birds are driven closer to the coast than normal. The most rewarding locations are the headlands and islands which reach out into the ocean and around which the seabirds need to pass. These include Cape Clear Island, County Cork; Carnsore Point, County Wexford; Loop Head, County Clare; The Mullet, County Mayo; Malin Head, County Donegal.

Bird observatories: Some headlands and islands are well known for the passage of migrant

songbirds and these have become known as bird observatories. The best locations are usually on long promontories or islands, stretching out into the sea. Best months are usually September or October, when falls of hundreds of migrants may occur in specific places. The birds, moving south in autumn, are funnelled down the coast and often rest in groups of trees and shrubs, awaiting the right wind and weather conditions to make the long sea crossing to the European continent. Bird observatories are often key places for bird ringing and the study of bird migration. The most consistently used locations in Ireland are Cape Clear Bird Observatory, County Cork, Great Saltee, County Wexford and Copeland Bird Observatory, County Down. Several other locations have been carefully watched in recent years. These include Loop Head, County Clare; Old Head of Kinsale, County Cork, Hook Head, County Wexford and Clogher Head, County Louth.

Winter waterbirds: From September to March, Irish coasts hold huge numbers of waders and wildfowl, which move south from their arctic nesting grounds to overwinter here. The typical estuarine species include brent goose, shelduck, wigeon, oystercatcher, ringed plover, godwits, curlew, redshank and dunlin. Coastal grassland, especially flooded areas will typically attract flocks of oystercatcher, curlew, redshank, lapwing and golden plover. More open beaches along the Atlantic hold flocks of sanderling while rocky shores are used by purple sandpiper, turnstone, oystercatcher and curlew. Offshore flocks of seaduck such as common scoter and individual great northern diver are relatively common. Western islands and headlands are good places to look for barnacle goose flocks. Some coastal farmland, such as the Wexford Slobs, holds large flocks of Greenland white-fronted goose, whooper swan and a wide range of ducks and waders. Grey heron and little egret are widespread on all types of coastal habitat. Among the best coastal wet-lands for viewing winter birds are Rogerstown and Malahide Estuaries, County Dublin; the North Bull Island, Dublin city; Wexford Wildfowl Reserve and Tacumshin Lake, County Wexford; Tramore Back Strand, County Waterford; Cork Harbour, County Cork; Castlemaine Harbour and Tralee Bay, County Kerry, Shannon/Fergus Estuary, County Limerick/Clare; Inner Galway Bay, County

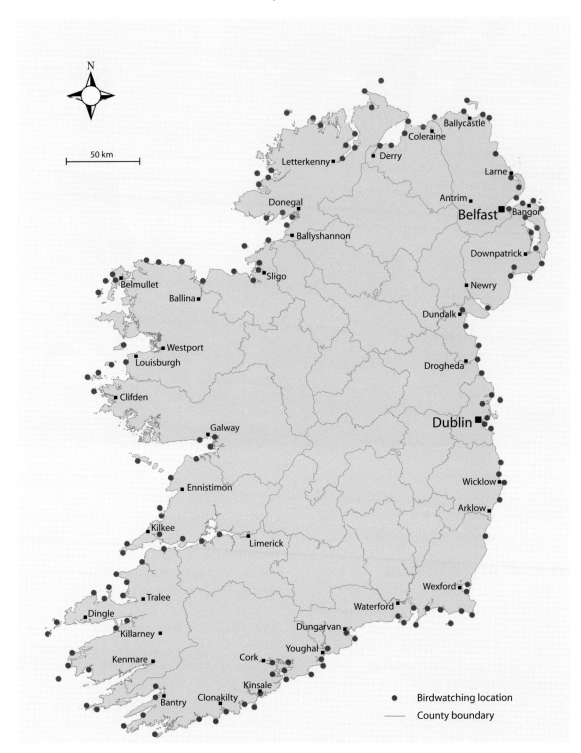

Map showing best birdwatching locations on the coast of Ireland.

(left) View of 'Fungi' the bottlenose dolphin from a cave near Dingle, County Kerry (Nigel Motyer); *dolphin watching in the Shannon Estuary* (Eddie Dunne).

Galway; The Mullet, County Mayo; Sligo Bay, County Sligo; Lough Swilly, County Donegal; Lough Foyle, County Derry; Strangford Lough and Carlingford Lough, County Down.

Whale and Dolphin Watching

Watching cetaceans (whales, dolphins and porpoises) in Irish waters is a relatively new activity, which parallels the international interest in these species. It requires patience, preparation and knowledge of what to look for. Good binoculars or a telescope are usually essential for land-based watching. Often, the only thing visible may be a small dorsal fin among distant waves. Watching cetaceans is best done from a boat but may also be rewarding from certain land viewpoints. The website of the Irish Whale and Dolphin Group www.iwdg.ie includes an on-line reporting scheme which allows the reader to check the latest sightings in any part of the coast.

Boat based whale-watching: The best-known cetacean in Ireland is the bottlenose dolphin, known as Fungi, which hangs around Dingle, County Kerry. Boat trips lasting one to two hours from Dingle Harbour are fairly certain to locate this friendly animal around the harbour mouth. Another solitary bottlenose dolphin has been present at Fanore, County Clare in recent years. The largest resident population of bottlenose dolphins in Ireland is found in the mouth of the Shannon Estuary. They can often be seen from the car ferry which crosses from Tarbert, County Kerry to Killimer, County Clare. Special dolphin-watching boat trips are available from Kilrush and Carrigaholt, County Clare, during the summer months.

Land-based whale watching: There are many good vantage points to watch the sea for passing cetaceans. These are mostly headlands or islands which jut out into the ocean and around which

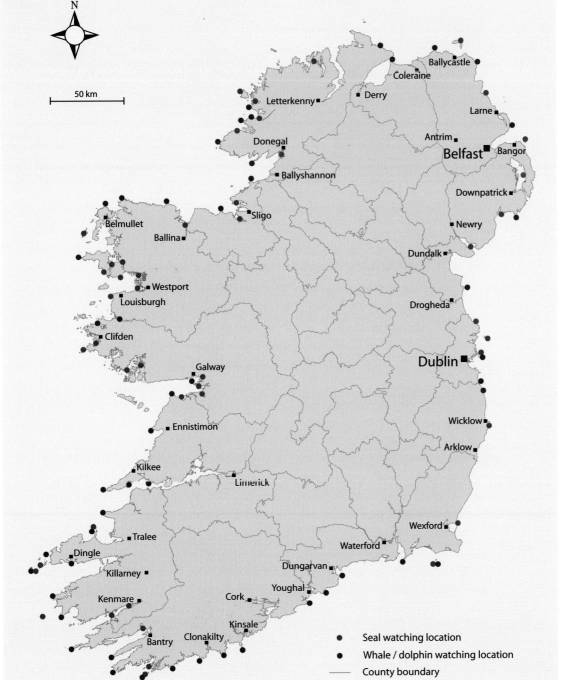

Map showing the best locations in Ireland to watch seals, whales and dolphins.

195

Seal watching from a tourist boat at Glengarriff, County Cork.

the animals are likely to swim. Whether or not they are seen from the land depends very much on sea conditions (best to watch when sea state is 3 or less and wind is under force 4) and light (best when the sun is behind the viewer).

Seal Watching

Watching seals in the wild is an interesting way to get to know these intelligent animals, as most other large mammals in Ireland are nocturnal. The main haul-out sites are fairly well known and their use by the two resident species, grey and common (harbour) seals, is predictable. However, individual seals may turn up on any part of the coast, or in harbours, especially if there is a source of food such as discards from fishing boats. Breeding (or pupping) sites are quite vulnerable to disturbance, and should not be approached during the pupping season (June-July for common seals and September-October for grey seals).

Often, the only visible part of the seal may be its head. The profile is quite distinctive for each species with common seals having a short, dog-like snout, and grey seals showing a longer horse-like profile. Closer encounters may allow a comparison of the nostrils, which are close together in the common seal but widely separated in the grey seal. The pelage (or fur coat) of the species is also quite distinctive as the common seal is covered with small spots and the grey seal with larger blotches (best seen on the underside).

Boat-based seal watching: Several places around the coast have common seal herds which are quite accustomed to close approaches by boats. These include Glengarriff, County Cork, Lissadel, County Sligo and Donegal Bay, County Donegal. At each location, there are dedicated boat trips 'to see the seals'. Most grey seal haul- outs are much more remote but there is a good chance of seeing some of these large animals on boat trips to the Great Blasket Island or Skellig Michael, County Kerry, Saltee Islands, County Wexford, Rathlin Island, County Antrim or the Inishkea Islands, County Mayo.

COMMON SEALS		GREY SEALS	
COUNTY	**SEAL HAUL-OUT**	**COUNTY**	**SEAL HAUL-OUT**
Cork	Glengarriff	Wexford	Raven Point/Wexford hbr
	Kenmare River		Saltee Islands
Clare	Ballyvaghan Bay	Cork	Cape Clear Island
Galway	Kinvara Bay	Kerry	Skellig Islands
	Oranmore Bay		Blasket Islands
	Kilkieran Bay		Magharee Islands
Mayo	Clew Bay	Galway	Slyne Head
	Achill Sound	Mayo	Inishkea Islands
Sligo	Ballasodare Bay		Achill Island
	Drumcliff Bay	Donegal	Slieve Toohy
Donegal	Inner Donegal Bay		Arranmore
	Gweebarra Estuary		Tory Island
	Dungloe Bay	Antrim	Rathlin Island
	Mulroy Bay	Down	Copeland Islands
Down	Strangford Lough	Dublin	Skerries Harbour
	Dundrum Bay		Lambay Island
	Carlingford Lough		Howth Harbour

Land-based seal watching: The best locations are listed in *Exploring Irish Mammals* by Tom Hayden and Rory Harrington.[6] Some good places to look for seals are given in the table below.

Coastal pathway in County Donegal.

Coastal Walks

There are numerous coastal locations where you can take an informal stroll or a longer, more challenging walk. A detailed guide is given in *Irish Coastal Walks* by Paddy Dillon.[7] The website www.irishsportscouncil.ie gives information on way-marked walks in Ireland. The Failte Ireland website www.walking.ireland.ie is helpful for those planning a walking holiday in Ireland. Some of the best coastal walks are listed overleaf.

Map showing best coastal walks and rock climbs in Ireland (Note: this does not imply right of access to private land).

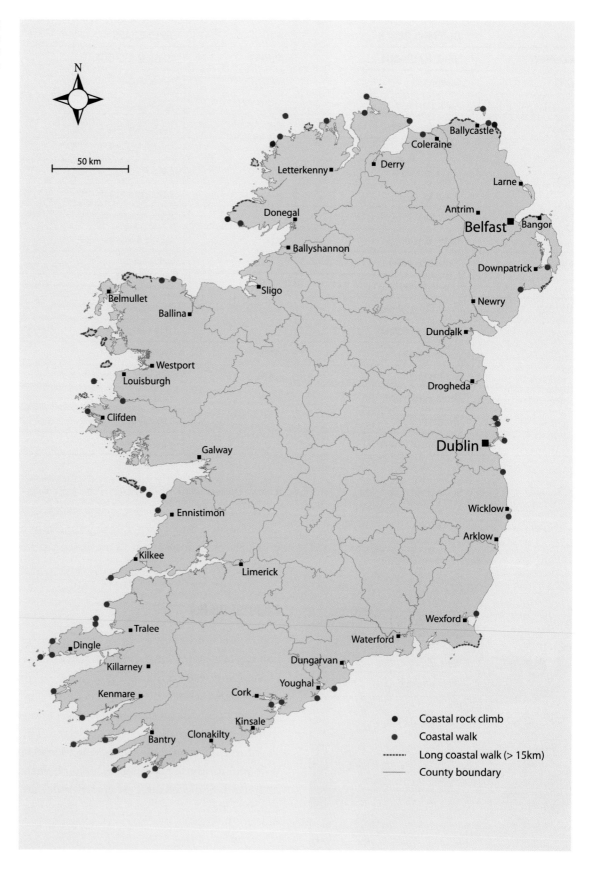

N

50 km

Ballycastle
Coleraine
Letterkenny
Derry
Larne
Donegal
Antrim
Belfast
Bangor
Ballyshannon
Downpatrick
Newry
Sligo
Dundalk
Belmullet
Ballina
Westport
Louisburgh
Drogheda
Clifden
Dublin
Galway
Wicklow
Ennistimon
Arklow
Kilkee
Limerick
Wexford
Tralee
Waterford
Dingle
Dungarvan
Killarney
Youghal
Kenmare
Cork
Kinsale
Bantry
Clonakilty

● Coastal rock climb
● Coastal walk
------ Long coastal walk (> 15km)
—— County boundary

COUNTY	WALK LOCATION	COUNTY	WALK LOCATION
Dublin	Donabate and Portrane	Galway	Inishbofin
	Howth Head	Mayo	Inishturk
Wicklow	Bray Head		Clare Island
Wexford	Raven Point		Minaun Cliffs
	Carnsore Point		Croaghaun and Achill Head
Waterford	Ardmore Head		Benwee Head
Cork	Great Island		Belderrig to Portacloy
	Sherkin Island		Downpatrick Head
	Cape Clear Island	Donegal	Slieve League
	Mizen Head		Glencolumkille
	Sheep's Head		Arronmore Island
	Bere Island		Bloody Foreland
	Dursey Island		Tory Island
Kerry	Derrynane Bay		Horn Head
	Valentia Island		Melmore Head
	Slea Head		Clonmany and Binnion
	Great Blasket Island		Malin Head
	The Three Sisters		Inishowen head
	The Magharees	Derry	Castlerock and Downhill
Clare	Kerry Head	Antrim	Causeway Coast Path
	Loop Head		Rathlin Island
	Cliffs of Moher		Fair Head
Galway	Inis Oirr		White Head and Black Head
	Inis Meáin	Down	North Down Coastal Path
	Inis Mór		Strangford Lough
	Omey Island		Killough and Ballyhornan
	Killary Harbour		Dundrum and Murlough

Rock Climbing on the Coast

Rock climbing is not for the faint-hearted but, for experienced climbers, some of Ireland's coastal cliffs provide spectacular locations to practice their sport. Popular locations include Fair Head, County Antrim; Gola Island and Malinbeg, County Donegal and the Burren Coast in County Clare. The website of the Mountaineering Council of Ireland (MCI) www.mountaineering.ie has some useful information including a list of climbing guidebooks. Some of these are available to download on-line at www.climbing.ie.

COUNTY	PORT	DESTINATION
Wexford	Kilmore Quay	Great Saltee
Cork	Baltimore	Sherkin and Cape Clear Islands
	Glengarriff	Garinish and seal watching
	Castletownbere	Bere Island
Kerry	Valentia	The Skelligs
	Dingle	Dolphin watching in Dingle Harbour
	Dunquin	Great Blasket Island
Clare	Kilrush, Carrigaholt	Dolphin watching in Shannon Estuary
	Doolin	Inisheer
Galway	Galway	Aran Islands
	Rossaveel	Inishmore
	Cleggan	Inishbofin
Mayo	Roonagh Quay	Clare Island
Sligo	Mullaghmore	Inishmurray
Donegal	Donegal town	Seal watching in Donegal Bay
	Burtonport	Arranmore Island
	Bunbeg, Magheroarty	Tory Island
Antrim	Ballycastle	Rathlin Island
Down	Donaghadee	Copeland Islands
Dublin	Skerries	St Patrick's Island
	Howth	Ireland's Eye
	Dun Laoghaire	Dublin Bay
	Dalkey	Dalkey island

The north harbour on Cape Clear Island, County Cork, which can be reached by daily ferry boat. The white house in the centre of the picture is the home of the Cape Clear Bird Observatory.

Boat Trips

There are many harbours and piers where boat trips can be taken to islands and other coastal destinations. Care should be taken before leaving to check that boat operators are licenced and carry the statutory safety equipment, including life jackets for all passengers. Especially popular locations are given in the table above.

Marine Biology and Aquaria

Among the best-studied areas for marine biology are Dublin Bay and Dalkey Sound, County Dublin; Cork Harbour, Kinsale Harbour and Lough Hyne, County Cork; Inner Galway Bay and Kilkieran Bay, County Galway; Clare Island, County Mayo; and Strangford Lough, County Down. There are several useful guides to seashore life and inshore marine life.[8,9]

Marine aquaria, which display a selection of native fish and other marine creatures, can be visited at Portaferry, County Down; Bray, County Wicklow; Dingle, County Kerry; Lahinch, County Clare; and Salthill, County Galway.

Rock pool-ing on the coast of County Donegal.

References

Introduction

1.   Carson, R. (1955) *The Edge of the Sea*. Houghton Mifflin Company. Boston.
2.   Mac an Iomaire, S. (2000) *The Shores of Connemara*. (translated from Irish by Padraic de Bhaldraithe) Tir Eolas. Galway.

Chapter 1 – Shape of the Shore

1.   Neilson, B and Costello, M.J. (1999) 'The relative lengths of intertidal substrata around the coastline of Ireland as determined by digital methods in a Geographical Information System'. *Estuarine and Coastal Shelf Sciences* 49, 501-508.
2.   Robinson, T. (1996) *Setting foot on the Shores of Connemara and other writings*. The Lilliput Press. Dublin.
3.   Kinahan, G.H. and McHenry, A. (1882) *A Handybook on the Reclamation of Waste Lands, Ireland*. Hodges Figgis. Dublin.
4.   Howe, M. (2003) 'Coastal soft cliffs and their importance for invertebrates'. *British Wildlife* 14: 323-331.
5.   Dorian, H. (2000) *The Outer Edge of Ulster: A memoir of social life in nineteenth-century Donegal*. Lilliput Press, Dublin.
6.   Mac an Iomaire, S. (2000) *The Shores of Connemara*. (translated from Irish by Padraic de Bhaldraithe) Tir Eolas. Galway.
7.   Fossitt, J.A. (2000) *A Guide to Habitats in Ireland*. The Heritage Council. Kilkenny.
8.   Connor, D.W., Brazier, D.P., Hill, T.O. and Northen, K.O. (1997) Marine Nature Conservation Review: marine biotope classification for Britain and Ireland. Vol. 1. Littoral biotopes. Vol 2. Sublittoral biotopes. Joint Nature Conservation Committee Report no. 230.
9.   Wilson, J.G. and Lawler, I. (1996) Irish marine habitats. In: *The Conservation of Aquatic Systems*. Ed. J.D. Reynolds. Royal Irish Academy. Dublin.
10. Fossitt, op. cit.
11. Erwin, D.G., Picton, B.E., Conor, D.W., Howson, C.M., Gilleece, P. and Bogues, M.J. (1990) Inshore marine life of Northern Ireland. Survey report to Conservation Branch DoE (NI). Belfast. HMSO.
12. Picton, B.E. and Costello, M.J. (eds.) (1997) BIOMAR biotope viewer: a guide to marine habitats, fauna and flora of Britain and Ireland. Environmental Sciences Unit. Trinity College, Dublin [Compact disc].
13. Wilson, op. cit.

Chapter 2 – Rocky Shores and Islands

1.   Howe, M. (2003) 'Coastal soft cliffs and their importance for invertebrates'. *British Wildlife* 14: 323-331.
2.   Brown, R. (1990) *Strangford Lough: The Wildlife of an Irish Sea Lough*. Institute of Irish Studies, Queens University. Belfast.
3.   Myers, A.A., Little, C., Costello, M.J. and Partridge, J.C. (1991) *The Ecology of Lough Hyne*. Royal Irish Academy. Dublin.

4. Bell, J.J. and Shaw, C. (2002) 'Lough Hyne: a marine biodiversity hotspot?' In: *Marine biodiversity in Ireland and adjacent waters* pp. 35-44. (ed. J.D. Nunn) Ulster Museum, Belfast.

5. Norton, T. (2002) 'And in the beginning … The pioneering ecological work at Lough Hyne'. In: *Marine biodiversity in Ireland and adjacent waters* pp. 1-4. (ed. J.D. Nunn) Ulster Museum, Belfast.

6. Kitching, J.A., Sloane, J.F. and Ebling, F.J. (1959) The ecology of Lough Ine VII. Mussels and their predators. *Journal of Animal Ecology* 28: 331-341.

7. Norton, T. (2001) *Reflections on a Summer Sea.* Century Books. London.

8. Keegan, B.F. and King, P. (1996) 'The fauna of Kinsale Harbour and approaches, south coast of Ireland'. In: *The Conservation of Aquatic Systems.* Ed. J.D. Reynolds. Royal Irish Academy. Dublin.

9. Myers, A. (2002) *New Survey of Clare Island. Volume 3: Marine Intertidal Ecology.* Royal Irish Academy, Dublin.

10. Green, M., Knight, A., Cartmel, S. and Thomas, D. (1988) 'The status of wintering waders on non-estuarine west coast of Ireland'. *Irish Birds* 3, 569-574.

11. Colhoun, K. and Newton, S.F. (2000) 'Winter waterbird populations on non-estuarine coasts on the Republic of Ireland: results of the 1997-98 Non-Estuarine Coastal Waterfowl Survey (NEWS)'. *Irish Birds* 6, 527-542.

12. Cabot, D. and West, B. (1973) 'Population dynamics of Barnacle geese in Ireland'. *Proceedings of the Royal Irish Academy* 73B, 176-188.

13. Cabot, D. and West, B. (1983) 'Studies on the population of Barnacle geese wintering on the Inishkea Islands, County Mayo'. I. Population dynamics 1961-1983. *Irish Birds* 2, 318-336.

14. Dornan, B. (2000) *Mayo's Lost Islands: The Inishkeas.* Four Courts Press. Dublin.

15. Merne, O.J. and Walsh, A (1994) 'Barnacle Geese in Ireland, spring 1993 and 1994'. *Irish Birds* 5, 151-156.

16. Cabot, D., Nairn, R., Newton, S. and Viney, M. (1984) *Irish Expedition to Jameson Land, North-East Greenland.* Barnacle Books. Dublin.

17. Berrow, S.D., Mackie, K.L., O'Sullivan, O., Sheppard, K.B., Mellon, C. and Coveney, J.A. (1993) 'The second international chough survey in Ireland', 1992. *Irish Birds* 5, 1-10.

18. Thompson, W. (1850) *The Natural History of Ireland.* Reeve. London.

19. Ussher, R.J. and Warren, R. (1900) *The Birds of Ireland.* Gurney and Jackson. London.

20. Merne, O.J. (1980) 'Irish seabird islands'. *British Birds* 73, 80-85

21. Cramp, S., Bourne, W.R.P. and Saunders, D (1974) *The Seabirds of Britain and Ireland.* Collins. London.

22. Lloyd, C., Tasker, M.L. and Partridge, K. (1991) *The Status of Seabirds in Britain and Ireland.* T. and A.D. Poyser. London.

23. Mitchell, P.I., Newton, S.F., Ratcliffe, N. and Dunn, T.E. (2004) *Seabird Populations of Britain and Ireland.* T. and A.D. Poyser, London.

24. Ussher, op. cit.

25. Praeger, R.L. ed. (1907) 'Contributions to the Natural History of Lambay, County Dublin' . *Irish Naturalist*, 26, 1-112.

26. Merne, O.J. and Madden, B. (1999) 'Breeding seabirds of Lambay, County Dublin'. *Irish Birds* 6, 345-359.

27. Brazier, H. and Merne, O.J. (1989) 'Breeding seabirds on the Blasket Islands, County Kerry'. *Irish Birds* 4, 43-64.

28. Mitchell, op. cit.

29. Newton, S.F. and Crowe, O. (2000) *Roseate Terns – The Natural Connection.* Maritime Ireland/Wales INTERREG Report No. 2. Marine Institute. Dublin.

30. Wernham, C.V., Toms, M.P., Marchant, J.H., Clark, J.A., Siriwardena, G.M. and Baillie, S.R. (eds.) (2002) *The Migration Atlas: movements of the birds of Britain and Ireland.* T. and A.D. Poyser, London.

31. Whilde, A. (1979) Auks trapped in salmon drift nets. *Irish Birds* 1, 370-376.

32. Merne, O.J. and Furphy, J. S. (1970) 'Irish sea seabird wreck'. *Irish Naturalists' Journal.*

33. Holdgate, M. (1971) 'The Seabird Wreck in the Irish Sea, Autumn 1969'. *The Natural Environment Research Council Publication Series C,* No. 4, 117.

34. Kiely, O. and Myers, A.A. (1998) 'Grey seal *(Halichoerus grypus)* pup production at the Inishkea Island Group, County Mayo, and Blasket Islands, Co. Kerry. *Biology and Environment* 98B, 113-122.

35. Kiely, O., Ligard, D., McKibben, M., Connolly, N and Baines, M. (2000) *Grey Seals: Status and Monitoring in the Irish and Celtic Seas.* Maritime Interreg Series no. 3. Marine Institute. Dublin.

36. Thomson, D. (1954) *The People of the Sea: A journey in search of the seal legend.* Turnstile Press.

37. Kingston, S., O'Connell, M. and Fairley, J.S. (1999) 'Diet of otters *Lutra lutra* on Inishmore, Aran Islands, west coast of Ireland'. *Biology and Environment'* 99B, 173-182.

38.   Murphy, K.P. and Fairley, J.S. (1985) 'Food and sprainting places of otters on the west coast of Ireland'. *Irish Naturalists' Journal* 21, 477-479.

39.   Kelly, P.A., Mahon, G.A.T. and Fairley, J.S. (1982) 'An analysis of morphological variation in the fieldmice *Apodemus sylvaticus* (L.) on some Irish islands'. *Proceedings of the Royal Irish Academy* 82B, 39-51.

40.   Fairley, J.S. (1984) *An Irish Beast Book: a natural history of Ireland's furred wildlife*. 2nd edition. Blackstaff Press. Belfast.

41.   Fairley, op. cit.

42.   Praeger, R.L. (1937) *The Way that I Went: An Irishman in Ireland*. Hodges Figgis. Dublin.

43.   Collins, T. (1985) *Floreat Hibernia: a bio-bibliography of Robert Lloyd Praeger 1865-1953*. Royal Dublin Society. Dublin.

Chapter 3 – Sand and Shingle Shores

1.   Carson, R. (1955) *The Edge of the Sea*. Houghton Mifflin Company. Boston.

2.   White, J. (1981) 'Notes on Irish Vegetation: No. 1 The vegetation of shingle in County Louth'. *Bulletin of the Irish Biogeographical Society* No. 5, 1-4.

3.   Pilcher, J. and Hall, V. (2001) *Flora Hibernica: The Wild Flowers, Plants and Trees of Ireland*. The Collins Press. Cork.

4.   Moore, D.J., Wilson, F.R.G., and Curtis, T.G.F. (in press). 'The shingle beaches of Ireland: An inventory, their geographical variation and an assessment of their conservation significance'. *Biology and Environment*.

5.   Wilson, J.G. and Emblow, C. (2002) 'Biodiversity of macrofauna on sandy and muddy shores'. In: *Marine biodiversity in Ireland and adjacent waters* pp. 5-14. (ed. J.D. Nunn) Ulster Museum, Belfast.

6.   Wilson, J.G. (1982) 'The littoral fauna of Dublin Bay'. *Irish Fisheries Investigations Series B (marine)* No. 26, 1-19.

7.   Seed, R. and Lowry, B.J. (1973) 'The intertidal macrofauna of seven sandy beaches of County Down'. *Proceedings of the Royal Irish Academy* 73B, 217-231.

8.   Healy, B. and McGrath, D. (1998) 'Marine fauna of County Wexford, Ireland: the fauna of rocky shores and sandy beaches'. *Irish Fisheries Investigations New Series* 2, 1-71.

9.   Quigley, M.B. ed. (1991) *A Guide to the Sand Dunes of Ireland*. European Union for Dune Conservation and Coastal Management. Galway.

10.   Curtis, T.G.F. (1991) 'A site inventory of the sandy coasts of Ireland'. Pp. 6-17. In: Quigley, M.B. ed. *A Guide to the Sand Dunes of Ireland*. European Union for Dune Conservation and Coastal Management. Galway.

11.   Ni Lamhna, E. (1982) 'The vegetation of saltmarshes and sand-dunes at Malahide, County Dublin. Studies on Irish Vegetation'. *Journal of Life Sciences, Royal Dublin Society* 3, 111-129.

12.   Dorian, H. (2000) *The Outer Edge of Ulster: A memoir of social life in nineteenth-century Donegal*. Lilliput Press, Dublin.

13.   Moore, J.J. and O'Reilly, H. (1977) Saltmarsh: vegetation patterns and trends. In: D.W. Jeffrey (ed.) *North Bull Island Dublin Bay: A modern coastal natural history* pp. 83-87. Royal Dublin Society. Dublin.

14.   Cabot, D. (1999) *Ireland: A natural history*. Harper Collins. London.

15.   Bassett, J.A. and Curtis, T.G.F. (1985) 'The nature and occurrence of sand-dune machair in Ireland'. *Proceedings of the Royal Irish Academy* 85B, 1-20.

16.   Crawford, I, Bleasedale, A. and Conaghan, J. (1998) *BioMar survey of Irish machair sites, 1996. Irish Wildlife Manuals, No. 3*. Dúchas, The Heritage Service.

17.   O'Briain, M. and Farrelly, P. (1990) 'Breeding Biology of the Little Tern at Newcastle, County Wicklow and the impact of Conservation Action 1985 1990. *Irish Birds* 4, 149-168.

18.   Nairn, R.G.W. (1979) 'The status and conservation of the common seal *Phoca vitulina* (L.) in Northern Ireland'. *Irish Naturalists' Journal* 19, 360-363.

19.   Wilson, S.C. and Montgomery-Watson, J. (2002) 'Recent changes on the pattern of harbour seal pupping in County Down, north-east Ireland'. *Irish Naturalists' Journal* 27, 89-100.

20.   Summers, C.F., Warner, P.J., Nairn, R.G.W., Curry, M.G. and Flynn, J. (1980) 'An assessment of the status of the common seal *Phoca vitulina vitulina* in Ireland'. *Biological Conservation* 17, 115-123.

21.   Viney, M. (2001). 'Edge of the tide: a natural history of beachcombing'. *British Wildlife* 12: 6, 381-387.

22.   Minchin, D. (1996) 'Tar pellets and plastics as attachment surfaces for *Lepadid cirripedes* in the North Atlantic Ocean'. *Marine Pollution Bulletin* 32: 855-859.

23.   Viney, M. op. cit.

24.   Nelson, E.C. (2000) *Sea Beans and Nickar Nuts*. BSBI Handbook No. 10. London.

25.   Minchin, D. and Minchen, C. (1996) 'The sea pea *Lathyrus japonicus* Willd. in Ireland, and an addition to the

flora of West Cork (H3) and Wexford (H12)'. *Irish Naturalists' Journal* 25: 165-169.

26. McGrath, D., Minchin, D. and Cotton, D. (1994) 'Extraordinary occurrences of the by-the-wind sailor *Valella velella* (L.) (Cnidaria) in Irish waters'. *Irish Naturalists' Journal* 24: 383-388.

Chapter 4 – Muddy Shores

1. O'Briain, M. and Healy, B. (1991) 'Winter distribution of light-bellied brent geese *Branta bernicla hrota* in Ireland'. *Ardea* 79, 371-326.

2. Curtis, T.G.F. and Sheehy Skeffington, M.J. (1998) 'The salt marshes of Ireland: an inventory and account of their geographical variation'. *Biology and Environment*. 98B, 87-104.

3. Sheehy Skeffington, M.J. and Wymer, E.D. (1991) 'Irish Salt Marshes – An Outline review'. Pp. 77-91. In: Quigley, M.B. ed. *A Guide to the Sand Dunes of Ireland*. European Union for Dune Conservation and Coastal Management. Galway.

4. O'Reilly, H. and Pantin, G. (1957) 'Some observations on the saltmarsh formation in County Dublin'. *Proceedings of the Royal Irish Academy* 58B, 89-126.

5. Nairn, R.G.W. (1986) '*Spartina anglica* in Ireland and its potential impact on wildfowl and waders: a review'. *Irish Birds* 3: 215-228.

6. McCorry, M. J., Curtis, T.G.F. and Otte, M.L. (2003) '*Spartina* in Ireland'. In *Wetlands of Ireland* (ed. M.L. Otte). University College Dublin Press.

7. Healy, B. (1973) 'Saltmarsh Fauna'. In: *North Bull Island Dublin Bay: A modern coastal natural history* (ed. D.W. Jeffrey). Royal Dublin Society. Dublin.

8. Healy, B. and Oliver, G.A. (1998) 'Irish coastal lagoons: summary of a survey'. *Bulletin of the Irish Biogeographical Society* 21, 116-150.

9. Deegan, B.M. and Harrington, T.J. (2004) 'The distribution and ecology of Schoenoplectus trigueter in the Shannon-Estuary'. Biology and Environment 104 B, 107-118.

10. Nairn, R.G.W., ten Cate, M.E. and N. Sharkey (2000) 'Long-term monitoring of wintering waterbirds in Inner Galway Bay', 1980/81 to 1999/2000. *Irish Birds* 6, 453-468.

11. Quinn, J.L. and Kirby, J.S. (1993) 'Oystercatchers feeding on grasslands and sandflats in Dublin Bay'. *Irish Birds* 5, 35-44.

12. Grant, J.D. (1982) A study of the winter feeding ecology of common wading birds of the North Bull Island, Dublin Bay. BSc Thesis, University College, Dublin.

13. Hutchinson, C.D. and O'Halloran, J. (1994) 'The ecology of Black-tailed Godwits at an Irish south coast estuary'. *Irish Birds* 5, 165-172.

14. Merne, O.J. (1985) 'The infauna of the Shannon and Fergus estuarine mudflats as a food resource for shorebirds'. MSc thesis. Environmental Sciences Unit. Trinity College, Dublin.

15. O'Briain, op. cit.

16. O'Briain, op. cit.

17. Mathers, R.G. and Montgomery, W.I. (1997) 'Quality of food consumed by overwintering pale-bellied Brent geese *Branta bernicla hrota* and wigeon *Anas penelope*'. *Biology and Environment* 97B, 81-90.

18. Hutchinson, C. (1979) *Ireland's Wetlands and their Birds*. Irish Wildbird Conservancy. Dublin.

19. Sheppard, R. (1993) *Ireland's Wetland Wealth*. Irish Wildbird Conservancy. Dublin.

20. Prater, A.J. (1981) *Estuary Birds of Britain and Ireland*. T. and A.D. Poyser. Calton.

21. Crowe, O. (2005) *Ireland's Wetlands and their Water Birds*. BirdWatch Ireland, Newcastle.

22. Crowe, op. cit.

23. Merne, op. cit.

24. Hutchinson and O Halloran, op. cit.

25. Whilde, A. (1983) 'The winter bird population of Inner Galway Bay'. *Irish Birds* 2, 278-293.

26. Nairn, op. cit.

27. Fox, A.D., Bell, M.C., Brown, R.A., Mackie, P. and Madsen, J. (1994) 'An analysis of the abundanc and distribution of Brent Geese and Wigeon at Strangford Lough, 1965/6 – 1988/9'. *Irish Birds* 5, 139-150.

Chapter 5 – Open Sea

1.   Hardy, A. (1956) *The Open Sea. Part I: The World of Plankton.* Collins. London.

2.   Hession, C., Guiry, M.D., McGarvey, S. and Joyce, D. (1998) Mapping and assessment of the seaweed resources (*Ascophyllum nodosum, Laminaria* spp.) off the west coast of Ireland. *Marine Resource Series* No 5. Marine Institute. Dublin.

3.   Praeger, R.L. (1937) *The Way That I Went: An Irishman in Ireland.* Hodges Figgis, Dublin.

4.   De Grave, S., Fazakerley, H., Kelly, L., Guiry, M.D., Ryan, M. and Walshe, J. (2000) A study of selected maerl beds in Irish waters and their potential for sustainable extraction. *Marine Resource Series* No. 10. Marine Institute, Dublin.

5.   De Grave, op. cit.

6.   Linnane, A., Ball, B., Munday, B., Browne, R. and Mercer, J.P. (2003) 'Faunal description of an Irish cobble site using airlift suction sampling'. *Biology and Environment: Proceedings of the Royal Irish Academy* 103B: 41-48.

7.   Mackie, A., Rees, E.I.S. and Wilson, J. (2002) 'The South-West Irish Sea Survey (SWISS) of benthic biodiversity'. In: *Marine Biodiversity in Ireland and Adjacent Waters.* Ed. J. Nunn. Ulster Museum. Belfast.

8.   Vermeulen, N.J. (1997) Hydrography, surface geology and geomorphology of the deep water sedimentary basins to the west of Ireland. *Marine Resource Series No. 2.* Marine Institute. Dublin.

9.   Praeger, op.cit.

10.   Praeger, op. cit.

11.   O'Sullivan, G. (2002) 'Ireland's cold water coral reefs: new horizons in Irish marine science'. *Sherkin Comment* Issue 31, 8-9.

12.   Hardy, op cit.

13.   Hardy, op cit.

14.   Mac an Iomaire, S. (2000) *The Shores of Connemara.* (translated from Irish by Padraic de Bhaldraithe) Tir Eolas. Galway.

15.   Raine, R. McMahon, T. and Rodan, C. (1993) 'A review of the summer Phytoplankton distribution in Irish coastal waters: A biography related to physical oceanography'. In *Biography of Ireland: Past, Present and Future.* 99-111 (eds. M.J. Costello and K.S. Kelly. publication of the Irish Biogeographical Society. No. 2.

16.   Hardy, op cit.

17.   Quigley, D.T.G. (2000) 'Ireland's marine fish fauna – an assessment of biodiversity'. In: *Biodiversity: The Irish Dimension* (ed. B.S. Rushton) pp. 59-75. Royal Irish Academy. Dublin.

18.   Quigley, op. cit.

19.   Ellis, J.R., Armstrong, M.J., Rogers, S.I and Service, M. (2002) 'The distribution, structure and diversity of fish assemblages in the Irish Sea'. In: *Marine biodiversity in Ireland and adjacent waters* pp. 93-114. (ed. J.D. Nunn) Ulster Museum, Belfast.

20.   Henderson, A.C., Flannery, K. and Dunne, J. (2003) 'Biological observations on shark species taken in commercial fisheries to the west of Ireland'. *Biology and Environment: Proceedings of the Royal Irish Academy* 103B: 1-8.

21.   Berrow, S.D. and Heardman, C. (1994) 'The basking shark *Cetorhinus maximus* (Gunnerus) in Irish waters – patterns of distribution and abundance'. *Biology and Environment* 94B, 101-108.

22.   Berrow, op. cit.

23.   O'Riordan, C.E. (1972) 'Provisional list of Cetacea and turtles stranded or captured on the Irish coast'. *Proceedings of the Royal Irish Academy* 72B, 253-274.

24.   Wernham, C.V., Toms, M.P., Marchant, J.H., Clark, J.A., Siriwardena, G.M. and Baillie, S.R. (eds.) (2002) *The Migration Atlas: movements of the birds of Britain and Ireland.* T. and A.D. Poyser, London.

25.   Pollock, C.M., Reid, J.B., Webb, A. and Tasker, M.L. (1997) *The distribution of seabirds and cetaceans in the waters around Ireland.* JNCC Report No. 267. Joint Nature Conservation Committee. Peterborough.

26.   Mackey, M., Ó Cadhla, O., Kelly, T., Aguilar de Soto, N. and Connolly, N. (2004) *Cetaceans and Seabirds of Ireland's Atlantic Margin. Volume 1 – seabird distribution, density and abundance.* Report on research carried out under the Irish Infrastructure Programme (PIP). CMRC, University College Cork.

27.   Ó Cadhla, O., Mackey, M., Aguilar de Soto, N., Rogan, E. and Connolly, N., (2004) *Cetaceans and Seabirds of Ireland's Atlantic Margin. Volume II – cetacean distribution and abundance.* Report on research carried out under the Irish Infrastructure Programme (PIP). CMRC, University College Cork.

28. Sharrock, J.T.R. ed. (1973) *The Natural History of Cape Clear Island*. T. and A.D. Poyser. Berkhamstead.

29. Berrow, S.D., Whooley, P. and Ferris, S. (2002) *Irish Whale and Dolphin Group Cetacean Sighting Review (1991-2001)*. Irish Whale and Dolphin Group.

30. O'Riordan, op. cit.

31. Fairley, J. (1981) *Irish Whales and Whaling*. Blackstaff Press. Belfast.

32. Berrow, S.D. and Rogan, E. (1997) 'Review of cetaceans stranded on the Irish coast, 1901-95'. *Mammal Review* 27, 51-76.

33. Rogan, E. and Berrow, S.D. (1996) 'A review of harbour porpoises, *Phocoena phocoena*, in Irish waters'. *Report of the International Whaling Commission* 46, 595-605.

34. Fairley, op. cit.

35. Rogan, op. cit.

36. Fairley, op. cit.

Chapter 6 – Living on the Coast

1. Gibbons, M. and Gibbons, M. (2004) 'Dyeing in the Mesolithic'. *Archaeology Ireland* 17 (4): 28-31.

2. Caulfield, S. (1988) *Céide Fields and Belderrig Guide*. Morrigan Book Company.

3. Caulfield, op. cit.

4. Cooney, G. (2000) *Landscapes of Neolithic Ireland*. Routledge. London.

5. Cooney, op. cit.

6. O'Sullivan, M. and Downey, L. (2004) 'Coastal promontory forts'. *Archaeology Ireland* 18 (2): 18-20.

7. O'Sullivan, A. (2001) *Foragers, farmers and fishers in a coastal landscape: An intertidal archaeological survey of the Shannon Estuary*. Discovery Programme Monograph No. 5. Royal Irish Academy. Dublin.

8. O'Sullivan, op. cit.

9. McErlean, T., McConkey, R. and Forsythe, W. (2002) *Strangford Lough: An archaeological survey of the maritime cultural landscape*. Blackstaff Press/Environment and Heritage Service. Belfast.

10. McErlean, op. cit.

11. Bradley, J. (1995) 'Scandinavian rural settlement in Ireland'. *Archaeology Ireland* 9 (3), 10-12.

12. Gibbons, M. (2004) 'The Longphort phenomenon in early Christian and Viking Ireland'. *History Ireland* 12(3): 19-23.

13. O'Brien, E. (1995) 'A tale of two cemeteries'. *Archaeology Ireland* 9 (3), 13-15.

14. McGill, L. (1992) *In Conal's Footsteps*. Brandon Books. Dingle.

15. Mason, A. (1967) *The Islands of Ireland*. Mercier Press. Cork.

16. Somerville-Large, P. (2000) *Ireland's Islands: Landscape, Life and Legends*. Gill and Macmillan. Dublin.

17. Clark, W. and Harvey, R. (2003) *Donegal Islands*. Cottage Publications. Donaghadee.

18. Mitchell, F. (1989) *Man and Environment in Valentia Island*. Royal Irish Academy. Dublin.

19. Pochin Mould, D.D.C. (1978) *Valentia: Portrait of an Island*. Blackwater Press. Dublin.

20. MacConghail, M. (1987) *The Blaskets: a Kerry Island Library*. Country House. Dublin.

21. Praeger, R.L. (1937) *The Way that I Went: An Irishman in Ireland*. Hodges Figgis. Dublin.

22. MacConghail, op. cit.

23. Clark, op. cit.

24. Aalen, F.H.A. and Brody, H. (1969) *Gola Island: The Life and Last Days of an Island Community*. Mercier Press. Cork.

25. Aalen, op. cit.

26. Dornan, B. (2000) *Mayo's Lost Islands: The Inishkeas*. Four Courts Press. Dublin.

27. Heraughty, P. (1982) *Inishmurray: Ancient Monastic Island*. O'Brien Press. Dublin.

28. Perry, K.W. and Warburton, S.W. (1976) *The Birds and Flowers of the Saltee Islands*. Belfast.

29. Long, B. (1993) *Bright Light, White Water. The Story of Irish Lighthouses and their People*. New Island Books. Dublin.

30. Anon. (2003) *For the Safety of All: Images and inspections of Irish lighthouses*. National Library of Ireland. Dublin.

31. Long, op. cit.

32. McErlean, op. cit.

33. Evans, E.E. (1957) *Irish Folk Ways*. Routledge and Kegan Paul. London.

34. MacPhilib, S. (2002) 'Traditional Fishing boats of the River Boyne Estuary'. *Ulster Folklife* 48.

35. Mac Cullagh, R. (1992) *The Irish Currach Folk*. Wolfhound Press. Dublin.

36. Rowe, D. and Wilson, C.J. (1996) *High Skies – Low Lands: An anthology of Wexford Slobs and Harbour*. Duffry Press. Enniscorthy.

37. Scott, R. (2004) *The Galway Hooker*. (4th edition) A.K. Ilen Company, Limerick.

38. Rowe, op. cit.

39. MacPolin, D. (1999) *The Drontheim: Forgotten sailing boat of the North Irish Coast*. (privately published).

40. Nixon, W.M. (1979) *To Sail the Crested Sea*. Irish Cruising Club. Dublin.

41. Nixon, op. cit.

42. Delaney, A.F. (1987) *The Water Wags 1887-1987*. Privately published. Dublin.

Chapter 7 – Harvesting the Sea

1. Moriarty, C. (1997) 'Fish and fisheries'. In: *Nature in Ireland: A scientific and cultural history* (ed. J.W. Foster) pp. 283-298. Lilliput Press. Dublin.

2. Mitchell, F. and Ryan, M. (1997) *Reading the Irish Landscape*. Town House. Dublin.

3. O'Neill, T. (1987) *Merchants and Mariners in Medieval Ireland*. Irish Academic Press. Dublin.

4. Went, (1959) 'Sprat or white-fish weirs in Waterford Harbour'. *Journal of the Royal Society of Antiquaries of Ireland* 89, 91-93.

5. Mac an Iomaire, S. (2000) *The Shores of Connemara*. (translated from Irish by Padraic de Bhaldraithe) Tir Eolas. Galway.

6. Somerville-Large, P. (2000) *Ireland's Islands: Landscape, Life and Legends*. Gill and Macmillan. Dublin.

7. Murphy, R. (1974) *High Island*. Harper and Row. New York.

8. Aalen, F. and Brody, H. (1969) *Gola Island: The life and Last Days of an Island Community*. Mercier Press. Cork.

9. Dornan, B. (2000) *Mayo's Lost Islands: The Inishkeas*. Four Courts Press. Dublin.

10. Fairley, J. (1981) *Irish Whales and Whaling*. Blackstaff Press. Belfast.

11. Ó Crohán, T. (1934) *The Islandman*. Talbot Press. Dublin.

12. Ó Crohán, op. cit.

13. MacCártaigh, C. (2001) 'Shark Hunting in Ireland'. *Maritime Life and Traditions* No. 13, 2-15.

14. Ó Crohán, op. cit.

15. MacCártaigh, op. cit.

16. Tyers, P. (ed) (1998) *Blasket Memories: The Life of an Irish Island Community*. Mercier. Cork.

17. Ó Crohán, op. cit.

18. Lavelle, D. (1976) *Skellig: Island outpost of Europe*. O'Brien Press. Dublin.

19. Evans, E.E. (1957) *Irish Folk Ways*. Routledge and Kegan Paul. London.

20. Ó Crohán, op. cit.

21. Ó Crohán, T. (1986) *Island Cross-Talk*. Oxford University Press. Oxford.

22. Mac an Iomaire, op. cit.

23. Thomson, D. (1954) *The People of the Sea: A Journey in Search of the Seal Legend*. Turnstile Press.

24. Wilkins, N.P. (2004) *Alive Alive O: The Shellfish and Shellfisheries of Ireland*. Tir Eolas. Kinvara.

25. Cummins, V., Coughlan, S., McClean, O., Connolly, N., Mercer, J., and Burnell, G. (2002) 'A assessment of the potential for the sustainable development of the edible periwinkle, *Littorina littorea*, industry in Ireland. *Marine Resource Series* No. 22. Marine Institure, Dublin.

26. Browne, T.J. (1903) *Report on the Shellfish Layings on the Irish Coast as Respects their Liability to Sewage Contamination*. Local Government Board for Dublin.

27. West, A.B., Partridge, J.K. and Lovitt, A. (1979) 'The cockle *Cerastoderma edule* (L.) on the south bull, Dublin Bay: population parameters and fishery potential'. *Irish Fisheries Investigations Series B (marine)* No. 20, 1-18.

28. Wilkins, N.P. (2001) *Squires, Spalpeen and Spats: Oysters and Oystering in Galway Bay*. Privately published.

29. Wilkins, op. cit.

30. Wilkins, N.P. (1989) *Ponds, Passes and Parks: Aquaculture in Victorian Ireland*. Glendale. Dublin.

31. Evans, op. cit.

32. Synge, J.M. (1907) *The Aran Islands*. Oxford University Press.

33. Evans, op. cit.

34. Heraughty, P. (1982) *Inishmurray: Ancient Monastic Island*. O'Brien Press. Dublin.

35. Ó Crohán, op. cit.

36. Robinson, op. cit.

37.   Robinson, op. cit.

38.   Evans, op. cit.

39.   McErlean, T., McConkey, R. and Forsythe, W. (2002) *Strangford Lough: An Archaeological Survey of the Maritime Cultural Landscape.* Blackstaff Press/Environment and Heritage Service. Belfast.

Chapter 8 – Respecting the Coast

1.   Neff, J. (1998) *Irish Coastal Habitats: A study of impacts on designated conservation areas.* Heritage Council. Kilkenny.

2.   Crawford, I., Bleasedale, A. and Conaghan, J. (1998) 'BioMar survey of Irish machair sites, 1996'. *Irish Wildlife Manuals, No. 3.* Dúchas, The Heritage Service.

3.   Madden, B., Cooney, T., O'Donoghue, A., Norriss, D.W. and Merne, O.J. (1998) 'Breeding waders of machair systems in Ireland in 1996'. *Irish Birds 6:* 177-190.

4.   Dorian, H. (2000) *The Outer Edge of Ulster: A memoir of social life in nineteenth-century Donegal.* Lilliput Press, Dublin.

5.   Quinn, A.C.M. (1977) *Sand Dunes: Formation, Erosion and Management.* An Foras Forbartha. Dublin.

6.   Dorian, op. cit.

7.   Orford, J., Cooper, A. and Smith, B. (1997) 'LOICZ: the Human factor as an influence on the Irish Coast'. In: *Global Change and the Irish Environment* (ed. J. Sweeney) pp. 88-107. Royal Irish Academy. Dublin.

8.   Rowe, D. and Wilson, C.J. (1996) *High Skies – Low Lands: An anthology of Wexford Slobs and Harbour.* Duffry Press. Enniscorthy.

9.   Orford, op. cit.

10.   Anon. (1992) *Coastal Management: A case for action.* Eolas/County and City Managers Association. Dublin.

11.   Anon. (1973) *Brittas Bay: a Planning and Conservation Study.* An Foras Forbartha. Dublin.

12.   Pilcher, J. and Hall, V. (2001) *Flora Hibernica: The Wild Flowers, Plants and Trees of Ireland.* The Collins Press. Cork.

13.   Sweeney, J. (1997) 'Global warming scenarios and their implications for environmental management in Ireland'. In: *Global Change and the Irish Environment* (ed. J. Sweeney) pp. 155-170. Royal Irish Academy. Dublin.

14.   Carter, R.W.G. and Johnston, T.W. (1982) Ireland – the shrinking island? *Technology Ireland 14* (3) 22-28.

15.   Sweeney, op. cit.

16.   Carter, R.W.G. (1991) 'Sea Level Changes'. In: *Climate Change: Studies on the Implications for Ireland.* (Ed. B.E. McWilliams) pp 108-150. Department of the Environment. Stationery Office. Dublin.

17.   Wilson, J.G. (1993) 'Climate change and the future for the cockle *Cerastoderma edule* in Dublin Bay – an exercise prediction modelling'. In: *Biogeography of Ireland: past, present and future* (eds M.J. Costello and K.S. Kelly) *Occasional publications of Irish Biogeographical Society 2,* 141-149.

18.   O'Gallachoir, B.P., Holmes, B., Lewis, A.W. and Thomas, G.P. (1996) Ocean wave energy research in Ireland. In: *Irish Marine Science 1995* (eds. B.F. Keegan and R. O'Connor). Pp. 495-508. Galway University Press. Galway.

19.   Brady Shipman Martin (1997) *Coastal Zone Management: A Draft Policy for Ireland.* Government of Ireland.

Chapter 9 – Enjoying the Coast

1.   Hailes, J. ed. (1999) *Underwater Ireland: Guide to Irish dive sites.* 2nd edition. Irish Underwater Council. Dun Laoghaire.

2.   Walsh, D. (2004) *Oileáin: A Guide to the Irish Islands.* Pesda Press. Bangor. Wales.

3.   Dunlop, N. and Green, P. (1992) *Sea Angling.* Gill and Macmillan. Dublin.

4.   Hutchinson, C. (1994) *Where to Watch Birds in Ireland.* Gill and Macmillan. Dublin

5.   Lloyd, C. (1981) *Birdwatching on Estuaries, Coast and Sea.* Severn House. London.

6.   Hayden, T. and Harrington, R. (2000) *Exploring Irish Mammals.* Town House. Dublin.

7.   Dillon, P. (1999) *Irish Coastal Walks.* Cicerone Press. Milnthorpe, Cumbria.

8.   Erwin, D. and Picton, B. (1995) *Guide to Inshore Marine Life.* (2nd edn.) The Marine Conservation Society. Immel Publishing. London.

9.   Challinor, H., Murphy Wickens, S., Clark, J. and Murphy, A. (1999) *A Beginner's Guide to Ireland's Seashore.* Sherkin Island Marine Station.

Appendix

Scientific names of plants and animals mentioned in the text

PLANTS

Common Name	Scientific Name
alder	*Alnus glutinosa*
bee orchid	*Ophrys apifera*
bell heather	*Erica cinerea*
bird's foot trefoil	*Lotus corniculatus*
blackthorn	*Prunus spinosa*
bladder campion	*Silene vulgaris*
bladder wrack	*Fucus vesiculosus*
bracken	*Pteridium aquilinum*
bramble	*Rubus fruticosus*
brown ribweed	*Alaria esculenta*
(dabberlocks)	
burnet rose	*Rosa pimpinellifolia*
carragheen moss	*Chondrus crispus*
channel wrack	*Pelvetia canaliculata*
common butterwort	*Pinguicula vulgaris*
common reed	*Phragmites australis*
cord grass	*Spartina anglica*
cottonweed	*Otanthus maritimus*
creeping bent grass	*Agrostis stolonifera*
creeping willow	*Salix repens*
cuvie	*Laminaria hyperborea*
daisy	*Bellis perennis*
dog lichen	*Peltigera canina*
dulse	*Palmaria palmata*
eelgrasses	*Zostera species*
glasswort	*Salicornia europea*
gorse	*Ulex europaeus*
grass of parnassus	*Parnassia palustris*
hawthorn	*Craetagus monogyna*
horned poppy	*Glaucium flavum*
ivy	*Hedera helix*
knotted wrack	*Ascophyllum nodosum*
lady's bedstraw	*Galium verum*
ling	*Calluna vulgaris*
lyme grass	*Leymus arenarius*
marram grass	*Ammophila arenaria*
marsh helliborine	*Epipactis palustris*
marsh orchid	*Dactyloriza species*
maerl	*Lithophyllum, Lithothamnion, Phymatolithon and Mesophyllum species*
oarweed	*Laminaria digitata*
oyster-plant	*Mertensia maritima*
pyramidal orchid	*Anacamptis pyramidalis*
red fescue	*Festuca rubra*
red seaweed	*Audouinella floridula*
red seaweed	*Corallina officinalis*
ribwort plantain	*Plantago lanceolata*
saltmarsh grass	*Puccinellia maritima*
saltmarsh rush	*Juncus maritimus, Juncus gerardii*
saltwort	*Salsola kali*
sand couch	*Elymus juncea*
sand sedge	*Carex arenaria*
scentless mayweed	*Triplospermum inodoratum*
sea beet	*Beta maritima*
sea bindweed	*Calystegia soldanella*
sea buckthorn	*Hippophae rhamnoides*
sea campion	*Silene vulgaris maritima*
sea heart	*Entada gigas*
sea holly	*Eryngium maritimum*
sea-kale	*Crambe maritima*
sea lavender	*Limonium humile*
sea lettuce	*Ulva lactuca*
sea pea	*Lathyrus japonicus*
sea plantain	*Plantago maritima*
sea purslane	*Halimione portulacoides*
sea rocket	*Cakile maritima*
sea sandwort	*Honkenya peploides*

sea spurge	*Euphorbia paralias*
seaside pansy	*Viola tricolor*
serrated wrack	*Fucus serratus*
silverweed	*Potentilla anserine*
spiral wrack	*Fucus spiralis*
stonewort	*Chara species*
sugar kelp	*Laminaria saccharina*
tangleweed	*Laminaria digitata*
tassleweed	*Ruppia maritima*
thrift	*Armeria maritima*
triangular club-rush	*Schoenoplectus triqueter*
white clover	*Trifolium repens*
wild thyme	*Thymus praecox*
wintergreen	*Pyrola rotundifolia*

INVERTEBRATE ANIMALS

Common Name	Scientific Name
acorn barnacle	*Semibalanus balanoides*
amphipod	*Corophium volutator*
amphipod	*Gammarus duebeni*
Baltic tellin	*Macoma baltica*
beadlet anemone	*Actinia equina*
blue-rayed limpet,	*Helcion pellucidum*
breadcrumb sponge	*Halichondria panicea*
brittlestar	*Ophiuroidea*
brittlestar	*Amphiura*
burrowing anemone	*Cerianthus lloydi*
by-the-wind sailor	*Velella velella*
cockle	*Cerastoderma edule*
common starfish	*Asterias rubens*
crawfish	*Palinurus vulgaris*
cuttlefish	*Sepia officianalis*
dead man's fingers	*Alcyonium digitatum*
dog whelk	*Nucella lapillus*
Dublin Bay prawn	*Nephrops norvegicus*
edible periwinkle	*Littorina littorea*
edible sea urchin	*Echinus esculentus*
feather star	*Antedon bifida*
flat periwinkle	*Littorina littoralis*
goose barnacle	*Lepas anatifera*
goose barnacle	*Lepas fascicularis*
heart urchin	*Echinocardium cordatum*
hermit crab	*Paguridae*
honeycomb worm	*Sabellidae*
horse mussel	*Modiolus modiolus*
jewel anemone	*Corynactis viridis*
laver spire shell	*Hydrobia ulvae*
limpet	*Patella species*
lion's mane jellyfish	*Cyanea lamarckii*
lugworm	*Arenicola marina*
masked crab	*Corystes cassivelaunus*
moon jellyfish	*Aurelia aurita*
mussel	*Mytilus edulis*
paddle worms	*Phyllodocidae*
peppery furrow shell	*Scrobiculara plana*

plumose anemone	*Metridium senile*
porcelain crabs	*Pisidia* or *Porcellana* species
Portuguese man-o-war	*Physalia physalis*
purple sea urchin	*Paracentrotus lividus*
ragworm	*Nereis diversicolor*
razor shell	*Ensis ensis*
rough periwinkle	*Littorina saxatilis*
sandhopper	*Talitrus saltator*
snakelocks anemone	*Anemonia viridis*
squid	*Sagittatus sagittatus*
sea fan	*Eunicella verrucosa*
sea scorpion	*Cottidae*
soft coral	*Parerythropodium coralloides*
striped venus shell	*Venus striatula*
tellin	*Tellina tenuis*
thick-lipped dog whelk	*Hinea incrassate*
topshells	*Trochidae*
variegated scallop	*Chlamys varia*

FISH

Common Name	Scientific Name
American barrelfish	*Hyperoglyphe perciformis*
ballan wrasse	*Labrus berggyylta*
basking shark	*Cetorhinus maximus*
black scabbard fish	*Aphanopus carbo*
blackspot grenadier	*Caelorhinchus caelorhinchus*
blenny	*Chirolophis ascanii*
blue shark	*Prionace glauca*
boarfish	*Capros aper*
butterfish	*Pholis gunnellus*
coalfish	
cod	*Gadus morhua*
dab	*Limanda limanda*
lesser spotted dogfish	*Scyliorhinus canicula*
eel	*Anguilla anguilla*
goby	*Gobius spp.*
Greenland halibut	*Reinhardtius hippoglossoides*
grey mullet	*Chelon labrosus*
herring	*Clupea harengus*
jellycat	*Anarhichas denticulatus*
long-rough dab	*Hippoglossoides platessoides*
mackerel	*Scomber scombrus*
mako shark	*Isurus oxyrinchus*
Norway pout	*Trisopterus esmarkii*
orange roughy	*Hoplostethus atlanticus*
plaice	*Pleuronectes platessa*
pollack	*Pollachius pollachius*
Porbeagle	*Lamna nasus*
rabbit fish	*Chimaera monstrosa*
red gurnard	*Aspitrigla cuculus*
shore rockling	*Gaidropserus mediterraneus*
sandeel	*Ammodytes tobianus* and
	Ammodytes lanceolatus
six-gilled shark	*Hexanchus griseus*
starry smoothhound	*Mustelus asterias*

snake blenny	*Lumpenus lumpretaeformis*
Spanish mackerel	*Scomber japonicus*
sprat	*Sprattus sprattus*
spurdog	*Squalus acanthias*
tope	*Galeorhinus galeus*
triggerfish	*Balistes carolinensis*
undulate ray	*Raja undulata*
witch	*Glyptocephalus cynoglossus*
wolf-fish	*Anarhichas lupus*
wreckfish	*Polyprion americanus*

REPTILES AND AMPHIBIANS

Common Name	Scientific Name
Hawksbill turtle	*Eretmochelys imbricata*
Kemp's ridley turtle	*Lepidochelys kempii*
Leathery turtle	*Dermochelys coriacea*
Loggerhead turtle	*Caretta caretta*
Natterjack toad	*Bufo calamita*

BIRDS

Common Name	Scientific Name
arctic tern	*Sterna paradisaea*
barnacle goose	*Branta leucopsis*
bar-tailed godwit	*Limosa lapponica*
black guillemot	*Cepphus grylle*
black-tailed godwit	*Limosa limosa*
brent goose	*Branta bernicla hrota*
chough	*Phyrrocorax phyrrocorax*
common gull	*Larus canus*
common tern	*Sterna hirundo*
cormorant	*Phalacrocorax carbo*
curlew	*Numenius arquata*
dunlin	*Calidris alpina*
fulmar	*Fulmaris glacialis*
gannet	*Morus bassanus*
golden eagle	*Aquila chrysaetos*
great black-backed gull	*Larus marinus*
great shearwater	*Puffinus gravis*
Greenland white-fronted goose	*Anser albifrons flavirostris*
greenshank	*Tringa nebularia*
grey heron	*Ardea cinerea*
guillemot	*Uria aalge*
herring gull	*Larus argentatus*
kestrel	*Falco tinnunculus*
kittiwake	*Rissa tridactyla*
lapwing	*Vanellus vanellus*
Leach's storm petrel	*Oceanodroma leucorhoa*
little egret	*Egretta garzetta*
little tern	*Sterna albifrons*
long-tailed skua	*Stercorarius longicaudus*
Manx shearwater	*Puffinus puffinus*
oystercatcher	*Haematopus ostralegus*

peregrine falcon	*Falco peregrinus*
pied wagtail	*Motacilla alba*
pomerine skua	*Stercorarius pomarinus*
puffin	*Fratercula arctica*
purple sandpiper	*Calidris maritima*
razorbill	*Alca torda*
red-breasted merganser	*Mergus serrator*
redshank	*Tringa totanus*
ringed plover	*Charadrius hiaticula*
rock dove	*Columba livia*
rock pipit	*Anthus petrosus*
roseate tern	*Sterna dougallii*
sanderling	*Calidris alba*
sandwich tern	*Sterna sandvicensis*
shag	*Phalacrocorax aristotelis*
shelduck	*Tadorna tadorna*
short-eared owl	*Asio flammeus*
snipe	*Gallinago gallinago*
sooty shearwater	*Puffinus griseus*
starling	*Sturnus vulgaris*
storm petrel	*Hydrobates pelagicus*
turnstone	*Arenaria interpres*
whimbrel	*Numenius phaeopus*
wigeon	*Anas penelope*
Wilson's storm-petrel	*Oceanites oceanicus*

MAMMALS

Common Name	Scientific Name
badger	*Meles meles*
blue whale	*Balaenoptera musculus*
bottlenose dolphin	*Tursiops truncates*
common (or harbour) porpoise	*Phocoena phocoena*
Cuvier's beaked whale	*Ziphius cavirostris*
false killer whale	*Pseudorca crassidens*
fox	*Vulpes vulpes*
grey seal	*Halichoerus gryphus*
harbour (or common) seal	*Phoca vitulina*
hedgehog	*Erinaceus europaeus*
house mouse	*Mus domesticus*
killer whale	*Orcinus orca*
long-tailed field mouse	*Apodemus sylvaticus*
northern right whale	*Eubalaena glacialis*
otter	*Lutra lutra*
pilot whale	*Globicephala melas*
Risso's dolphin	*Grampus griseus*
Sowerby's beaked whale	*Mesoplodon bidens*
stoat	*Mustela erminea*

Index

Illustrations are shown in bold